Creative Advertising

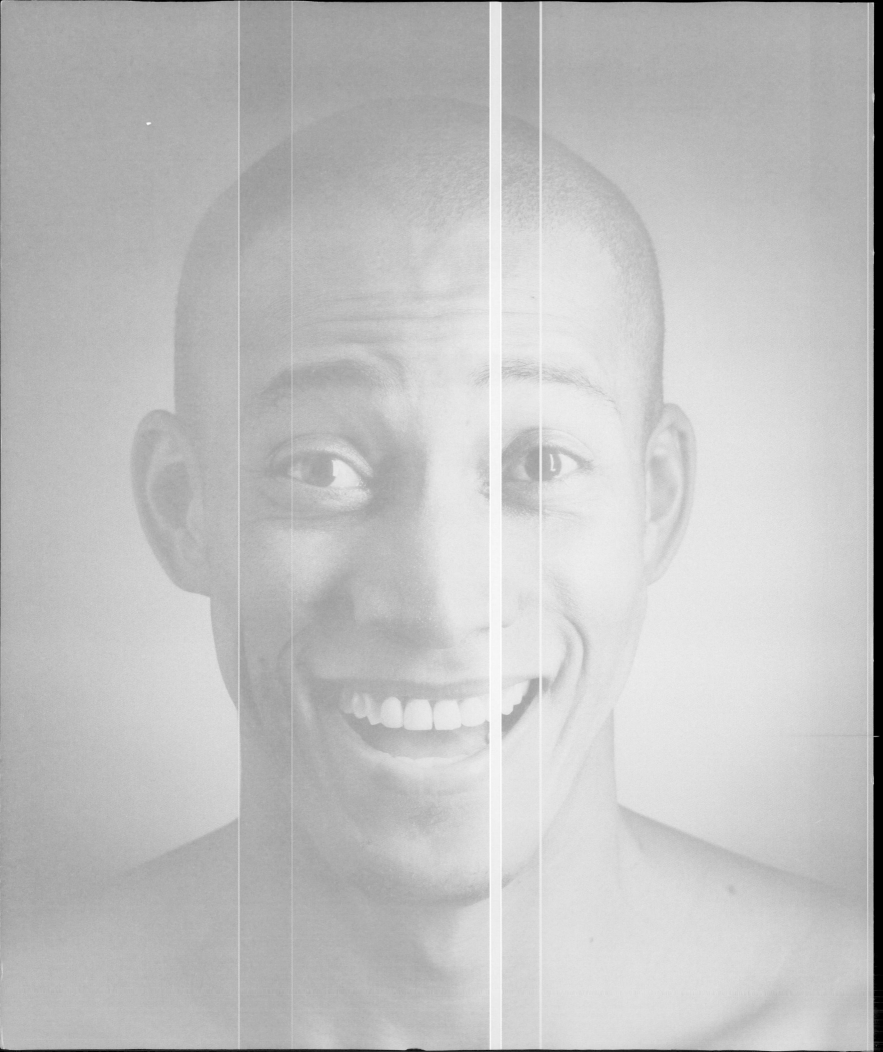

MARIO PRICKEN

Creative
Advertising

IDEAS AND TECHNIQUES FROM THE WORLD'S BEST CAMPAIGNS

Thames & Hudson

Translated from the German *Kribbeln im Kopf*
by Mary Whittall

Author

Mario Pricken
www.idea-engineering.com

Design

Christine Klell

Photography

Christian Postl

First published in the United Kingdom
in 2002 by Thames & Hudson Ltd,
181A High Holborn, London WC1A 7QX

First published in hardcover in the United States
of America in 2002 by Thames & Hudson Inc.,
500 Fifth Avenue, New York, New York 10110

© 2002 Thames & Hudson Ltd, London and
Thames & Hudson Inc., New York

Original edition © 2001
Verlag Hermann Schmidt, Mainz

First published in paperback 2004
Reprinted in 2005

British Library Cataloguing-in-Publication Data
A catalogue record for this book is available
from the British Library

Library of Congress Catalog Card Number
2001096432

ISBN-13: 978-0-500-28476-8
ISBN-10: 0-500-28476-8

ACKNOWLEDGMENTS

My thanks go to all the people whose
support made this unusual book possible.
First of all, of course, I must thank the
advertising agencies who allowed me
to use their material, as well as the many
creatives who gave me hundreds of hours
of their time, Professor Walter Lürzer
for his support, and of course Verlag
Hermann Schmidt, my publishers, for
their unstinting confidence in me.
Special thanks to my parents,
who always gave me the best
they possibly could.

CONTENTS

What this book can do   8

PART 1
DREAMTEAM: A FRAMEWORK FOR GREAT CREATIVE PERFORMANCE

1.01   DreamTeam, a basis for every meeting   12
1.02   Your brief creates space for a motivated team   14
1.03   Switch on all five senses   15
1.04   Go into meetings with a clear goal   16
1.05   Always separate the ideas phase from the evaluation phase   18
1.06   Avoid idea killers   19
1.07   Use doodles to visualize your ideas   20
1.08   Grab ideas and run with them   22
1.09   Look for the positive in other people's ideas   23
1.10   Make mistakes and have fun doing it   24
1.11   Stick with it, the best ideas are yet to come   25
1.12   Develop your sense of humour   26
1.13   Wait before evaluating ideas   27
1.14   Select ideas creatively   28
1.15   Turning ideas into action   29

PART 2
THE KICKSTART CATALOGUE: FINDING IDEAS THAT COMMUNICATE

2.01   Introducing the KickStart catalogue   32
2.02   The KickStart catalogue   34
2.03   Without words   40
2.04   Mixing and matching   45
2.05   Comparative juxtaposition   50
2.06   Repetition and accumulation   55
2.07   Exaggeration   58
2.08   Turn it right around   62
2.09   Omission and suggestion   66
2.10   Paradoxes and optical illusions   71
2.11   Provocation and shock tactics   74
2.12   Playing with time   81
2.13   A change of perspective   85
2.14   Spoofs and parodies   90
2.15   Symbols and signs   94
2.16   Come and play   101
2.17   Telling stories   106
2.18   Absurd, surreal, bizarre   112
2.19   Take it literally   118
2.20   Change the product   122
2.21   Alternative uses   128
2.22   Double meanings   133
2.23   Play with words   138

2.24	In the beginning was the word	143
2.25	Reframing: a key to creative thinking	148
2.26	Metaphor and analogy	154
2.27	Break out of the frame	164
2.28	Alternative media	172

PART 3

COPY WITH PUNCH: USING WIT AND HUMOUR

3.01	Structuring jokes	182
3.02	A practical guide to joke-making:	
	constructing and disrupting frames of reference	184
3.03	Developing punchlines	188
3.04	Adapting and using existing punchlines	190
3.05	Make the most of black humour	193
3.06	Unintentional humour and situation comedy	197
3.07	Blue humour	200

PART 4

CLASSIC CREATIVE TECHNIQUES

4.01	The morphological matrix	206
4.02	Osborn's checklist	214
4.03	Visual synectics	222

PART 5

VISUALIZATION: MOVIES IN YOUR MIND

5.01	Tools for professional dreamers	226
5.02	Synaesthesia	228
5.03	Controlling the pictures in your mind	229
5.04	Aids to visualization	230
5.05	Brainfloating	231
5.06	Develop ideas through storyboarding	232

PART 6

INTERVIEWS AND RESOURCES

6.01	Walter Lürzer, Professor, University of Applied Art, Vienna	236
6.02	PJ Pereira, Creative Director, New Media Agency Agênciaclick	238
6.03	Johan Kramer, Kesselskramer Advertising Agency	241
6.04	K.C. Tsang, Executive Creative Director, BBDO Hong Kong	244
6.05	Stefan Sagmeister, Graphic Designer	250
6.06	The team behind this book	254
6.07	List of agencies	256

This is a handbook for brilliant ideas. Its ambition is both provocative and optimistic: it aims to provide an insight into the alchemy of creative thinking. It promises to shed light on the strategies of top creatives and increase your understanding of the patterns that underlie great ideas. Many people think promises like these can't possibly be true. Others pin their hopes on them as the answer to all their prayers. Both groups are advised to be a little sceptical, but also to follow their curiosity. Anyone that is open to new approaches has a chance of experiencing the effect of these methods and techniques for themselves.

After countless conversations with creative people, it became clear to me that they all learnt their skills in completely individual ways and that most of the time they are not conscious of the complex internal processes that take place when they are hunting for solutions, designing a layout or creating a campaign idea. That isn't such an unusual concept, because it's a well-known fact that we do the things we do best unconsciously. Think of what it's like when you ride a bicycle, use a mobile phone or read a book. We no longer need to give any thought to the complex mental processes that are involved if we are to perform these tasks to the best of our ability. We've already learned them, and we carry them out automatically, without thinking about them, using specific learned patterns of behaviour. The same thing can be observed in creatives, who for the most part are not aware of how concrete their processes are when they develop a great idea.

I wanted to learn more about these processes, because advertising is a competitive business! First of all, I wanted to work out the brainstorming methods of top creatives which allow them to produce brilliant ideas. Second, I want to guarantee that these brilliant ideas will blow the minds of target groups. Although creativity remains unfathomable in many respects, the methods in this book are a first important step towards making the intuitive use of creative strategies openly available as a tool for teams in advertising agencies.

The book you have in your hands now is a kind of manual for the brain. But instead of the newest theories from research into creativity, you will find concrete instructions which you can use in practical situations. We can't say whether the academic theories are right or not. In day-to-day practice, what works is all that counts. This is a relevant book that provides fresh knowledge about what professionals do in practice, in a form that allows you to try out the techniques for yourself. This is not a book that teaches you how to do your job better, but I hope that it will help you to have great ideas and a lot of fun.

Idea engineering

The techniques presented here form the substance and the structure of the training exercise I call 'idea engineering'. I developed this exercise through my professional practice, and by applying it in agency work I have turned it into a extremely efficient tool. To do this, I studied the thought strategies of advertising professionals and formalized them in new ways, or combined them with proven creative techniques. A systematic analysis of more than ten thousand outstanding ad campaigns has brought to light the structures that top creatives use to develop brilliant ideas. The outcome is that your team will find tools in this book that they can use to expand their own skills and thought strategies in daily professional practice. Greater choice creates more flexible thinking and leads faster and more efficiently to the Big Idea – and you will have a lot more fun along the way!

THE BASIC PREMISES OF IDEA ENGINEERING

The following premises are simply the fruits of my experience. They are not theories to which you must swear allegiance, nor are they the only truth. I just want to invite you to experiment with the 'brain tools' and creative techniques given here, and to add to them or alter them in the light of your own experience. You can even let me know how you get on with them, and about any relevant discoveries you make, at **www.idea-engineering.com**. The basic assumptions below are at the foundation of all the methods described in this book, and sum up what creativity means to me.

- This book is aimed at agency teams and professionals in the communications industry.
- This book is a cookbook for practical creativity, not just a compendium of theories.
- Methods and techniques for developing concepts and campaign ideas are at its core.
- This book does not discuss issues of good or bad advertising.
- It does not contain advice on designing creative layouts or composing copy.
- The book covers the distance from the initial briefing to the evaluation of ideas.
- The list of methods (the KickStart catalogue) does not claim to be exhaustive.
- All the campaigns illustrated were chosen on subjective grounds and are illustrated as examples of all the possible variations within a category.
- All the campaigns illustrated are examples selected from countless alternatives and should not be taken as models for plagiarism!
- Use this book intuitively and have fun with it – find out what helps you to develop great ideas and enjoy doing it.

- The foundation for creativity is in the individual, and so these methods and techniques are to be taken only as usual tools and stimuli, to give you more freedom of choice and so enhance and liberate your creative skills.
- There is no one right way to be creative. Creativity is a living process with many possible strategies, and the creative outcomes to which they lead will depend on the context and the individual.
- If one person has learnt how to develop really creative ideas, it stands to reason that everyone else can.
- Creativity demands abundance, which is why the objective is to increase the possible choices, and so improve flexibility.
- Don't confuse the menu with the meal: theoretical knowledge will do nothing to increase your creativity. Try the methods out, experiment with them in your work. Whatever you learn from the experience will nourish you and become part of your strategies in future.
- If something doesn't work for you, stop using it and try something else.
- Have fun!

1

PART 1   **DREAMTEAM: A FRAMEWORK FOR GREAT CREATIVE PERFORMANCE**

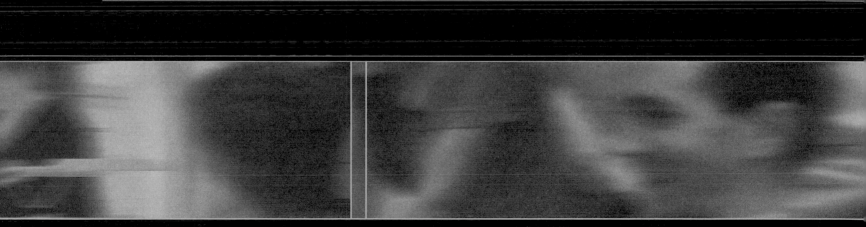

DreamTeam is a list of fifteen rules of creative teamwork that form the foundation of all the methods described in this book. Whichever creative technique you're using, take the DreamTeam rules as the framework whenever you're working as a team. They provide the creative space to let the imagination fly and launch all the team members on their way to original ideas.

From 'Aha' to 'Ha ha'

When you introduce DreamTeam as the new culture for meetings in your agency, pay particular attention to the following points. All team members must be equally well-informed and prepared to stick to the rules. Someone who has only heard about some of the DreamTeam rules, but doesn't actively live them in the team, puts a brake on the group process. Just knowing about the rules is like reading the menu instead of eating the meal. The menu doesn't nourish you, and knowing the rules is

pointless if that knowledge is not used to the full within the team. Next, you need to get all the parts of the agency with which you work on-side and informed about the basic DreamTeam principles. In this way you build up the necessary understanding from every department to get the support you need for your project. This is because the effects of DreamTeam often reach way beyond meetings and begin to influence areas such as client meetings, briefs, art buying or collaboration between different departments. Experience shows that you need to familiarize your team with the DreamTeam rules step by step. It's particularly effective to call meetings just for this purpose, where the team can try out the rules under stress-free conditions by performing simple set tasks. You will see initial distrust turning into 'aha' and finally into 'ha ha'. DreamTeam creates the optimal group climate for the team to start looking for that Big Idea in a relaxed frame of mind and having a lot more fun than you might expect.

'In the factory   we make cosmetics;   in the drugstore   we sell hope.'

DreamTeam: a toolkit for agency professionals

Agency professionals, particularly the 'old pros' with their long experience, should learn how to use the DreamTeam tools in the company of other people in a playful atmosphere, in order to refine their team-working skills and build up creativity, the key qualification. The following fifteen points are both rules for the game of top-quality creative performance and strategies that can be used as highly effective methods of communication in meetings.

What results can you expect from the DreamTeam rules?

- They produce a bigger catch of valuable ideas.
- They give the team a creative boost.
- They build structured freedom and prevent sessions of destructive chaos.
- They foster faith in the team and enhance motivation.
- They allow a brilliant 'group brain' to develop.
- They promote all sorts of fun and increase individual creative potential.
- They save time, money and nervous energy in the hunt for ideas.

The brief acts as the ignition for the team of creatives and so it has a big influence on motivation and space in all the meetings that follow. Write a brief like a love letter to the product, and let your imagination run free. Create an environment where your team can work enthusiastically. There are two kinds of information in most briefs: the kind that restricts the team's creative search-field, and the kind that enlarges the search-field for potential ideas and stimulates the imagination.

RESTRICTING THE SEARCH-FIELD

The restrictive elements of a brief should be kept in the background during the creative phase. These parameters will only come into force at the stage when ideas are being developed and evaluated, in order to establish whether an individual idea meets the project specifications. Restrictive components might be, for example:

- Budget constraints
- The client's ideas and wishes
- Style requirements
- Marketing information
- Previously rejected concepts

ENLARGING THE SEARCH-FIELD

In the first brief, you should put most emphasis on the parameters that will stimulate the imagination, give detailed information about the product and so provide the largest possible hunting ground for ideas. Elements that could enlarge the search-field might include:

- Benefit, USP
- Reason Why
- Tone or mood
- Product information profile
- Target group etc.

'If your advertising goes unnoticed, everything else is academic.' William Bernbach, DDB

The best ideas take time. The more you think about the product, analyse it, examine it from every angle – play with it, in other words – the more freely great ideas will flow. Give your team all the information you can get hold of. Best of all, bring the product to the first meeting, or take the whole creative team to visit the client, so that their own experience of the product or service activates all their senses. If that's not possible, then videos, CD-ROMs, photos or other media can be useful triggers. The key factor is that physically coming face to face with the product itself can stimulate all five senses and have a positive and inspiring effect on the process of generating ideas.

These ads for John West and Centella Queen show the kind of great ideas that come from direct, playful engagement with the product. The solution to the task is already there in the product. Your five senses are the tools you use to shape the idea.

Client John West
Agency Leo Burnett Ltd, London
Creative Direction Nick Bell, Mark Tutssel
Art Direction Richard Connor
Copy Julie Adams
Photo Andy Roberts

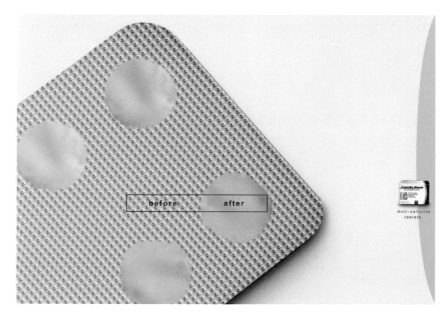

Campaign for anti-cellulite tablets
Client Centella Queen
Agency Grey Worldwide Argentina, Buenos Aires
Creative Direction Carlos Pérez, Fernando Militerno
Art Direction Fernando Militerno
Copy Carolina Morano, Matias Corbelle
Photo Millennium

'Creative without strategy is called art. Creative with strategy is called advertising.'
Jef I. Richards,
University of Texas
Advertising Department

If you engage with the product intensively and start a creative meeting with a goal already clearly formulated, then you're already more than halfway there. The goal and the solution are like a question and answer. Only a good question will result in a satisfactory answer. Einstein summed this up brilliantly when he said that if he was going to be killed and had just one hour to find out how to save his life, he would spend the first fifty-five minutes looking for the right question. Once he'd found the question, it would take only five minutes to work out the right answer.

○ WHAT DOES A GOAL ACHIEVE?
Formulating the goal in advance reduces a complex brief to a clear strategy, a single-minded proposition. It ensures that all team members target the same goal and end up with ideas that will communicate a clear message.

○ The goal is in clear view throughout the meeting: it isn't restrictive but acts as a focal point, leading to a clearly defined objective. It helps to prevent chaos in sessions and time-wasting discussions about how to interpret the brief.

○ Expressed in the form of a question (How can we achieve X?) the goal makes the team members begin an active mental search process, and so acts as a stimulus.

○ A goal keeps the team on track during the meeting and prevents them from getting snarled up in other ideas from which it's hard to get back to the task in hand.

EVERYBODY IS NOBODY
If you define the target group in a brief as 'everybody', you'll end up addressing nobody. The same applies to the other brief parameters: emphasizing everything in a brief is emphasizing nothing. Working out a goal with a central statement, or single-minded proposition, is a great boost to inventing ideas. Here are some possible ways to define a single-minded proposition.

ASK YOURSELF THE FOLLOWING QUESTIONS
○ Can the brief be reduced to a central denominator?
○ What are we actually looking for?
○ Can the objectives be collated in an overall concept?
○ What is the strategy?

EXAMPLES OF GOALS
Goals should always be formulated as questions, because they automatically spark off an active inner search process in the team members, directed towards finding an answer. Here are some sample goal types, which all team members ought to write down at the start of a meeting.

Example 1
Standard formulation, leaving a lot open
How can we show in a line of print copy that the new TB lens is the toughest camera lens currently on the market?

Example 2
Formulation directed towards a specific line of thought
How can we show humorously and provocatively in a line of print copy that the new TB lens is the toughest camera lens currently on the market?

Example 3
Standard formulation, leaving space
How can we communicate straightforwardly in a direct mailing that the new GR 300 drill is the first to provide a reliable sensor that gives advance warning of electric cables and water pipes in walls?

Example 4
Formulation directed towards a specific line of thought
How should we frame a direct mailing so as to convey the following message in the form of a game? The new GR 300 drill is the first to provide a reliable sensor that gives advance warning of electric cables and water pipes in walls.

Of course it isn't always possible to achieve a clear and straightforward definition of the goal at the first attempt. Often it is only while you are formulating the goal that you realize that the brief does not describe the product fully, that the target group is not defined precisely enough, or that there is no clear strategic positioning.

The following example, based on an actual case, shows what a subtle instrument goal formulation can be in helping to obtain a clear view of the actual goal or strategy.

1. The problem:

The service department of a business discovers that a lot of faults in the appliance are caused by users not reading the instructions properly, or failing to understand them.

2. This produces the provisional goal:

How can the text and graphics in the manual be made easier to understand and better suited to the user's needs?

3. Questions leading to a new formulation of a problem:

What is the real underlying problem? What is it behind the problem as first set that needs to be targeted?

4. The answers to these produce a series of new possible goal definitions:

- How can we ensure that users can see for themselves whether or not they've understood the instructions properly?
- How can we ensure that users will always read the instructions first?
- How can we ensure that reading the instructions and using the appliance for the first time go hand in hand?

Make room for creative added value. To a mathematician, 1 + 1 = 2. An imaginative person ignores the rules and opens up exciting new perspectives: 1 + 1 = 11.

Ideas need imagination more than knowledge, so it's important to keep the stage when ideas are being generated strictly separate from the stage when they're being evaluated. In the first part of the meeting, make space for uninhibited creativity without premature criticism. Even more, this is the stage when people should set their imaginations free to roam, and no limits should be set on creative game-playing.

If there are too many idea killers at large, some team members will withdraw into passivity or there will be endless and emotional arguments which will undermine any kind of creativity. Other team members will start to think to themselves 'Best not make a mistake, don't take risks'. And that is tantamount to thinking 'Mustn't make a fool of myself'. You end up with the very thing you wanted to avoid. These are the fears that lead inevitably, at most creative meetings, to compromises and shallow ideas.

CHOOSE THE RIGHT MOMENT FOR CRITICISM

It's only at the later, evaluation stage that it is justified to raise factors such as the brief criteria, and this is also the time for introducing professional know-how or criticism, so that raw ideas can be developed in a climate of constructive discussion. To prevent unconventional ideas being 'evaluated away' and prematurely discarded, the team should keep asking the same question: 'How can I improve this idea, what can I do to make it work after all?'

IDEA KILLERS IN THE TEAM

How would you like your ideas to be received at the next creative meeting? Sabotaged, sniggered at or simply ignored? Idea killers have one thing in common: they always work! Everything from the verbal stun-gun to the wry twitch at the corner of somebody's mouth is capable of trampling down the first little shoot of an idea. Sadly, in many teams, old familiar phrases like 'That won't work' and 'The client would never accept that' are still part of the meeting culture. Studies have shown that session members spend almost 70 per cent of their time running down colleagues' suggestions.

IDEA KILLERS IN YOUR OWN HEAD

Often the killer phrases of our colleagues do less damage than the little voice inside our own heads, whispering 'Forget it, it doesn't work!' Our own idea killers are particularly deadly because we are often not conscious of them. They are the product of exaggerated expectations we have of ourselves, or of the belief that we have to come up with ideas that are brilliant from the word go – a strategy almost certainly doomed to failure.

FOUR EFFECTIVE ANTIDOTES TO KILLER PHRASES

→   *Turn killer phrases into constructive feedback*

Ideas are almost never born perfect. Give them a chance to grow by introducing this rule in the team: if you can't avoid a critical comment during the ideas phase, first mention two aspects of the idea that you think are good. Then the criticism will be more acceptable when it comes, and may even lead to improvement of the original idea.

→   *Stop killer phrases in their tracks*

If fear of criticism is inhibiting team members from introducing really wild ideas, the following little trick will help: announce your own ideas with the words 'The craziest thing I can think of is... ' or 'I know it sounds silly, but might it be worth thinking about...'. That way you're taking the wind out of your critics' sails from the outset.

→   *Idea killers? Ridiculous!*

Once they've been identified as such, idea killers lose any lethal force in meetings. If everyone knows them, they can even raise a laugh in the group. Take the time, with the whole team, to think of as many idea killers as you can. Include all those that you yourself or others in the team have used. Make a note of them and put them where everyone can see them until the end of the session. You'll be amazed at how well this works.

→   *The 10 best responses to idea-killer phrases*

1. Nothing will come of that.

   Not if you just dismiss the idea, it won't.

2. Let's just wait and see what happens.

   What, until everyone else has overtaken us?

3. That doesn't work!

   But it's a great idea.

4. We do things differently!

   So, no change there.

5. This mailshot idea doesn't work!

   But what if...?

6. That's ridiculous!

   So what if it is?

7. We'll come back to your idea.

   All right. When?

8. The client will never accept that!

   Give it a chance!

9. What's so original about that?

   The fact that no one else has thought of it.

10. Anyone could come up with that.

    Exactly.

Your idea must be visual if it's really going to take root in other people's heads. Often it only takes a quick scribble, a few lines to bring the idea to life. Think about it: your ideas are mostly internal images that only you can see. A doodle releases the idea from your head and so raises your chances of enthusing others.

THREE ARGUMENTS IN FAVOUR OF DOODLES

○ Doodles are an essential means of communication, enabling the others in the team to see, and therefore understand, the images in your head.
○ Doodles reinforce the associations of internal images and so trigger new ideas in a playful way.
○ Doodles enable teams to develop raw ideas in gradual stages and so prevent good ideas from being killed off prematurely.

Tip

NOT ALL GOOD IDEAS FIT ON A MATCHBOX

The following experiment shows how important doodles can be: take a few outstanding ads and sum up their concept in one pithy sentence. Explain the ideas to someone who doesn't know the ads, and wait to see if they strike a spark in that person. After a few tries you'll see that even brilliant ads don't always succeed when summed up in a pithy sentence. And that's exactly what happens to ideas in meetings. Words are often not enough; it takes a doodle to produce that 'Aha!' experience.

Packaging for cosmetics samples.
A card insert is fitted inside the
outer acetate case.

Client Cheil Insync
Agency Arnell Group, New York
Art Direction Judith Asfour, Peter Arnell, Susan Conway
Source Lürzer's Archive Special, Packaging Design 1

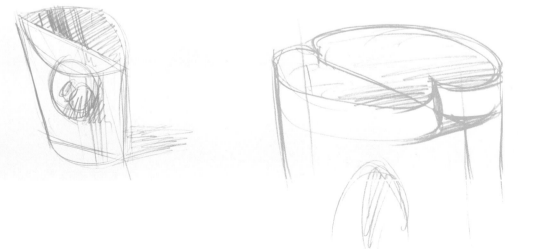

This teaser campaign introduces a new tractor with an innovative design and high-tech features.

Client CASE Corporation
Agency Cramer-Krasselt, Milwaukee
Creative Direction Pat Knapp
Art Direction Dan Koel
Copy Adam Albrecht

*'You have a Euro. I have a Euro.
We swap them. You have my
Euro and I have yours. Neither
of us is any better off. But now
imagine that you have an
idea and I have an idea.
We swap them. Now we've
both increased our store of
ideas by 100 per cent.'
A. S. Gregg*

Almost nothing inhibits the creative process more than clinging
obsessively to one single idea – namely, your own. Don't think of your
teammate as a rival in a competition for the best idea but as the supplier
of raw material for your next ideas. It doesn't even matter whether you
think his ideas are good or not – just use them as triggers or stimuli for
your own associations. The important thing is that you pick up the ideas,
develop them further and hand them back. Ideally, your teammate should
have the same attitude: each new idea you supply him with becomes the
raw material for ideas of his own. If you carry on consistently with this
new principle, a kind of ping-pong ensues, in which you catapult each
other into an emotional state resembling a creative trance! With each
new round of ping-pong, you and your ideas will get even better.

PING-PONG WITH IDEAS

Ping-pong with ideas, as described above, is best practised by two players.
A lot of brilliant two-person teams in advertising work on this principle.

A key factor is picking a partner you trust 100 per cent. Concentrate on
getting a rapid flow of ideas during the game, don't criticize, follow your
instincts and let yourselves be carried along by spontaneity.

Exercise

LOOK FOR THE POSITIVE IN OTHER PEOPLE'S IDEAS

If you want to promote the flow of ideas in the team, look for the positive aspects of other people's ideas. Even if you don't get anywhere with an idea at first, ask yourself: 'What's in it that we can use?' There will always be some aspect you can build on. Replace your inner CRITIC with an inner CREATIVE and exploit all the possibilities from this new perspective. Take the idea's good point and improve it by developing and cultivating the seed of the idea. This strategy makes you extremely flexible and always opens new perspectives. You can learn to think 'What if...?' and this will develop in time into an inner attitude which will open doors to new ideas instead of closing them.

THINKING 'WHAT IF...'

What's the good side if your house burns down tomorrow? What would be the advantages of losing your job tomorrow? Anything that looks like a catastrophe at first, may reveals a whole, surprising series of positive aspects on a second look. Develop the play of ideas a little more and the tragic loss of your house opens the door to new freedom, new opportunities, a new future.

Thinking 'What if...' is a conceptual switch, a change of perspective. You look at the very same thing from a different perspective. And you can be sure that there are hundreds of other standpoints that you've never envisaged. To broaden your spectrum, try putting yourself in someone else's shoes, in your thoughts, and occupy their position. What positive aspects would your best friend see? Your aunt? Mick Jagger? A beggar? A child? A blind man?

'To swear off making mistakes is very easy. All you have to do is swear off having ideas.'
Leo Burnett, quoted in 100 LEO's, Chicago.

Before he made a light bulb that worked, Edison discovered more than 1600 ways how not to make a light bulb. One of Madame Curie's blind alleys is what we know today as radium. And Columbus was in fact looking for India. Mistakes are a basic learning principle, accompanying all great discoveries and often leading to brilliant ideas. Get rid of the compulsion to come up with nothing but good ideas that are ready to use! Say everything that occurs to you, no matter how silly it sounds – it could be the raw material for a brilliant idea. People who think they should only speak up at a meeting when they have the one true correct answer are putting themselves under enormous pressure and smothering all creativity in the bud. So make mistakes and enjoy it! What you need as a stable basis is confidence in the team and a mutual agreement that meetings can end in failure.

Exercise

A FOOL'S FREEDOM

What's the worst mistake you could make in a meeting? What would you learn from it? The greatest fear of many people is making a mistake and looking silly in front of other people. Learn to live with this fear, by making a fool of yourself deliberately but staying in control. Put yourself in a ridiculous position by making an abstruse suggestion, and exaggerate it to the point where you have to laugh at yourself. By doing so you achieve a degree of inner freedom that allows you to leave familiar paths behind and let your imagination run free.

STICK WITH IT, THE BEST IDEAS ARE YET TO COME

If you throw in the towel after the first round and accept the first ideas that come up, you're giving up the chance of really brilliant ideas. Ninety minutes more, and you penetrate reservoirs of ideas that reveal solutions you won't find in any handbook, ideas that are really new and unique. Stay with it, follow your ideas to the bitter end, try to work out as many different solutions as possible. Meetings take a cyclical course. After a first phase of producing ideas, your team may fall into a deep silence. Don't let it make you uneasy, and whatever you do don't end the session.

You can safely assume that many of the participants are just immersed in an internal search process. Apart from that, the first cycle usually produces only a few basic ideas – shallow, second-hand ones that you've all heard before. It often takes only one sentence to set the process moving again and plunging into the second phase with a lot of new ideas. Here the chance of developing far better ideas is already much higher. Since several such phases are possible, stay with it, in order to go even deeper into the pool of untouched ideas.

Fiery Fries. **BURGER KING**

These two brilliant ads are examples of the many campaigns on the theme of 'fiery food'. If you wanted to communicate the idea of hot and spicy food today, you would need to break new ground and plunge into the realms of untouched fantasy. That's why the rule is: stick with it in meetings, and look beyond the first easy ideas that come up, ideas you've seen somewhere before.

Client Burger King
Agency Saatchi & Saatchi, Singapore
Creative Direction Andy Clarke
Art Direction Andy Clarke
Photo Shaun Pettigrew

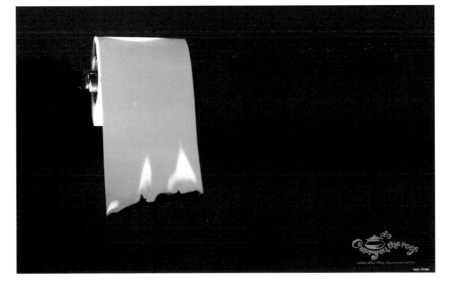

Client 'Curry on the Roof' Restaurant
Agency Mudra Communications Ltd, New Delhi
Creative Direction Freddy Birdy
Art Direction Naved Akhtar
Illustration Soumitra Dasgupta
Photo Madhukar Soma

Humour is the healthy way of creating a 'distance' between one's self and the problem, a way of standing back and looking at a problem with perspective.

Humour reveals new aspects. Humour disarms, relaxes, and releases happiness hormones. It's also infectious, so it's one of the most important creative tools for teams looking for great ways to communicate ideas. Don't just make jokes at other people's expense, however. Instead, look out for a really funny topic in meetings – yourself. Learn to laugh at yourself. Anyone who can see what's absurd and laughable about himself gains a new freedom and gives the team a creative boost.

Really good campaign ideas flourish in a group climate where humour cn flow. Looking at this witty ad by DM9 of Brazil, you can almost feel the fun they had developing it.

Push-up Bra valisère

www.valisere.com.br   lingerie

Client Valisère
Agency DM9 DBB, São Paulo
Creative Direction Manır Fadel
Art Direction Mariana Sá
Photo Andre Andrade

WAIT BEFORE EVALUATING IDEAS

When you leave a successful meeting with a few really good ideas and a feeling of euphoria, wait a while before assessing the ideas. Step back a little and don't fall too much in love with the first, seemingly irresistible ideas. Sleep on it and next day look at the sketches with a critical eye: does the idea work? Does it have a real emotional kick? Is the concept clear and comprehensible? Show your first ideas to other people, so that you can read from the feedback whether you've hit the bull's eye or if you are the only one who understands it. Don't forget: a good idea speaks for itself and can usually be conveyed in a few scribbles. Less good ideas need elaborate concepts to persuade or even be understood.

It's often worthwhile to distribute the minutes with all the doodles and ideas to every team member the next day. Ask people to take another look at the ideas, improve or add to them, or take them a step further. At this point everyone has gained a little distance from the initial task and the goal will be clearer. Even more importantly, overnight each team member's unconscious mind will have had the chance to get acquainted with the problem, and experience has shown that more potentially exciting solutions will present themselves.

Sometimes the really interesting ideas are simply eliminated or talked out during the evaluation phase. Anything unusual, wild, uncomfortable, or harder to translate into action, gets dropped. At this stage, you need to make new ideas from old, in order to save potentially great initiatives. There are already more than enough old, familiar ideas that have simply been rehashed. Remember: as a rule, people tend to prefer what they know, because anything really new strikes them as too risky.

Tip

DEVELOP NEW IDEAS FROM OLD

Your meetings have assembled a host of isolated ideas and bits of ideas, and now you can fit them together as your fancy pleases, like when you start a jigsaw puzzle. At this stage, individual, way-out scraps of ideas should not be evaluated away but integrated into existing initiatives. The only ideas that increase the opportunities for really original solutions are the 'wild', 'silly' or 'leftfield' ones.

Ask yourself this question: how can the basic ideas best be combined, either to optimize them or obtain an entirely new idea? You're now entering a sort of second creative phase. Develop a concept out of the original ideas which takes the other aspects into account (you will need to invent bridging ideas to cover the gaps). The individual elements should be moulded, refined and enriched.

THREE WAYS TO EVALUATE AND SELECT IDEAS

In the final analysis, there are three ways to reach a decision about which of the basic ideas should be worked up for presentation:

○ Democratically: The team leader invites every member of the meeting to give a score to the ideas they think are best and deserve to be worked up for presentation. The idea with most points wins.

○ Use the brief as a yardstick: The main criteria from the client's brief are used as the yardstick for assessing which ideas have reached the objectives.

○ Creative Director or Art Director: Depending on the agency culture, it is of course possible that the creative director or art director will be the one to decree which of the starter ideas will be developed for presentation.

The path to mediocrity begins by treating tender shoots as if they were already full-blown ideas. Leaving isolated strokes of genius out of the calculation, only hard work can turn good ideas into great ones. What this means is scrutinizing, reworking, rejecting, improving, adjusting, scrutinizing again, and finally reworking yet again.

It's the task of the art department to develop the concept in as many different ways as they can, in order to find the best one. Good-quality doodles are usually enough for this. Only the largest number of possible variations creates a chance for a really great campaign! The same applies to copy, of course. Develop a lot of headlines, not just one.

○ How can Art Direction provide optimal support for the concept, or reinforce what it says by visual means?

○ What does the basic idea need, for the solution to hit the bull's eye?

○ What could I change to give the idea a stronger emotional kick?

○ What weak points does the idea have, what seems implausible? How can I improve it?

○ Is the idea to the point? What works better?

○ What can I substitute or alter to improve the idea? Add new elements or change the copy, develop new headlines?

○ What do I need to do to make the idea so appealing that people will be happy to see it more than once?

Art direction brings an idea to life, determining whether it gives the campaign the boost that it needs or weakens it by going off on the wrong course. Here are two excellent examples of ideas being translated into action.

Kills bugs fast.

Client Porsche
Agency Goodby, Silverstein & Partners, San Francisco
Creative Direction Jeff Goodby, Rich Silverstein
Art Direction Todd Grant
Copy Jeff Goodby
Photo Clint Clemens

Client Fatbrain.com
Agency GMO/Hill Holliday, San Francisco
Creative Direction Wendy Erwin Sigler
Art Direction Terry Rietta; Sharon Azula
Illustration Rich Borge

2

ABOUT THIS SECTION OF THE BOOK

The first thing you will find in this chapter is the KickStart catalogue, a compilation of over 200 questions which will inject excitement into meetings. There is no discussion within the catalogue itself about what is good or bad advertising, nor are there tips on how to improve layout or copy. What the catalogue does have to offer are strategies likely to promote great ideas for campaigns. In the second part, you will find sample ads for each category of the catalogue, illustrating the kind of ideas these questions can trigger. Most of these international campaigns received awards at major festivals and they should NOT be plagiarized! I selected all the examples illustrated on subjective criteria. In almost every category, you will also find exercises and tips intended to help you develop proficiency with some of the techniques by learning the basics in a kind of induction course.

WHAT'S THE IDEA BEHIND IT?

To compile the catalogue, I isolated the communication patterns of more than 10,000 first-class, award-winning campaigns using print, TV, web and direct marketing, and put all the information together to form a new creative technique. The result enables you to try out effective communication models and brilliant strategies for yourself. At the same time, the catalogue provides tools you can use systematically to expand and improve the methods and techniques that people in your agency work with every day.

A TOOLKIT FOR THE BRAIN

Systematic analysis of the work produced by top creatives reveals certain patterns and strategies in their thinking. Some creatives' strength lies in analogy, while others always try to induce a change of perspective, and others develop ideas by turning everyday situations on their heads. One thing is clear in every case: even the best creatives use only part of the spectrum of possible ways of thinking. If your strengths lie, for example, in the field of metaphor or comparative juxtaposition, then you probably don't combine or reframe things very often. You will probably find that you are familiar with some of the categories and already use them intuitively, while others are new to you and will extend your versatility, enabling you to develop outstanding ideas. This catalogue is a toolbox containing an inexhaustible supply of new brain tools which anyone can use to expand their own strategies. It doesn't give a lecture on how to do things but simply leads users into areas they may never have considered before.

WHEN TO USE THIS TECHNIQUE

The KickStart catalogue is incredibly useful when you are looking for new and unusual campaign ideas for the press, TV and cinemas, events, promotions, packaging, web banners, brochures or direct mailing.

WORK WITH A GOAL IN MIND

Before you use this tool for the first time, make sure that you and your team have a clear goal in front of you. This is especially important when using the KickStart catalogue, because if you don't know your goal, then either you will stumble upon it by accident or reach it by a roundabout route, leaving you drained of nervous energy, or you won't reach it at all. Take the time to formulate your goal, as described in Part 1 of this book. Make sure everyone in the team has the goal clearly in sight and use it as a compass throughout the whole process of looking for ideas.

MAKE YOUR TEAM A DREAMTEAM

The DreamTeam rules in Part 1 of this book are an invaluable basis for teams working with this catalogue. But the KickStart catalogue can also be used to good effect on its own. The rules remain the same: take one question after another, stay on one question for as long as possible, and avoid evaluating your ideas too early.

How to use the KickStart catalogue

1. Formulate your goal and make sure all the team members have it clearly in sight: How can we achieve X with a line of copy?

2. One member of the team should (a) ensure the team keeps to the rules and note down the suggested ideas without any comment, and (b) keep reminding the team of the KickStart questions. It is best if the person who called the meeting takes this role.

3. Now pick one question from the catalogue at random and put it to the team. What idea does the question suggest to you, what associations does It conjure up? Even if the flow of ideas seems rather sluggish at first, stay with it. You'll be surprised by what happens once your team gets going. It's possible for one question to be so productive that the team will spend over an hour on one theme. The longer the better, because that's the only way the team will dig down deep to where the newest, most unusual ideas can be found.

4. When you've exhausted the first question, choose another one. If the team's attention starts to flag during the meeting, or wanders from the subject, remind everyone of the goal again and repeat the current KickStart question at frequent intervals.

5. Of course, you don't have to use all the KickStart questions. Work with the catalogue only until you have assembled enough raw ideas.

6. It may well happen that after several months of working with the KickStart catalogue, you will notice that you have begun to use many of the strategies and techniques automatically and no longer need the catalogue in meetings.

Evaluating and developing ideas

If everything has gone well, you ought to have a substantial collection of raw ideas by the end of a meeting. Guided by the basic DreamTeam rules, try to develop your basic ideas and tentative solutions in doodle form. Do this before going on to evaluate the ideas and finally select the best.

Double whammy

In practice, many creatives treat the KickStart catalogue like a school test: they begin at the beginning and work their way through to the end. This method doesn't work – in fact, it's a sure-fire way to kill all creativity. Use the catalogue intuitively, and choose any question that appeals to you out of any section. I have also noticed that people tend to work with just one KickStart question at a time, never with two at once. Yet that's precisely what can make it exciting! Why not go for a double whammy – for example find a shocking idea and show it without text. Or, how would your ad look if you found a metaphor and then overstated it wildly? What if you altered the product with the intention of making the target group laugh? You see, using two questions at once from different categories makes questions twice as exciting and may also produce ideas with twice as much punch.

Using international campaigns as examples

On the pages that follow, each category of KickStart questions is accompanied by excellent examples from international campaigns. Next to these examples, you will find additional KickStart questions intended to show you the kind of ideas those strategies can lead to. Of course each of these campaigns is only one of countless possibilities. Experience has shown that the KickStart questions often lead to completely new realms of ideas, often very different from the examples given here. And that's a good thing, because in the end these technique are designed to open fresh sources of inspiration in the heads of your team.

Tip

WITHOUT WORDS

- How could the USP be depicted without words?
- Are there scenes or situations in which the product benefit could be conveyed without words?
- How can the benefit be portrayed in one picture?
- How might the USP be communicated in a silent film?
- How can the benefit be summed up without words in a simple picture?
- How could a story be told in simple sign language?

MIXING AND MATCHING

- How can the product be combined with something else in order to make the USP clearer?:
    - Mix the two together?
    - Collage?
    - Selection?
    - Rearrangement?
    - Combine several objects to make one?

- How can the problem and solution be combined to make the product message unambiguously clear in a single picture?

COMPARATIVE JUXTAPOSITION

- What before-and-after comparison could underline the product benefit?
- What can the product be compared with, to make the benefit obvious at a glance?
- What kind of juxtaposition could represent both the problem and the solution in surprising, provocative or humorous terms?
- How can the benefit be communicated by comparing the product with something from a completely unrelated context?

REPETITION AND ACCUMULATION

- How can the product benefit be emphasized by repetition?
- How can repetition attract attention, and represent the problem situation in a witty, provocative or exaggerated way?
- How can the benefit be reinforced by an accumulation of problem situations?

EXAGGERATION

- What exaggeration could represent the benefit more forcefully?:
    - What can be added?
    - Make it bigger? Longer? Heavier? Thicker?
    - Give it added value?
    - Increase the number of components?
    - Multiply by two? By twenty?
    - The sky's the limit?

- What reduction, no matter how extreme, could represent the USP more forcefully?:
    - What can it do without?
    - Make it more compact?
    - Smaller? Shorter? Flatter?
    - More aerodynamic? Lighter?
    - Can the parts be shown separately?

TURN IT RIGHT AROUND

- How can the benefit be depicted by inverting something familiar into its opposite?:
    - Convert the benefit into a disadvantage?
    - Show the negative instead of the positive?
    - Achieve the opposite of the USP?
    - Turn it upside down? Reverse roles?
    - Change the perspective of the people involved?
    - Switch cause and effect?

Omission and suggestion

- What could replace the product? Who or what could take its place in order to focus on the USP?
- How can attention be attracted by omissions in headlines, copy, spoken dialogue or TV spots?
- What can be reduced or removed to emphasize the benefit?
- How can the product be reduced to its essentials?
- How can the product, packaging or benefit be represented, or replaced, by suggestion?

Paradoxes and optical illusions

- How can a paradoxical or contradictory statement emphasize the benefit of a product or service?
- How could an optical illusion represent a product feature visually?
- How can an optical illusion attract attention by making the target group play a game?

Provocation and shock tactics

- How can the product or its benefit be depicted provocatively?
- What has no one else ever associated with this product?
- What would no one dare to say about the product?
- Can you break a taboo, or provoke the target group by other means, to draw attention to the product message?
- How can you use a provocative allusion or double meaning to make the target group think?
- How could the product be depicted to have an especially horrifying or funny effect?
- How could it be made to scandalize or provoke?
- How can shock be used to dramatize the product benefit?

Playing with time

- What effects does time have on the product or the user?
- How will the product change the user's future?
- What possibilities does it open up? How will it affect the way the user now views the past?
- How might the user have had to solve problems previously without the product?
- Where does the new product take the user?
- What can be used from anywhere in history to throw positive light on the USP?
- How can the product be associated with historical events in a way that emphasizes its benefit?
- What vision of the future or futuristic image can help to make a product feature visible at a glance?

A change of perspective

- How can the product be presented from the viewpoint of other creatures, things or events associated with it?
- How can playing with extreme close-up or extreme distance communicate something about the product or service?
- How can the product reveal new perspectives to the target group?
- How can the benefit be presented from the viewpoint of things or creatures affected by it?

Spoofs and parodies

- What opportunities for spoofing or parody does the product offer?

  → *1. Spoofs:* What legends, stories, fairy tales, movie plots, other ads, TV shows etc. can be spoofed by changes of time, place and tone, to put across an idea?

  → *2. Parodies:* What stereotypes, clichés or behaviour patterns can be parodied in connection with the product?

Symbols and signs

- How can the product benefit be represented more simply by symbols or signs?
- How can symbols and signs convey a complete message without words?
- Are there signs or symbols which will communicate a message if inverted or altered?
- What symbols and signs can be combined to generate a new meaning, representing the product advantage?
- What sign language can be used to convey the product message without words?

Come and play

- What kinds of games can you use to get your target group involved: riddles, DIY instructions, something to make (fold/roll up/glue together/look for/draw); quizzes, board games, optical illusions, party games, anything else you can think of?

- What could you do to the medium (press, poster, direct mail, banner etc.) to turn it into a toy?

- What witty, provocative or intriguing instructions could you use to get your target group to play?

Telling stories

- What everyday situations could you develop around the product to show its advantages in the best light? What sort of story could involve the product as best friend or partner? In what everyday situation could it attract attention in a provocative way? In what situation could it become a star, a lifesaver or a helper? In what everyday story could it make people laugh?

- Which of the following dramatic styles would be best for presenting the product strength in an everyday situation or story?
  Horror
  Thriller
  Adventure
  Slapstick
  Comedy
  Action
  Costume
  Love story
  Drama
  Soap opera
  Documentary
  News
  Chat show

Absurd, surreal, bizarre

- What is the most surreal or absurd idea that would put the brand or benefit centre-stage?
- What absurd or bizarre ideas can the product be associated with?
- What is the most bizarre use for the product?
- What stylistic conventions can you use to spin the most absurd story possible around the product?
- What is the best way to represent the benefit within a surreal or fantastic situation?

Take it literally

○ What images do you get if you take descriptions of the product benefit literally?

○ What ideas or statements about the product can be taken literally in order to generate witty, satirical or flippant visual images?

○ What idioms or verbal metaphors can be taken literally?

○ How can slogans, common expressions, keywords or text associated with the product be converted literally into pictures?

○ What slang phrases, metaphors or turns of phrase could be translated literally into a visual image that will get the product or service noticed?

○ Are there any names, acronyms, slogans or other verbal concepts that can have a double meaning if taken literally?

Alter the product

○ How could the product be depicted differently to best communicate its benefit?:

    Change its shape?

    Change its use?

    Change its location?

    Combine it with things from nature or technology?

    Alter the way it looks, moves, sounds, smells?

    Can you change anything else?

○ How could the product be altered to communicate the benefit at a metaphorical level?

○ How could the product be altered to communicate one particular feature by overstatement?

Alternative uses

○ Where else could the product be used so as to communicate its USP clearly?

○ Can you imagine ways in which the product can be used in new and different contexts?:

    By other people or target groups?

    In unexpected situations?

    In a different environment?

○ How could the product itself represent its benefit or the problem situation?

○ What unorthodox ways of using the product would give a striking demonstration of its USP?

Double meanings

○ What opportunities for ambiguity, double meanings or wordplay are there in the words you use to describe the benefit?

○ How can the benefit be illustrated in a picture with a double meaning?

○ What verbal ambiguities emerge from the brief, in slogans or taglines, product descriptions, or from discussion in meetings?

○ Describe the product, without naming it, in such a way as to produce double meanings of the following types:

    Obscene

    Sexually suggestive

    Provocative

    Attacking (the rival product)

    Playful

    Reckless

    Paradoxical

    Witty

Play with words

○ How can you play with the typography to represent the USP in an effective visual image?

○ How can words, symbols or logos be integrated into the picture without using the usual typographic techniques?

○ How can the central advertising message be reinforced by altering the typography?

○ How can words be integrated into the picture in an unusual way, attracting attention and underlining the central advertising statement?

IN THE BEGINNING WAS THE WORD

With the following KickStart questions, get help from reference books:
dictionaries of quotations, popular idioms, sayings, proverbs or graffiti.

○ What sayings or proverbs does the product or its USP make you think of?

○ What sayings might other people think of: your grandparents,
politicians, housewives, etc.?

○ Can you make these sayings or proverbs seem unfamiliar, or take on a
new meaning that involves the USP? For example: Truth will pout;
Where there's a will, I'm away; Every crowd has a silver lining.

○ Can the proverb be turned into its opposite? For example, 'The early
bird catches the worm' could be 'The early bird misses the worm'.

○ What quotations does the product suggest to you? What quotations
from other areas: politics, art, everyday life, the media? What quotations
from current celebrities might be borrowed?

○ Can you think of any appropriate graffiti? Are there any famous passages
of dialogue from films, plays or novels, or well-known running gags
from TV series that you could use?

→ *Everyday language*

Listen to how people talk: what common jargon, dialect or slang phrases
would describe the product perfectly?

How would the ordinary man in the street describe the USP? Or someone
cool? What slang does it suggest to you? Run through the following
examples:

An old lady

A lawyer

A child

One of the target group, etc.

→ *Taglines*

○ What tagline can you develop around your goal or the product?
Formulate the tagline like a book title and try to derive ideas from it.
Sample 'titles' could include:

'The Art of Travel'

'100 Ways to Build a House'

'The Shortest Route to Money'

'Make your Home a Castle'

→ *Wordplay*

○ Can you construct rhymes, puns or other kinds of wordplay from the
product or brand, which will underline the USP? Collect terms relating
to the product or its benefit and try them out as answers to the
following questions:

○ What sounds like the terms that describe the product? Can wordplay,
puns, rhymes or other verbal jokes be developed from them? Can
they be combined or rhymed with words from foreign languages?

○ What contradictions do descriptions of the product provoke?
What images occur to you if you think about oxymorons like
'eloquent silence', 'bittersweet'?

○ Can compound terms be split up and used in meaningful new
combinations with other product descriptions?

○ Can these compound terms be reversed? For example, 'heartsweet'
from 'sweetheart'?

○ Give the product a nickname, or find a pet name for it. Spell the name
wrong! Invent a word for the USP.

REFRAMING

- How can you alter the frame or context from within which events are seen, and so change their meaning?
- Is there a larger or different frame or context within which the product will acquire a new and positive value?
- Is there a context in which seemingly negative aspects acquire a positive meaning?
- Is there another context within which the product would be startling or surprising?
- Can you attach a new label with positive overtones to forms of behaviour, events or objects, in order to reveal new and interesting perspectives?

METAPHOR AND ANALOGY

- What metaphors or analogies can be found in nature or technology that will represent the brand or benefit at a glance: the brand is like X?

- What can the product or its USP be compared with?
  What looks like it or works on a similar principle?
  What parallels can be drawn?
  What visual images do these metaphors and analogies suggest?
  What other ideas does the product suggest?
  What could you take as a model?

- How can you represent a new product by comparing it with something familiar, so that the benefit is immediately obvious?
- How can metaphor or analogy present a problem situation so that it can be seen at a glance and needs no explanation?

BREAK OUT OF THE FRAME

- How can the advertising medium be actively involved in the message, in order to make the benefit immediately apparent?
- How can the context of the medium be integrated into the message in a meaningful way?
- How can standard media be altered to give the benefit more impact?
- How can the medium be involved in the message in a playful and intelligent way?

ALTERNATIVE MEDIA

- How could an outsize installation be used to tell a story about a product in the open air or in a large space?
- How can an outdoor site be used in a fun way to attract and involve the attention of passers-by?
- How can an advertising message be integrated into an everyday location in an attention-grabbing way?
- What everyday objects could be used for advertising, to put the message across in an amusing or original way?
- What unconventional ad formats could be used to grab your target group's attention?
- What familiar places or objects can you use for your ad to attract attention in a provocative way?

As the following examples show, stories can be told in an effective way without using words. Key elements are deployed in the picture in such a way that they say more about the product than is actually seen. Many of these pictorial messages work because they invite the viewers, by omission or suggestion, to complete the story for themselves, using their own store of experience. Viewers are motivated to work out the meaning in their own heads, which leads to a positive 'Aha' experience. These examples show that non-verbal advertising doesn't always have to use metaphorical pictorial language. Look at these ads and try to work out which factors put the message across, without using either words or pictorial metaphors.

Client Mercedes-Benz
Agency Leo Burnett Ltd, London
Creative Direction Nick Bell
Art Direction Mark Tutssel
Photo Russell Porcas

KickStart question: How can a positive aspect of the product be suggested without words?

Client Bic
Agency TBWA Hunt Lascaris, Johannesburg
Creative Direction Clare McNally
Art Direction Jan Jacobs
Photo David Prior

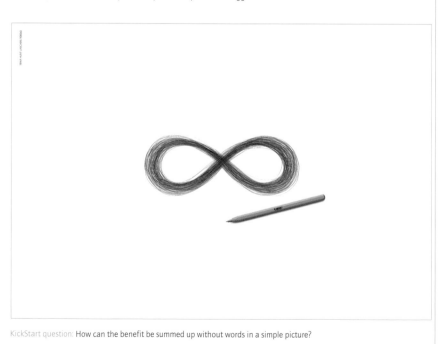

KickStart question: How can the benefit be summed up without words in a simple picture?

This campaign for bottled beer uses the tagline
'Reassuringly Expensive'.
Client Interbrew UK – Stella Artois
Agency Lowe Lintas, London
Creative Direction Charles Inge
Art Direction/Copy Mick Mahoney, Andy Amadeo
Photo Jenny van Sommers

KickStart question: How can simple images tell
a story which is left to the viewer to complete?

Client Ford
Agency Ogilvy & Mather, Amsterdam
Creative Direction Willem van Harrewijen
Art Direction Jeroen Peters, Kees Rijken
Photo Boudewijn Smit

De Maverick 4x4.

KickStart question: How can the benefit be portrayed without words, and without showing the product?

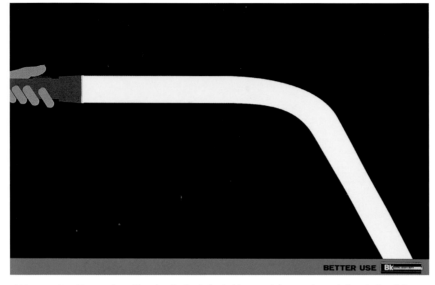

Client Bk Batteries
Agency Grey Worldwide, Shanghai
Creative Direction Bok, Larry Ong
Art Direction Bok, Larry Ong
Illustration Bok
Source Lürzer's Archive 4/2000

KickStart question: How can the problem situation be depicted without words in a way that underlines the benefit?

Client Pepsi
Agency BBDO Canada, Toronto
Creative Direction Michael McLaughlin,
Jack Neary, Scott Dube
Art Direction Scott Dube
Copy Ian MacKellar
Photo Philip Rostron

KickStart question: How can the appeal of a product be depicted effectively without words?

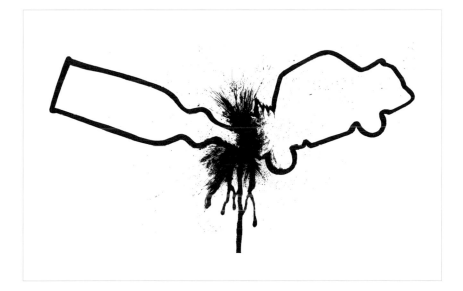

Client Don't Drink & Drive
Agency Leo Burnett, Warsaw
Creative Direction Darek Wojciechowski
Art Direction Darek Wojciechowski
Illustration Darek Wojciechowski

KickStart question: How can a simple visual image depict a problem situation strikingly?

Exercise

SIGNS AND PICTOGRAMS

In the following exercise, try to translate simple statements, commands and information into a pictorial language that can be internationally understood. The aim is to reduce a message to a sign or a pictogram by minimizing the information, as in the examples on the left. Notice that it's not always possible to summarize a message in a simple picture without words. But use the exercise to train your ability to convert statements quickly into non-verbal symbols – this will boost your creativity. Incidentally, the strategy is also very helpful when you are trying to come up with real ideas for logos, intended to communicate something about a company or what it does.

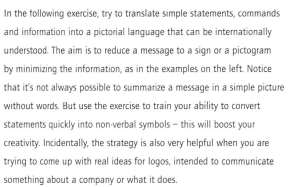

A PICTURE IS WORTH A THOUSAND WORDS

The object of this little exercise is to display the central advertising statement about a product at a glance and without using words. It's best to start by working out a goal with a single-minded proposition. For example: 'How can we show without words that this new sports car accelerates faster than any other car?' In practice, the goal is always dependent on the parameters of the brief and ought to be targeted around the product's strategic positioning.

With this single-minded proposition in mind, and following the DreamTeam rules, start looking for a pictorial way to represent 'acceleration'. The key question is: 'What are the key features of "acceleration" and how can they be represented pictorially, without words?' Here again, you should develop as many ideas as you can – don't give up after the first ten.

You can also extend this exercise to TV spots. How can the product's usefulness be depicted in a story without words? Think of the era of silent movies and how ingenious the actors had to be to convey complex situations and feelings without words. Jokes which don't need words are another fruitful source of non-verbal stories to tell.

Client Renault Portuguesa
Agency Publicis, Lisbon
Creative Direction Filipe Lourenço
Art Direction Paulo Martins
Copy Nuno Jerónimo
Photo Renault Stock Image

The goal of these KickStart questions is to represent the central advertising statement clearly and convincingly by combining or associating different things. This method of developing visual advertising messages is one of the most frequently used today and offers infinite possibilities. Try it for yourself – there are no limits in your imagination.

'Creativity is meaning through synthesis.' Dr Myron Allen

Client Johnson's
Agency DPZ Propaganda, São Paulo
Creative Direction Rui Branquinho
Art Direction Claudia Issa
Photo Roberto Donaire

KickStart question: How can the problem and solution be combined to make the product message unambiguously clear in a single picture?

Client GM
Agency Mullen Advertising Inc., Wenham, MA
Creative Direction Stephen Mietelski
Art Direction Mike Ancevic
Photo Bruce Peterson, Stuart Hall

KickStart question: What different things can be linked together to show the benefit in a picture?

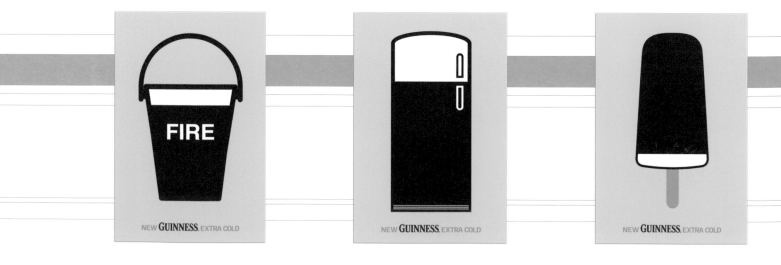

Client Sony
Agency Del Campo Nazca Saatchi & Saatchi,
Buenos Aires
Creative Direction Estaban Pigni
Art Direction Mariano Favetto
Photo Daniel Ackerman
Illustration Mario Franco

KickStart question: What can be associated
with the product to communicate its features
on a metaphorical level?

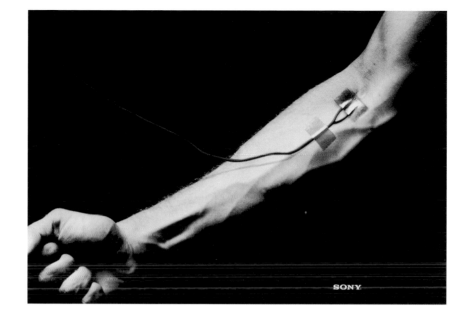

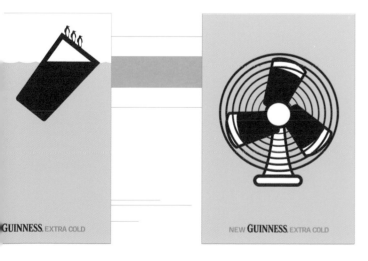

Client Guinness
Agency Abbott Mead Vickers BBDO, London
Creative Direction Peter Souter
Art Direction Jeremy Carr
Copy Jeremy Carr
Illustration John Rogers

KickStart question: What can be associated with the
product to emphasize its special features?

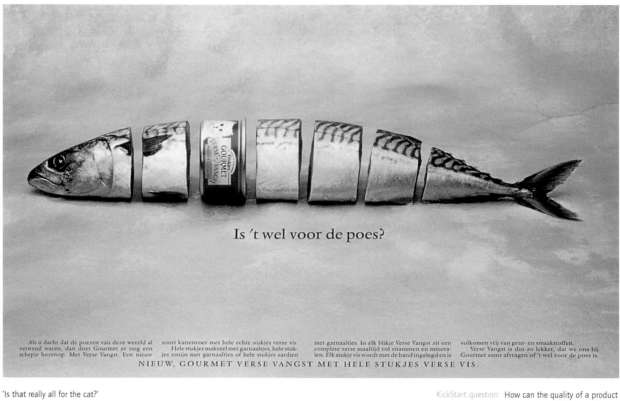

Is 't wel voor de poes?

Als u dacht dat de poezen van deze wereld al   soort kattenvoer met hele echte stukjes verse vis.   met garnaaltjes. In elk blikje Verse Vangst zit een   volkomen vrij van geur- en smaakstoffen.
verwend waren, dan doet Gourmet er nog een   Hele stukjes makreel met garnaaltjes, hele stuk-   complete verse maaltijd vol vitaminen en minera-   Verse Vangst is dus zo lekker, dat we ons bij
schepje bovenop. Met Verse Vangst. Een nieuw   jes tonijn met garnaaltjes of hele stukjes sardien   len. Elk stukje vis wordt met de hand ingelegd en is   Gourmet soms afvragen of 't wel voor de poes is.

NIEUW, GOURMET VERSE VANGST MET HELE STUKJES VERSE VIS.

'Is that really all for the cat?'   KickStart question: How can the quality of a product
Client Gourmet   be represented by combining things?
Agency Lowe Lintas, Amsterdam
Creative Direction Machteld van der Gaag
Peter van der Wijk
Art Direction Joep de Kart
Photo John Parker

TOBACCO KILLS MORE THAN HEROINE AND COCAINE **TOGETHER.**

Client Fundação Portuguesa de Cardiologia   KickStart question: What two things can be combined to make a third?
Agency Young & Rubicam Portugal, Lisbon
Creative Direction Jorge Teixeira, Luis Christello
Photo Ana Urban

Client Coca-Cola
Agency McCann-Erickson, Madrid
Creative Direction Juan Nonzioli
Art Direction Rebeca Díaz
Photo Sara Zorraquino

KickStart question: What things can be combined to represent the benefit in a humorous way?

Client Kelty Cubbs
Agency BOC Advertising, Portland, OR
Designer Jeff Pollard
Art Direction Dan Cox
Illustration Jeff Pollard

Client American Sommelier Association
Designer Jon Rohrer, Flux Labs, Philadelphia
Art Direction Jon Rohrer, Prilla Rohrer
Illustration Jon Rohrer

Client Michigan Humane Society
Designer Lynn Simoncini, Lori Soenen
Art Direction Lynn Simoncini;
Bozell Detroit

Pet
Education
Center

COMBINATION AS A CREATIVE STRATEGY

One of the most important creative strategies is to combine two concepts or objects that were previously unconnected, so as to produce something completely new. The result should be a simple, unambiguous advertising message. For example, try to combine the following elements in such a way as to make the benefit immediately apparent: the product, parts of the product, people from the target group, the product's raw materials, the original problem, the benefit, the context, plants, packaging, or people who have nothing to do with it. The less the things you combine have to do with each other originally, the more exciting and surprising the result will be. Treat it as a game and try absolutely everything.

Exercise

'The difference between before and after equals the value of the product.'

Comparative juxtapositions such as 'before and after' are undoubtedly some of the classics of advertising. But as the examples on the following pages demonstrate, there's always space for brilliant ideas. The questions in this section are intended to dramatize the product by means of comparative juxtaposition of the benefit and the problem situation. The comparison doesn't always have to be obvious, however; it can also refer to something quite remote, and so generate a certain tension, rather similar to the effect of a joke.

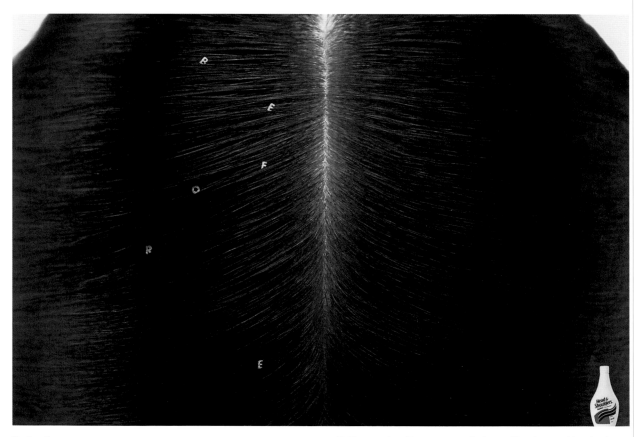

'B-e-f-o-r-e'
Client Head & Shoulders
Agency Saatchi & Saatchi, Singapore
Creative Direction Craig Davis
Art Direction Edmund Choe
Photo The Shooting Gallery

KickStart question: How can comparative juxtaposition show a problem situation and its solution?

Client Lee
Agency Fallon Worldwide, Minneapolis
Creative Direction Buck Holzemer
Art Direction Bob Barrie
Photo Chad Peterson

KickStart question: How can the benefit be
shown in a picture, using comparison?

Campaign for the women's lingerie
department of a major store
Client El Corte Inglés
Agency Publicis Casadevall Pedreño & PRG,
Barcelona
Creative Direction Xavi García
Art Direction Ramón Roda, Maico García
Copy Xavi García
Photo Sisco Soler

KickStart question: How can the product be
represented humorously, using comparative
juxtaposition?

Double billboard for a laundry firm
Client 5àSec Laundry Services
Agency Opal Publicidade S.A., Portugal
Creative Direction & Art Direction
Susana Salvado Leal, José Luiz Dantas

KickStart question: How can playful use
of the medium create a comparative
juxtaposition that communicates the benefit
in an unambiguous way?

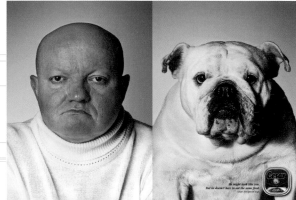

'She might look like you, but she doesn't have to eat the same food.'
Client Effem, Cesar
Agency Almap, BBDO Comunicações, São Paulo
Creative Direction Roberto Pereira, Marcello Serpa
Art Direction Luis Sanches, Valdir Bianchi
Photo Manolo Moran

KickStart question: How can a comparison that focuses on the high quality of the product seize viewers' attention?

Client Vileda
Agency Leo Burnett, Lisbon
Creative Direction Gezo Marques
Art Direction João Ribeiro, Leandro Alvarez
Photo Picto

KickStart question: How can the benefit be communicated by comparing the product with something from a completely unrelated context?

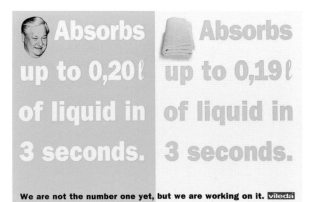

'Before' and 'After'
Client Bio
Agency New Deal DDB, Oslo
Creative Direction Erik Hersoug
Art Direction Morten Kristiansen
Photo Denise Grünstein, Anders Thessing

KickStart question: How can the benefit be communicated by a metaphorical comparison?

This witty TV spot compares a cartoon hero
with naked reality.
Client Cartoon Network
Agency Wieden & Kennedy, London
Creative Direction Toni Barry
Art Direction Anthony Sperduti
Director Ringan Ledwidge
Production Harry Nash

Ad for a computer game which offers
two coupons to choose from
Client Command & Conquer
Agency Banks Hoggins O'Shea FCB, London
Creative Direction Rob Fletcher
Art Direction Rob Fletcher
Copy David Alexander
Photo Zed Nelson

KickStart question: How can comparative
juxtaposition be used to reinforce
the benefit?

Client Sunsations Sunglass Company
Agency Fallon Worldwide, Minneapolis
Creative Direction Tina Hall
Art Direction Bob Brihn
Illustration Craig Perman

After.
(you don't wanna see before)

SUNSATIONS SUNGLASS COMPANY

Technique

COMPARATIVE JUXTAPOSITION AS A SOURCE OF IDEAS

To tap into new sources of inspiration for comparisons, you can use the following method to compose typical pairs of opposites, like 'before and after', which can then be used to stimulate advertising ideas. First of all, you should once again work out a goal and make a note of the key terms that describe the benefit.

For example, the most obvious terms for a pair of fashion sunglasses might be the following: fashionable, vision, dark, attractive, value for money, eye-catching, exclusive, and so on. Now list the pairs of opposites:

- fashionable – old-fashioned
- vision – blindness
- dark – dazzling
- attractive – ugly
- value for money – expensive
- eye-catching – inconspicuous
- exclusive – mass-produced

Now use these opposites in the team as stimuli in the search for ideas. Let yourselves be inspired by the tension between the antitheses and give your imagination a chance to lift off. If these pairs of words don't give you enough of an impulse, use terms that take you onto an abstract plane. The following list might work just as well for the topic of 'fashion sunglasses', and could be extended to include several thousand pairs of opposites if necessary.

→ *A few comparative opposites:*

- winner – loser
- New York – Beijing
- heaven – hell
- accelerator – brake
- wrinkled – smooth
- beautiful – ugly
- functioning – broken
- animal – human
- commonplace – rare
- cheap – expensive
- sunshine – rain
- past – future
- yes – no

Repetition attracts the most attention when it's enhanced by a puzzling variation. This kind of variation is achieved by disrupting a regularly repeated pattern: for example, when there is a stain on a clean piece of fabric, the viewer's perception is jolted and their attention is focused on that spot. Repetition and accumulation can of course also be used to tell stories, overstate the benefit, or present new proofs of the USP in concrete terms. Let the KickStart questions in this section inspire you to find new ways of communicating your product message. The examples on the following pages show only a small part of what can be achieved through repetition and accumulation.

Variations in visual patterns attract attention. You can also reach the other senses by disrupting a repetitive pattern in a similar way.

'There is one pleasure you can enjoy as many times as you like. No limits.'
Client Nestlé
Agency McCann-Erickson, Barcelona
Creative Direction Josep M. Ferrara
Art Direction Xavi Cubero
Copy Josep M. Ferrara, Sergi Zapater
Photo Josep Maria Roca

KickStart question: How can repetition be used to show the benefit visually?

'Tibet is occupied. By China. Your concern can keep Tibet alive. Swiss-Tibetan Friendship Society.'
Client Free Tibet
Agency Euro RSCG, Zurich
Creative Direction Frank Bodin
Art Direction Dany Bieri

KickStart question: How can repetition attract attention and represent the problem situation in a striking way?

La nouvelle Renault Espace invente la climatisation personnalisée

'The new Renault Espace introduces personal air-conditioning.'

Client Renault
Agency Publicis, Brussels
Creative Direction Gilles de Bruyère
Art Direction Fred Dawlat,
Jean-Marc Wachsmann
Photo Frank Uyttenhove

KickStart question: How can repetition of a metaphor be used to portray the benefit in a picture?

Campaign for a brand of surfing wear and equipment

Client Nobrand
Agency BBDO CNUAC, Shanghai
Creative Direction Tony Liu
Art Direction Tony Liu, Tao Lei
Photo H. Richard Johnston, Jeff Divine,
Ron Whitby

KickStart question: How can accumulation or repetition depict the product image in an attention-grabbing way?

CHOISIR VISUAL, C'EST DÉJÀ Y VOIR CLAIR.

350 OPTICIENS EN FRANCE

'If you choose Visual, you're already seeing more clearly.'
Campaign for a chain of French opticians.

Client Visual
Agency Euro RSCG Scher Lafarge, Paris
Creative Direction Jean-Christophe Royer
Art Direction Christophe Caubel
Photo Malcom Venville

The 'Fitness for Health' logo uses the repeated symbol for a heartbeat to lead directly into a symbol for jogging.

Agency Good Dog Studio
Designer Richard Barnes

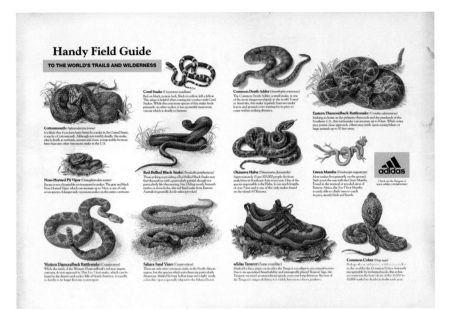

Client Adidas
Agency Leagas Delaney, San Francisco
Creative Direction Matt Rivitz
Art Direction Steve Mapp
Illustration Barbara Ambler

KickStart question: How can
the benefit be reinforced by an
accumulation of problem situations?

A meteor
virus
aerial killer
bad-ass alien is about to destroy the world.

Bruce Willis
Kevin Costner
Mel Gibson
Arnold Schwarzenegger tries to save mankind,

but he's stopped by a corrupt senator
the CIA
the FBI
the Mafia.

Fighting against the trauma of Vietnam
alcoholism
technology
the corrupt senator's seductive secretary,

he's able, after blowing up the mother ship
the comet
the whole neighborhood
the corrupt senator's car,

to save the world.

And, at the end, he gets a kiss from Julia Roberts
kiss from Meg Ryan
kiss from Sandra Bullock
hug from the President of the USA.

Cult
Hey, see an original movie.

Client Cult Movies
Agency Almap, BBDO Comunicações,
São Paulo
Creative Direction Eugenio Mohallem,
Marcello Serpa
Art Direction José Carlos Lollo
Copy Cassio Zanatta
Photo Eduardo Rodrigues

KickStart question: How can you use
accumulation to grab attention and
advertise the product in an
entertaining way?

Exaggeration in the depiction of features of the product, problem situations or solutions can grab the viewer's attention and emphasize the benefit. With the following KickStart questions, use distortion and overstatement to develop great ideas. Make sure that the message is clear and simple, to avoid any misunderstandings that would lead the target group to make negative associations. Don't have any qualms about exaggerating things, but do it with a wink so that the credibility of your message doesn't suffer.

Client Volkswagen South Africa
Agency Ogilvy & Mather Rightford
Searle-Tripp & Makin, Cape Town
Creative Direction Greg Burke
Art Direction Jonathan Lang
Copy Wynne Lubbe
Photo Jan Verboom

WIDESCREEN TV | **THOMSON**

Client Thomson
Agency Impiric, Singapore
Art Direction Koh Kuan Eng
Copy Evelyn Tan, Amish Mehta
Photo John Clang

KickStart question: How can the benefit be shown at a glance by making something radically larger or smaller?

Client Epson
Agency OgilvyOne Worldwide, Bangkok
Creative Direction Gumpon Laksanajinda, Wisit Lumsiricharoenchoke
Art Direction Saravuth Sadsananaud
Illustration Kamarart
Photo Isara Studio

KickStart question: How can the effects of one product feature be exaggerated in order to emphasize the benefit in a witty way?

THE ALL NEW ⊕ TOYOTA LANDCRUISER. NOW WITH V8 POWER.

Client Toyota Motor Corporation
Agency Saatchi & Saatchi, Sydney
Creative Direction Michael Newman
Art Direction Paul Bennell, Jay Furb
Photo Simon Harsent

KickStart question How can exaggeration
be used to show the benefit in a way that
is both witty and attention-grabbing?

Client Onergy
Agency SSC & B Lintas, Mumbai
Creative Direction Vikram Gaikwad
Art Direction Raj Kamble
Photo Prasad Naik

KickStart question How can the benefit
be exaggerated through suggestion?

Onergy
For enhanced vigour and vitality.

'The kind of suspension only Citroën
know how to make.'
Client Citroën
Agency Benjamens van Doorn
Euro RSCG, Amsterdam
Creative Direction Aad Kuyper
Art Direction Cor den Boer
Photo Peter Boudestein

KickStart question How might
exaggerated evidence support the
ad's claims for the benefit?

'Engine Benefits: Phenomenal towing power.'
Client Polaris
Agency Carmichael Lynch Inc., Minneapolis
Creative Direction Glen Wachowiak
Art Direction Brian Kroening
Photo Phil Aarrestad

KickStart question What could be
exaggerated to prove the benefit?

Client Snack Ventures Europe
Agency Tiempo/BBDO, Barcelona
Creative Direction Siscu Molina
Art Direction Jordi Comas
Photo Leandre Escorsell

KickStart question How can the effects of
a product feature be exaggerated so much
that words are unnecessary?

Doing the opposite of what people expect not only opens the door to new and interesting ideas, it can also lead to surprises. Stand things on their heads and do the opposite of the usual, put the last thing first, turn something inside out, make a big thing small or vice versa, make beauty look ugly and ugliness beautiful. Take features of the product, its benefit, packaging, or function, and turn them into their opposites. Work with these KickStart questions in the team and you may think of things that are completely different from the examples shown: it doesn't matter as long as you have fun and come up with great ideas.

The Vitamin Supplement for Animals with Nutritional Deficiencies.

Client FCL Laboratories
Agency TBWA, Barcelona
Creative Direction Xavi Munill
Art Direction Tomas Descals

Client Whiskas
Agency BBDO Portugal, Lisbon
Creative Direction Jorge Teixeira
Art Direction Marco Dias
Copy Vasco Condessa
Photo Miguel Fonseca da Costa,
Nuno Calado

KickStart question: How can a benefit
be represented by showing the opposite
of what people expect?

Charity campaign for the protection of
the Brazilian rainforests
Client S.O.S. Mata Atlântica
Agency F/Nazca S&S, São Paulo
Art Direction Marco Aurélio Monteiro
Copy Wilson Mateos
Photo Rodrigo Ribeiro

KickStart question: How can a problem
situation be dramatized by switching
cause and effect?

'You'll also get money from us ... when
nothing happens to you.' Campaign for
an insurance company.
Client Schweizerische Mobiliar
Agency Publicis, Zurich
Creative Direction Jean Etienne Aebi
Art Direction René Sennhauser
Copy Matthias Freuler
Photo Nicolas Monkewitz

KickStart question: How can the benefit
be illustrated at a glance by standing the
situation on its head?

'4 Chips'
Client Heinz
Agency Leo Burnett, Paris
Creative Direction Christophe Coffre,
Nicolas Taubes
Art Direction Pascal Hirsch
Copy Axel Orliac, Laurent Drevet
Photo Pascal Hirsch

KickStart question: How can the benefit be
illustrated by transposition and exaggeration?

'Undressed'
Client Levi Strauss & Co
Agency Bartle Bogle Hegarty, London
Creative Direction Bruce Crouch
Art Direction Shawn Sutoles,
Matthew Saunby
Copy Adam Chaippe, Shawn Preston
Production Outsider Ltd, London

KickStart question: How can an everyday
situation be reversed to produce a new
and surprising result?

Client Lexus
Agency Saatchi & Saatchi, London
Art Direction Greg Martin
Copy Mike McKenna
Director Peter Thwaites
Production Gorgeous Enterprises, London

KickStart question How can reversal produce
an unexpected twist in a story and reinforce
the product image?

A young boy cycles through the neighbourhood, through the garden gate and
up to the house where the new Lexus is parked. Reverently, he gets off his bike,
approaches the car with sponge and bucket, and begins to wash and polish it with
great zeal, one piece at a time. He does not miss the radiator grille, the tyres or
the wing mirrors. We see the neighbour cast a swift glance on the scene from the
house. When he's done, the boy surveys his work with pride and goes to the door to
ring the bell. The door opens, a man appears and the boy looks at him expectantly.
But instead of receiving a well-deserved payment, the boy puts his hand in his
pocket, takes out a banknote, and presses it gratefully into the man's hand.

A pair of young lovers are wrestling naked on the couch when she begins to pull
a rolled-up sock over his foot (it almost looks like a condom). In the next frames,
the couple proceed to dress each other, one piece of clothing after another, in a
highly erotic way. They are standing there clothed when the door suddenly opens
and the parents enter the room unexpectedly, naked. They are shocked to discover
their daughter with a man, fully dressed. At the last moment, the mother puts her
hand protectively over her small son's eyes.

Pauses give music life, covering up can be more erotic than baring all, and jokes often rely on missing lines that the listener has to supply. If you want to underline or emphasize something, you can often do it by omission. The fact that information is missing involves the viewers by forcing them to play an active part in uncovering what is hidden. The questions in this section use omission and suggestion to generate excitement and attention.

INCOMPLETE INFORMATION

The optical illusion on the right shows how we supply missing information almost automatically, using either existing knowledge or our imaginations. What is omitted ought to challenge the viewer, but not enough to stop

them from completing the picture. In spite of giving minimal information, the circles invite the viewer's imagination to provide a three-dimensional 'phantom image' of a cube. Many people also get the impression that the cube is in front of the grey circles.

Client Louwman & Parqui
(Toyota The Netherlands)
Agency Adera Nederland,
Amsterdam
Creative Direction
Maarten van der Spoel,
Michael van Heusden
Art Direction
Michael van Heusden
Photo Jaap Vliegenthart

illenniu

It just won't be complete without

Client Mars
Agency FHV/BBDO, Amsterdam
Creative Direction Marcel Groen
Art Direction Martijn Andriessen,
Martijn Vandewerf

KickStart question: How can attention be
attracted through omissions in headlines,
copy, spoken dialogue or TV spots?

The address of a dentists' surgery appears in
the gap between the teeth.
Client Campos/Kurzhals
Agency Publicis Casadevall Pedreno & PRG,
Barcelona
Creative Direction Xavi Garcia
Art Direction Ramón Roda
Photo Ramón Eguiguren, Antón Eguiguren

KickStart question: How can omission be used to
underline the usefulness of a product or service?

Campaign for a sushi restaurant
Client Jappa Sushi
Agency Young & Rubicam Portugal, Lisbon
Creative Direction Jorge Teixeira, Luis Christello
Art Direction Marcelo Medeiros
Copy João Castanho
Photo Paulo David

KickStart question: How can omission contribute
to the description of the product or a service?

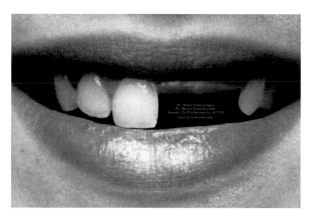

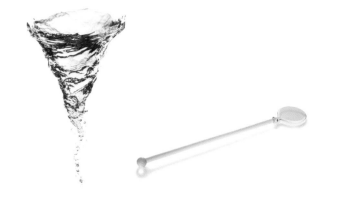

NO IMPERFECTIONS

Client UDV, Smirnoff
Agency J. Walter Thompson, London
Creative Direction Jaspar Shelbourne
Art Direction Ken Grimshaw
Copy John Donnelly
Photo Gary Bryan

KickStart question: How can omission be used to excite the imagination or stimulate curiosity?

Client Philip Morris
Agency TBWA Werbeagentur GmbH, Berlin
Creative Direction Tommy Mayer, Rainer Bollmann
Art Direction Martina Traut, Roland Gehrmann
Photo Hans Kroeskamp

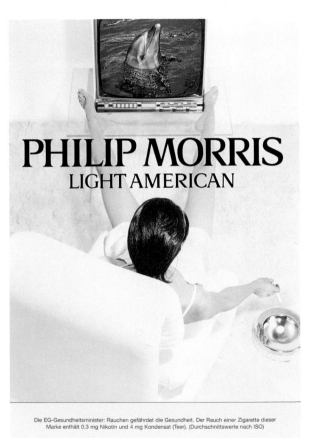

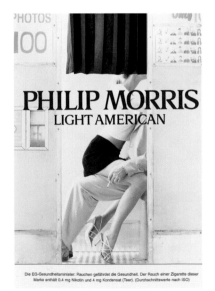

Die EG-Gesundheitsminister: Rauchen gefährdet die Gesundheit. Der Rauch einer Zigarette dieser Marke enthält 0,4 mg Nikotin und 4 mg Kondensat (Teer). (Durchschnittswerte nach ISO)

Die EG-Gesundheitsminister: Rauchen gefährdet die Gesundheit. Der Rauch einer Zigarette dieser Marke enthält 0,3 mg Nikotin und 4 mg Kondensat (Teer). (Durchschnittswerte nach ISO)

KickStart question: How can the product, packaging or benefit be represented, or replaced, by suggestion?

Campaign for liquid hand soap and towels
Client Lava
Agency Phillips-Ramsey Company, San Diego
Creative Direction Tony Durket
Art Direction Nathan Naylor
Copy Art Bradshaw
Photo Paul Beauchamp

KickStart question: How can suggestion or omission
represent the benefit in a striking image?

Client Japan Lighting Design
Agency Dentsu Inc., Tokyo
Creative Direction Yuji Tokuda
Art Direction Yuji Tokuda
Photo Takashi Seo

KickStart question: How can suggestion
or omission portray the benefit in an
aesthetically pleasing or other unusual way?

'Freezer by Noah' / 'Freezer by Dracula'
Client Bacardi/Martini
Agency BBDO Portugal, Lisbon
Creative Direction Pedro Bidarra
Art Direction Marco Dias
Copy Rui Bernardo
Photo João Palmeiro

KickStart question: How can suggestion
be used to tell a story about a product?

Campaign for a correction roller
Client Penol
Agency Geelmuyden Kiese, Oslo
Creative Direction Kristian Haagen
Art Direction Rikke Fabricius,
Kristian Haagen
Copy Rikke Fabricius, Kristian Haagen
Illustration Chris Gosling

KickStart question: How can omission be
used to give information about the product
in a witty or provocative way?

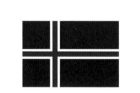

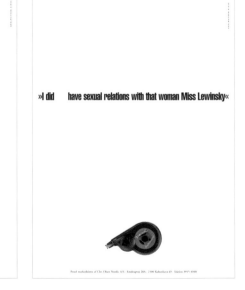

»I did   have sexual relations with that woman Miss Lewinsky«

If you really enjoy theoretical models, here's an attempt to represent paradox in a way anyone can understand, in one sentence: a paradox is when the very existence of a thing negates the conditions that make that existence possible: 'I'm lying!'

How about another explanation? A paradox is a statement which, although proceeding from logical and truthful premises, nevertheless ends in a contradiction. Somewhat easier to take in is the category of 'hidden command', which fits into the same general field as paradox. In order to obey the command 'Do NOT imagine a big, black sheepdog!', you must do exactly what it tells you not to: you conjure up the image of a big black sheepdog in your head, only to negate or obliterate it afterwards. 'Dilemma situations' also belong in this area. These appear to offer alternatives, but no matter what you do they always lead to the same conclusion. One splendid example is the mother who gives her son two ties for his birthday. The next day the son puts one of them on and goes to visit his mother proudly wearing it, but when she sees it, all she says is 'Oh, I see, you don't like the other one'. Could you find a way out of that dilemma? Here are a few more examples of paradox:

- I can resist everything except temptation.
- Eubulides the Cretan says all Cretans are liars.
- The intoxication of sobriety.
- Everything begins where everything ends.
- Laughter is a serious matter.
- Only the present lasts for ever.
- Moderation should not be taken to excess.
- Living means dying.
- There are no mistakes in this book except this one.

'I don't care to belong to any club that will have me as a member.'
Groucho Marx

'Buildings cleaned'
Client Werner Tomasi, plasterers
Agency Michael Conrad & Leo Burnett, Frankfurt
Creative Direction Uwe Marquardt, Kerrin Nausch
Art Direction Michael Schacht
Copy Jens Kessinger
Typography Uwe Marquardt

Campaign for surfing equipment
Client Nobrand
Agency BBDO Shanghai

KickStart question: How can a paradoxical
or contradictory statement reinforce the
product image?

Annoy the neighbour.
Turn it down.

fm 102

Client Jfm
Agency Leagas Delaney, London
Creative Direction Roger Pearce
Art Direction David Hieatt, Tony Barry

KickStart question: How can a paradoxical
or contradictory statement emphasize the
benefit of a product or service?

*Some of these examples
are not paradoxes in the
strictest sense but could be
colloquially called paradoxes
because they contain an
internal contradiction.*

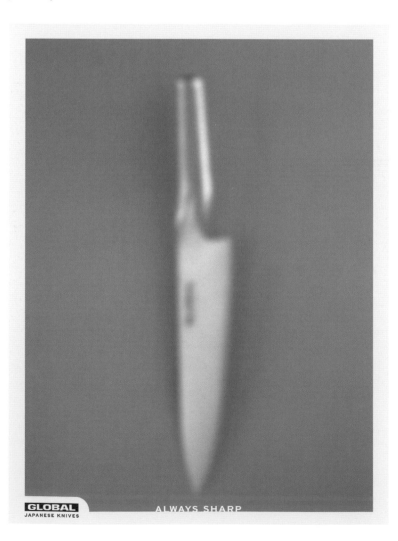

GLOBAL
JAPANESE KNIVES
ALWAYS SHARP

Client Global
Agency Bates Scandinavia, Copenhagen
Creative Direction Jacob Blom
Art Direction Jens Thomsen, Calus Mollebro
Photo Christian Stahr

KickStart question: How can a paradox
drive the benefit home?

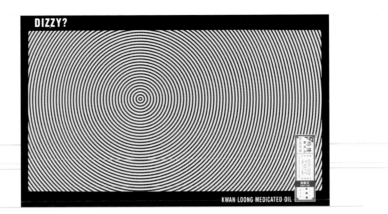

'No one will complain about your loud muffler again.'
Campaign for car stereo equipment.
Client Nitro Jensen
Agency Hoffman York, Milwaukee
Creative Direction David Hanneken,
Mike Ancevic, Gary Stepniak
Art Direction Mike Ancevic

KickStart question: How could an optical illusion
represent a product feature visually?

Client Kwan Loong Medicated Oil
Agency Batey Ads, Singapore
Creative Direction Kash Sree, Scott Lambert
Art Direction Kash Sree, Scott Lambert
Illustration Martin Lim

Shaking this ad makes the Martini
logo visible.
Client Bacardi Martini
Agency McCann Erickson, Geneva
Creative Direction Frank Bodin
Copy Carine Bluemlein

KickStart question: How can an optical
illusion attract attention by involving
the target group in a game?

There are no paradoxes or
negations in nature. It is
language which creates them
in our heads. I have included
optical illusion in this section
as a non-verbal counterpart
to paradox, because it too
generates ambiguities,
impossible images or other
forms of paradoxical deception
in the viewer's head.

*'If you slaughter a holy cow
you get a wonderful steak.'*

Attention is in short supply nowadays, so if you want people to notice
your campaign, be provocative! Provoking means challenging, inciting,
stimulating. But be careful: being seen is not the same as being looked at.
Provocation takes you across a frontier, but it requires skill and will only
lead you to your goal if you think about what you're doing: for example,
drawing attention to social issues, or warning people of dangers.
The following examples show a broad spectrum of possible variations
and areas where shock and provocation are appropriate.

Campaign for ladies' underwear
Client She-Bear
Agency TBWA Hunt Lascaris, Johannesburg
Creative Direction Richard Bullock, Reed Collins
Art Direction Kevin Watkins
Photo Gillian Lochner

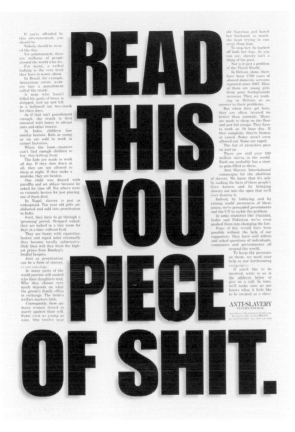

READ THIS YOU PIECE OF SHIT.

What have you got against condoms? Do they make it itch?
For the zilionth time cover up.

ILGA PORTUGAL
Gay and Lesbian Centre

Client ILGA (International Lesbian
and Gay Association)
Agency Ogilvy & Mather, Lisbon
Creative Direction José Manuel Abrantes
Art Direction Pedro João Oliveira
Copy Miguel Rego

KickStart question: How can you use a
provocative allusion or double meaning
to make the target group think?

Campaign for a human rights organization
Client Anti-Slavery International
Agency Saatchi & Saatchi, London
Creative Direction Michael Campbell
Art Direction Vanessa Rosser

KickStart question: Can you break a taboo,
or provoke the target group by other means,
to draw attention to a social issue?

Client REM REM
Agency Courage/BDDP, Copenhagen
Creative Direction Claus Suytte
Art Direction Peter Stenbaek
Photo Martin Juhl

KickStart question: What shocking images or
statements can you use to give the product a
certain image or attract more attention to it?

WHY KILL TIME, WHEN
YOU CAN KILL YOURSELF?

SUICIDE IS THE ULTIMATE WASTE OF TIME. TIME IS A PRECIOUS COMMODITY. ALL REMREM TIME PIECES REFLECT NOT ONLY THE VALUE OF TIME, BUT ARE ALSO A TRIBUTE TO LIFE. WWW.REMREM.COM

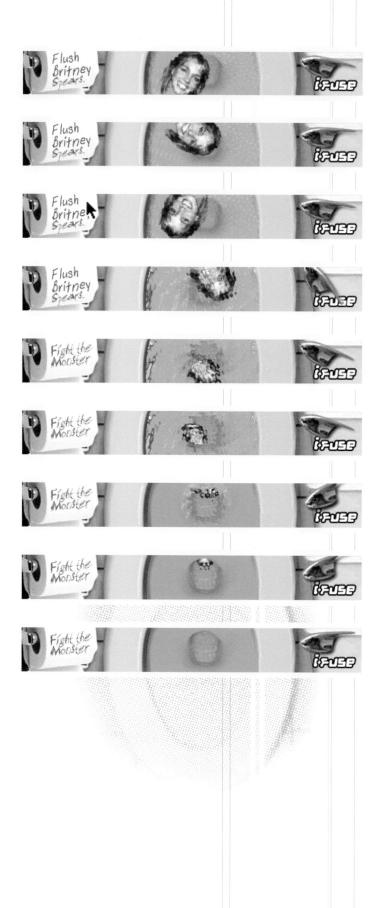

This animated web banner by iFuse gives the target group the chance to flush the famous popstar Britney Spears down the toilet at the click of a mouse.
Client iFUSE
Agency Freestyle Interactive, San Francisco
Art Direction Regan Honda
Engineer Ryan Olson
Producer Kim Askew

KickStart question: What provocative image can you come up with to polarize and so win the sympathy of a specific social group?

Client Shampoo Planet
Agency BDDP GGT Advertising, London
Creative Direction Johan Kramer
Art Direction Erik Kessels
Photo Miriam Jeurissen
Source Lürzer's Archive 5/1995

KickStart question: How can shocking questions or statements be used to put the service or product centre-stage?

Campaign for a shoe brand, using amputees as models
Client Shoebaloo
Agency KesselsKramer, Amsterdam
Creative Direction Johan Kramer
Art Direction Erik Kessels
Photo Miriam Jeurissen

KickStart question: How can provocative presentation of the product increase attention?

Client Companion Animal Placement
Agency Suburban Advertising, Jersey City
Creative Direction Eric Aronin
Art Direction Dave Laden
Photo Ashton Worthington
Source Lürzer's Archive 2/1997

KickStart question: What provocative statements might help you to communicate the benefit more clearly?

That's the great thing about pets.

They really don't care.

Adopt today.
(201) 653-7202   (212) 673-7295

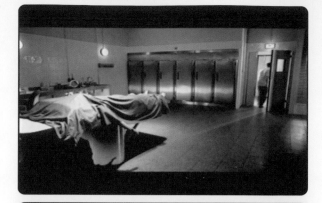

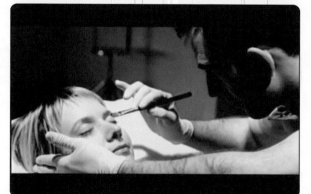

A man in a green smock is giving a beauty treatment to a blonde with a peaceful smile on her face in a neon-lit room. First he blow-dries her hair, then manicures her nails and freshens up her make-up. While Al Green's 'Let's Stay Together' plays in the background, he chats animatedly about events of the day, and the whole scene creates the impression of a session in a beauty parlour. At frequent intervals we catch a glimpse of an Accurist wristwatch. When he's finished, he peels off his rubber gloves, turns off the music and leaves the room. Only now does the viewer realize that the girl is dead and the room is a mortuary. In the last shot her arm with the wristwatch on it slips out from under the cover.

'Beauty Parlour'
Client Accurist Accu
Agency TBWA GGT Simons Palmer, London
Creative Direction Ben Short
Art Direction Cameron Short
Production Maguffin
Director Pete Cornish

KickStart question: How can provocation or shock tactics be used to present the product effectively in a story?

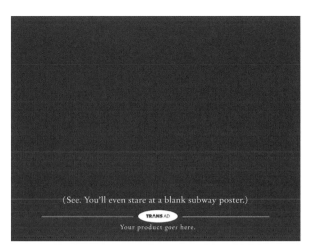

Client Trans Ad
Agency Roche Macaulay & Partners, Toronto
Creative Direction David Rosenberg
Art Direction Gerald Schoenhoff

KickStart question: What provocative claims could
you use to present the benefit convincingly?

Campaign for a menswear brand
Client John Pearse
Agency Doner Cardwell Hawkins, London
Creative Direction Paul Cardwell
Art Direction Paul Surety
Copy Mark Rudd
Photo Graham Fink

KickStart question: How can the product
be given a specific image by provocative
presentation?

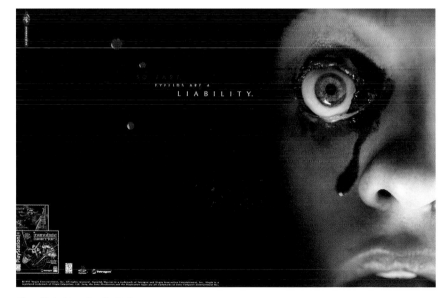

Client Virgin Interactive, PlayStation
Agency Wongdoody Inc., Seattle
Creative Direction Tracy Wong
Art Direction Michael Ivan Boychuk
Copy Craig Hoit
Photo Randy Albritton

KickStart question: How can shock be
used to dramatize the benefit?

BE PROVOCATIVE – DO SOMETHING UNUSUAL

Some rules are so successful that they are almost immune to criticism.
This is where provocation helps. Provoke people in meetings by targeted
rule-breaking. Imagine you're working on a TV spot for a detergent –
what five fundamental rules of product presentation could you
deliberately break? Make a note of the things that occur to you
and use them as a source of new ideas for your commercial.

Campaign for a chain of fitness centres
Client Gold's Gym
Agency Jack, Los Angeles
Creative Direction Jack Fund
Art Direction Jack Fund
Photo Tom Nelson
Source Lürzer's Archive 5/2000

PROVOCATION AS A SOURCE OF IDEAS

As a rule in meetings, people look for ideas that describe the product in
superlatives. That way of thinking often leads into a dead-end, because
sooner or later you run out of superlatives and the ideas all start to look
the same. This next technique is outstandingly effective at reinvigorating
meetings and opening exciting new avenues of ideas: at the next meeting,
invite the entire team to talk about taboos, the things advertisers would
never say publicly about a product or consumers. In other words, say all
the bad and negative things about the product and express consumers'
worst thoughts, too – their anxieties, doubts or anger. The objective is
to bring emotions into play which will spur team members into heated
debate and new ideas, using provocative statements as a stimulus.

Try saying the unsayable and thinking the unthinkable about the product.
Exaggerate your ideas to a ridiculous extent, add a few noughts to every
number. Think about the wildest things that pop into your mind, and you
will often hit the nail on the head. These questions should give your team
the necessary impetus to stir up a little controversy and emotion in the
meeting. Spend enough time with each question to give the team
the chance to forge ahead into really new territory.

- What would be especially horrifying or funny in association with
  the product or campaign?
- How could we make it a scandal?
- What damage might it do, what are the dangers?
- Who might be frightened by it? Why?
- What would you never do with the product, under any circumstances?
- Who might be provoked by it, and how?
- What might a child make of it, how would they think and feel?

Make the effects of time visible. Imagine the product on a line stretching from the past to the present, and on to the future. How will time alter the product? Or how will the product affect humanity and human history? Take the product back into the distant past, or put it in a time machine.

What eras could be connected with it, or what fashions (the twenties, seventies or nineties) give you the raw material for ideas? The KickStart questions in this section can only show you a tiny fraction of the possibilities, which are as infinite as time itself.

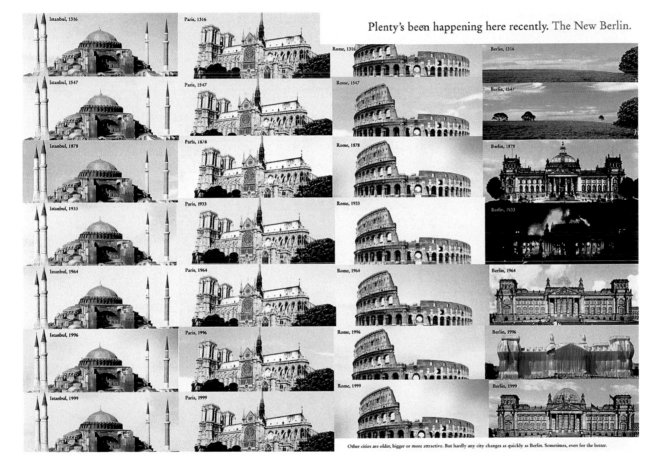

Client   City of Berlin
Agency   Scholz & Friends, Berlin
Creative Direction   Sebastian Turner
Art Direction   Lutz Plümecke
Copy   Robert Krause, Nina Havlicek

Daisy sofa. $1250.

An eclectic collection of upholstered furnishings. 877.290.1502

robin bruce

Ricky slipcover sofa. $1200.

An eclectic collection of upholstered furnishings. 877.290.1502

robin b

Client Robin Bruce Line, Rowe Furniture
Agency ADWORKS Inc., Washington, D.C.
Creative Direction Mark Greenspun
Art Direction Bill Cutter
Copy Mark Greenspun
Retouching Slingshot Studios

KickStart question: What elements from
different historical periods could show the
benefit in a positive light?

This campaign tells the story of worn Rockport shoes. The label on each shoe gives information about the owners, the circumstances in which they wore the shoes, what the wearers especially liked about them, and so on.

Client   Rockport
Agency   Leo Burnett, Chicago
Creative Direction   Paul Meyer, Kit Cramer
Art Direction   Mark Figliulo, K.C. Arnwong
Photo   Chuck Shotwell
Source   Lürzer's Archive 2/1996

KickStart question: How can the effects of time be represented to underline the benefit?

Campaign for the charity Oxfam and its second-hand clothing stores
Client   Oxfam
Agency   BMP DDB Ltd, London
Creative Direction   Patrick McClelland
Art Direction   Grant Parker

Client   Lee
Agency   Fallon Worldwide, Minneapolis
Creative Direction   Scott Vincent
Art Direction   Ellen Steinberg
Photo   Ann Elliott Cutting

KickStart question: How can the benefit be emphasized by playing with past, present and future?

Client Knorr
Agency Bates Ireland, Dublin
Creative Direction Ian Doherty
Art Direction Grant Parker

KickStart question: How could the
benefit be enhanced by giving it
historical associations?

Left: 'A babe of the twenties';
right: 'A babe of the Chambourcy
Diet generation'.
Client Chambourcy
Agency DPZ Propaganda, São Paulo
Creative Direction Adriana Davini
Art Direction Rodrigo de Almeida
Retusche Luisa Petit, J. R. Duran

KickStart question: How can the benefit
be enhanced by comparison with other
eras or fashions?

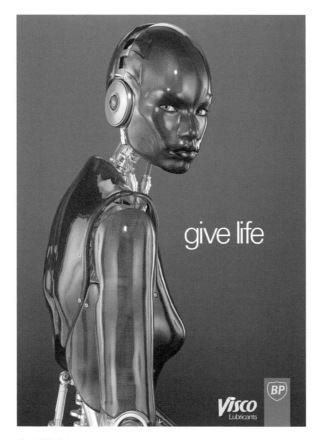

Client BP Lubricants
Agency Doner Cardwell Hawkins, London
Creative Direction Paul Cardwell
Art Direction Lee Ford
Copy Damian Simor
Photo Simon Emmett

KickStart question: What vision of the future or
futuristic image can help to make a product
feature visible at a glance?

A change of perspective is first of all an excellent way to generate a creative impulse during the process of looking for ideas, and secondly it can be used in advertising to show the target group new or interesting perspectives on the product. The examples on the following pages show a small selection of brilliant variations on the idea.

There are two ways to use changes in perspective as a creative tool. First, they can be used spatially, by showing objects or situations from unusual viewpoints: bird's eye view, extreme close-up, extreme distance, detached from space and time, from outer space, or simply from every possible angle. The second way is to imagine yourself leaving your body and slipping inside other people, objects or animals. Many creatives symbolically take on other identities to get a creative boost from the new point of view. Walt Disney, for example, used to 'become' the figure he was currently drawing, going so far as to speak, gesture and stand like the character in his imagination.

It seems rather good.

Client Vaasan Bakeries
Agency Paltemaa Huttunen
Santala TBWA, Helsinki
Art Direction Unto Paltemaa
Copy Markku Ronkko
Photo Horst Neumann

Client Irn-Bru
Agency The Leith Agency, Edinburgh
Creative Direction Nikki Mitchell
Art Direction Mats Persson
Photo Evan Myles

KickStart question: How can the product
be presented from the viewpoint of other
creatures, things or events associated with it?

The leaf advertises the botanical gardens in Frankfurt
and is also a map, showing the nearest metro station (U)
and bus stop (H).
Client Palmengarten Frankfurt
Agency Lesch & Frei GmbH, Frankfurt
Creative Direction Wolfgang Hanfstein
Art Direction Thomas Schneider

KickStart question: How can playing with extreme
close-up or extreme distance communicate something
about the product or service?

'Be here'. This campaign for Penguin Books invites viewers to look at the world from other people's point of view.
Client Penguin Books
Agency Mustoe Merriman Herring Levy, London
Creative Direction Simon Hipwell
Art Direction Dean Hunt
Photo Raymond Depardon

KickStart question: How can a playful invitation to try a new perspective demonstrate the product's features?

Campaign for a theme park
Client Playland
Agency Palmer Jarvis DDB, Vancouver
Creative Direction Chris Staples
Art Direction Ian Grais
Copy Alan Russell

Client Smirnoff Vodka
Agency Lowe Howard-Spink, London
Creative Direction Gary Anderson
Art Direction Tony Miller
Photo Paul Arden
Source Lürzer's Archive 6/1996

KickStart question: How can the product reveal new perspectives to the target group?

Aruba now on non-stop flights by TAM.

ARUB

Client Aruba
Agency Lew, Lara Propaganda, São Paulo
Creative Direction Margit Junginger
Photo Evan Myles

KickStart question: How can a change of
spatial perspective show a new way of looking
at things, and so underline the benefit?

Polo L. £8290 [VW]

Surprisingly ordinary prices [VW]

Client VW
Agency BMP DDB Ltd, London
Creative Direction Clive Pickering
Art Direction Neil Dawson
Photo Paul Reas

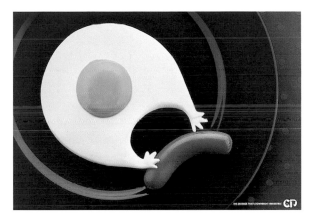

'CP. The sausage that's downright irresistable'.

Client CP
Agency Result Advertising, Bangkok
Creative Direction Aussanee Augsornnugul, Akanit Jackson
Art Direction Suthisak Sucharittanonta,
Chanchai Chavanont
Photo Pakarnwit Vathakanon

KickStart question: How can a playful change of
perspective focus the target group's attention?

KickStart question: How can exaggeration help to
present the benefit from the viewpoint of things
or creatures affected by it?

Creative Technique

CHANGING PERSPECTIVE THROUGH IDENTIFICATION

A dog remains a dog, and a daisy can't be anything but a daisy;
only human beings can alter their identity, or change their point
of view by slipping into the roles of others. If you're crazy enough,
you can experiment with what prophets, oracles and medicine men
have done since prehistoric times: assume the identity of animate
and inanimate things, in order to gather new knowledge from their
perspective. Throw yourself into the part of the creature or object
involved in the theme of the campaign. You can try it on your own,
or invite the whole team to take part. Take it seriously and use all five
senses! For example, for an ad campaign, you could take the role of
a product, the client, a sales assistant, the packaging, or a shelf in
the shop. Now try and develop solutions from the perspective of these
people or objects. It's important that the group should already have
some experience of applying these methods and so won't find them
silly or ridiculous.

*'There are two alternatives
with parody: either be better
than the original or leave it
alone.' Martin Flossmann*

To make the most of a parody or spoof, you need a well-known original, which could be taken from television, cinema, advertising, literature, music, politics or art. It could be a cartoon character, a brand, a slogan, a storybook hero or a logo. Change it to make it conflict with its original function and character, give it a new meaning. But make sure that it doesn't lose touch with its essential features, because the comic effect will to some extent depend on the pleasure of recognizing the original underlying the parody.

Client Oslo Gay & Lesbian Festival
Agency Bates Reklamebyrå, Oslo
Creative Direction Bendik Romstad
Art Direction Anne Gravingen
Illustration Bjürn Brochmann

Give him the best!

'Only the best for Fred'
Client Anheuser-Busch, Budweiser Beer
Agency DDB Chicago
Creative Direction Don Pogany
Art Direction Chuck Taylor
Copy Vinny Warren
Director Rent Sidon

KickStart question: How can a
parody or spoof help to develop an
entertaining story round the product?

A beautifully shot film shows a handsome,
healthy dog frolicking with his master in an
atmospheric park setting. The viewer can
admire his glossy coat and his powerful body
and the voiceover supports the impression that
this is yet another commercial for dogfood:

'Fred is great. He always wants to play. Just look
at him go! He's got so much energy. But he sure
can work up quite a thirst.'

When man and dog arrive home they go
straight to the kitchen. As the man takes a cold
Budweiser from the fridge the camera turns to
the dog and it's suddenly revealed that he's the
speaker. Now he talks directly to camera and
explains that his master deserves the best, and
that's why he always gives him Budweiser.

The Beetles

Client Harald A. Møller, Volkswagen
Agency Bates Reklamebyrå, Oslo
Art Direction Kenneth Hansen
Copy Frode Karlberg
Photo Knut Bry

KickStart question: What can be parodied
to give the product a particular image?

Christmas campaign for a shoe store
Client Shellys
Agency Mustoe Merriman Herring Levy, London
Creative Direction Ben Jones
Art Direction Rob Nielsen
Photo Robert Steele

KickStart question: How can a parody or spoof attract attention and present the product effectively?

Any food tastes supreme with

Client Heinz
Agency Leo Burnett Ltd, London
Creative Direction Steve Chung
Art Direction Rob Nielsen

KickStart question: What kind of parody or spoof could represent the benefit in an entertaining but unambiguous way?

Campaign for children's rights
Client Save The Children, Sweden
Agency Manne & Co., Stockholm
Art Direction Oskar Bård
Copy Peter Laurelli
Illustration Annelie Karlsson

KickStart question: How can a parody or spoof be used to communicate social issues unambiguously?

'A sign is something that stands for something else.'

A symbol is a visual image that stands for an object, a concept or a situation. The drawing of a stylized car next to a spanner represents a car workshop, a cigarette with a line across it means 'No Smoking'. The meaning of some signs derives from a causal connection – smoke is a sign of fire. Another function of many symbols is to convey information that can't be expressed in words. They often represent global forces: for example, the American flag, the cross, the hammer and sickle, the star of David. These symbols form a universal language which knows no frontiers, yet at the same time carries different associations or emotions depending on the viewer. The following KickStart questions should encourage your team to explore the wide field of symbols and signs to the full and use them for effective communication.

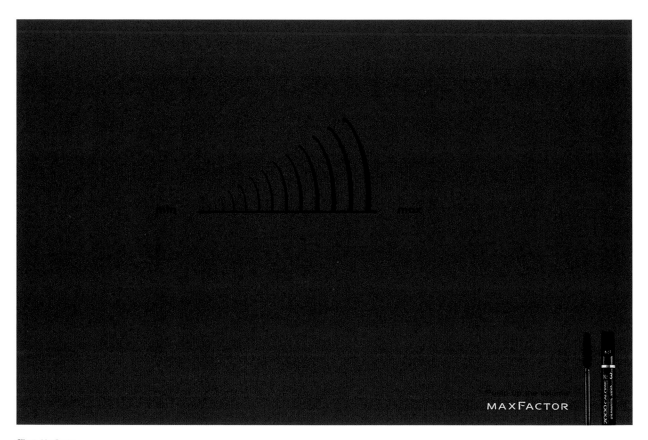

Client MaxFactor
Agency Leo Burnett, Lisbon
Creative Direction Gezo Marques
Art Direction João Ribeiro
Illustration Gezo Marques

FOR A PROPER MEAL _ _ _ _ _ CUT CORNERS.

Campaign for ready-meals in pouches
Client Tyne
Agency D'Arcy, London
Creative Direction Matt Wheeler
Art Direction David Chidlow
Photo Dick Marsh
Illustration David Fulfaric

KickStart question: How can the product benefit be represented more simply by symbols or signs?

This poster for Amnesty International asks for active support in its campaign against human rights abuses.
Client Amnesty International
Designer Tadeusz Lewandowski

KickStart question: How can symbols and signs convey a complete message without words?

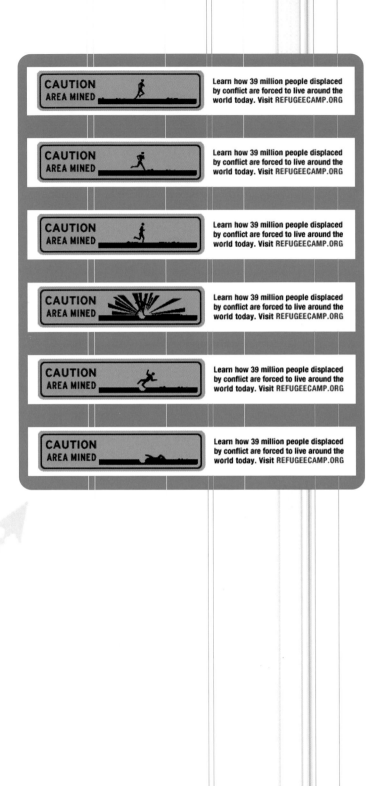

Banner campaign for war refugees
Client Médecins sans Frontières
Agency TBWA/Chiat/Day, New York
Creative Direction Doug Jaeger

KickStart question: What sources of symbols or signs can be used to communicate a message?

Campaign for an information helpline for pregnant women
Client Madalena Teixeira
Agency Nova Publicidade, Lisbon
Creative Direction Pedro Monteiro
Art Direction Nuno Levezinho
Copy Alexandre Bezerra

KickStart question: Are there signs or symbols which will communicate a message if inverted or altered?

SOS Pregnancy:
21 395 21 43
The information line that answers all your questions.

'The fastest delivery service on the Net.'
Campaign for an Internet shopping site.
Client americanas.com
Agency DM9 DDB, São Paulo
Creative Direction Aaron Sutton
Art Direction Sergio Gordilho
Photo Marco Cesar

KickStart question: What sources of symbols
or signs can be used to demonstrate a benefit
vividly and effectively?

Client The Canadian Paraplegic Association
Agency Butler, Shine & Stern, Sausalito
Creative Direction John Butler, Mike Shine
Art Direction Brad Wood
Copy Ryan Ebner

KickStart question: What well-known symbols
or signs can be adapted to make the message
clear at a glance?

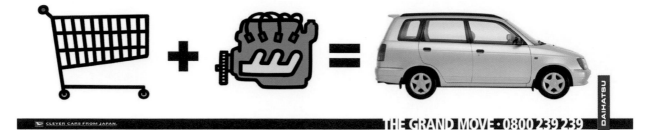

Client Daihatsu
Agency Banks Hoggins O'Shea FCB, London
Creative Direction Rob Fletcher, David Alexander
Art Direction Richard Dennison
Copy Markham Smith
Illustration David Webster

KickStart question: How can symbols be used
to tell a story about the benefit?

Client Columbia Brewery Co.
Agency Bryant, Fulton & Shee, Vancouver
Creative Direction Rick Kemp
Art Direction Lisa Francilia
Copy Dan Scherk
Photo Montizambert Photography
Illustration Mike McCartie

KickStart question: Where can you find sources
of symbols or signs that will present the product
in an unusual context?

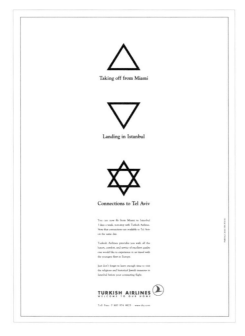

Client Turkish Airlines
Agency Pars-McCann-Erickson, Istanbul
Creative Direction Ugur Cakir
Art Direction Mete Ozkar
Copy Ali Yavuz

KickStart question: What signs or symbols
can be combined to generate a new meaning,
representing the product advantage?

Introducing ultra slim watches. **TITAN** SLIM

Client Titan Slim
Agency Ogilvy & Mather, Bangalore
Creative Direction Paul Vinod
Art Direction Manmohan Anchan
Photo N. Sugathan

KickStart question: How can symbols
or signs present the benefit strikingly
and at a glance?

'Egypt. Amaze your eyes.'

Client Egypt
Agency Publicis FCB, Brussels
Creative Direction Eric Jamez
Art Direction Eric Jamez

KickStart question: What sign language
can be used to convey the product
message without words?

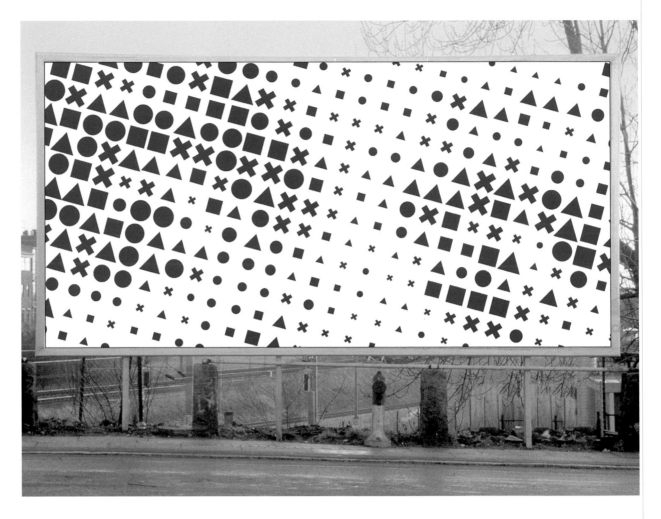

This poster for Playstation uses the four symbols
from the keys to make a pattern. The effect can
only be seen at a distance, when the pattern
becomes a pair of eyes.
Client Sony Playstation
Agency TBWA, London
Creative Direction Nigel Roberts
Art Direction Paul Belford
Illustration Paul Belford

KickStart question: How can symbols or signs
be combined to generate something new which
will become the product message?

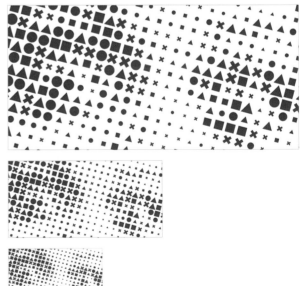

There are hundreds of ways to awaken the urge to play games in both
children and adults. Remind your target group of the games they played
when they were kids, set them riddles and puzzles, or challenge them
to a contest. All games have one thing in common: they only work when
the player takes an active part and is prepared to devote some attention
to it. So don't make your game too complicated or too simple, but let
people experience a sense of triumph that will produce an 'Aha!'
or a 'Yes!' These examples are just a small selection of the ways
in which you can grab the target group's attention by getting
them involved in a game.

This advertising campaign lets readers peel off
one of the dogs from the margin and put it in
the picture, to find out whether it's the right
dog for them.
Client   NCDL
Agency   TBWA London
Creative Direction   Paula Jackson, Nick Hine
Art Direction   Paula Jackson, Nick Hine
Photo   Matt Harris
Retouching   Seven Soho

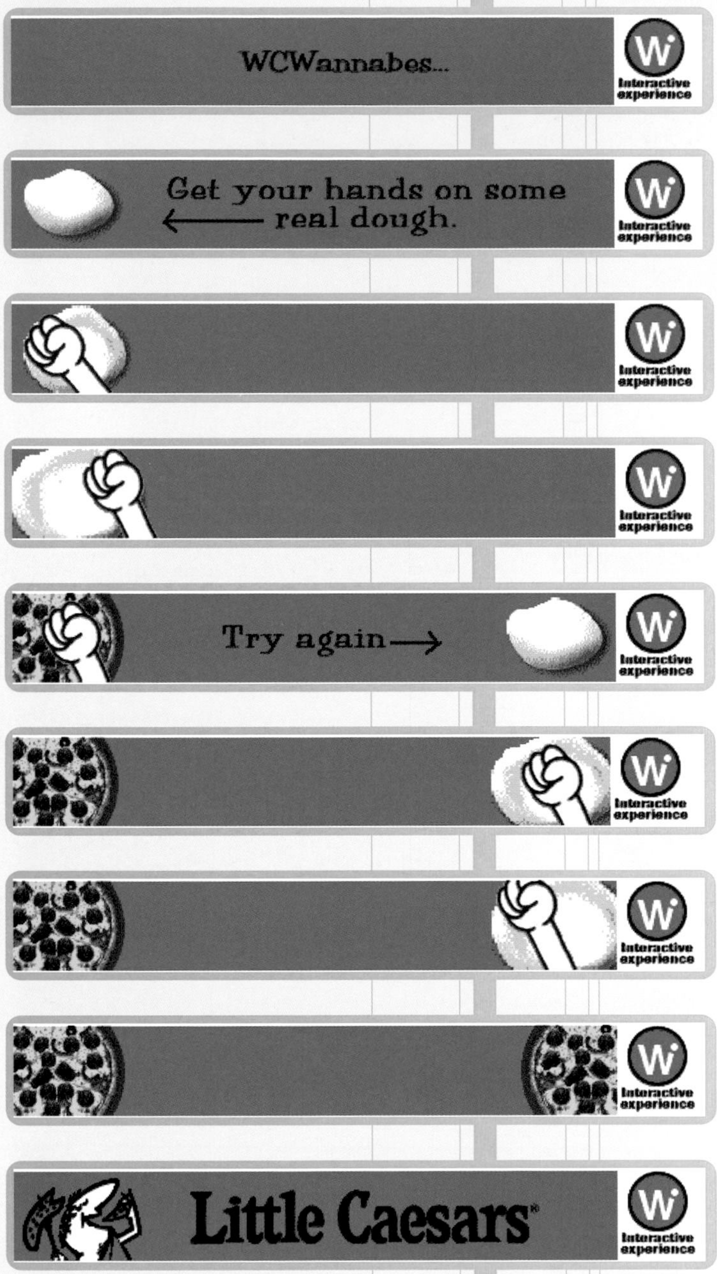

WCWannabes...

Get your hands on some real dough. ←

Try again →

Little Caesars

When you move your mouse across this web banner, the cursor becomes a hand. You can then bash the ball of dough and turn it into your own pizza.

Client Little Caesars
Agency FCB Worldwide, Detroit
Creative Direction Husam Ajluni
Art Direction Geoffrey Gates, Peter Arndt
Programming DragonFly Studios

KickStart question: How can you involve the target group in a game that puts the product centre-stage?

This banner campaign lets viewers have fun by playing a nine-hole game of golf.

Client Sun Microsystems
Agency Freestyle Interactive, San Francisco
Art Direction Leftfield, Karim Sanjabi
Production Kim Askew
Engineer Steve Von

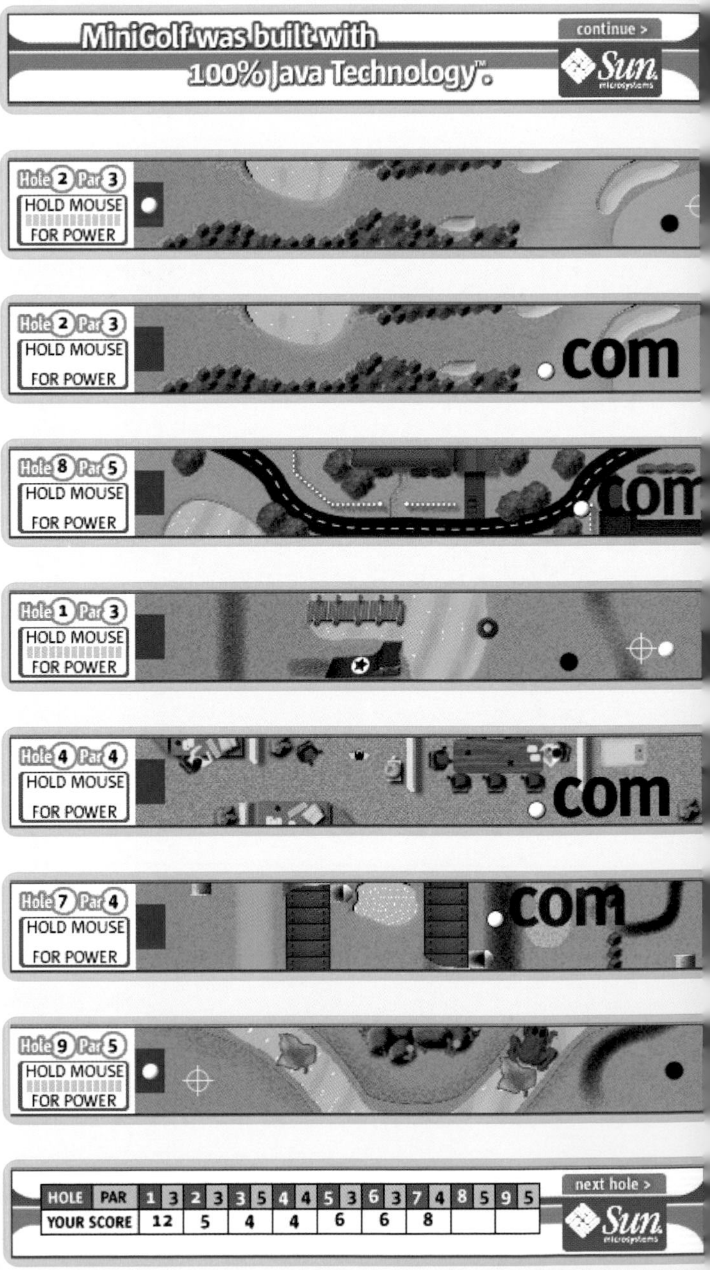

MiniGolf was built with 100% Java Technology. continue > ◆Sun microsystems

Hole 2 Par 3 HOLD MOUSE FOR POWER

Hole 2 Par 3 HOLD MOUSE FOR POWER .com

Hole 8 Par 5 HOLD MOUSE FOR POWER com

Hole 1 Par 3 HOLD MOUSE FOR POWER

Hole 4 Par 4 HOLD MOUSE FOR POWER .com

Hole 7 Par 4 HOLD MOUSE FOR POWER com

Hole 9 Par 5 HOLD MOUSE FOR POWER

HOLE	PAR	1	3	2	3	3	5	4	4	5	3	6	3	7	4	8	5	9	5	next hole >
YOUR SCORE	12	5		4		4		6		6		8								◆Sun microsystems

On the right is the back page of a magazine with an ad for Vapona insecticide. Rolling up the magazine gives you both the shape of a spraycan and a way to swat flies in the traditional manner.

Client Vapona/Sara Lee
Agency Leo Burnett Ltd, London
Art Direction Adam Staples, Paul Miles
Copy Adam Staples, David Harrison
Photo Piet Johnson

KickStart question: How can an invitation to play focus attention on the product?

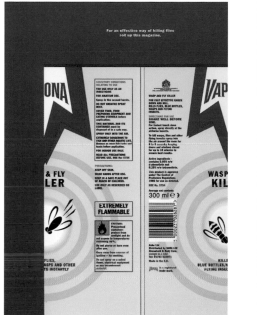

Campaign for a temp agency
Client Todays
Agency Gilliatt Paris, Dallas
Creative Direction Brad Walk
Art Direction Chuck Paris

KickStart question: How can you involve the target group and draw their attention towards the benefit?

A plastic bag was stuck to this double-page ad, containing a sheet
of stickers to make the picture more exciting.

Client Audi
Agency Limbo, London
Creative Direction Simon Antenen
Art Direction Michael Cavers
Photo Jean-Luc Bernard
Source Lürzer's Archive 5/1997

KickStart question: How could an ad
be designed to invite the reader to play
a game and so pay more attention?

'Pin this up and bang your head here.
If this reminds you of your job, read on.'
Client Todays
Agency Gilliatt Paris, Dallas
Creative Direction Chuck Paris
Art Direction Brad Walk

KickStart question: What witty, provocative
or intriguing instructions could you use to
get your target group to play?

Zo soepel stuurt stuurbekrachtiging op de Auto van het Jaar.

Ford

'That's how light the power steering
is on the Car of the Year.'
Client Ford
Agency Ogilvy & Mather, Amsterdam
Creative Direction Denis Baars,
Ferry van Tongeren
Art Direction Krijn van Noordwijk
Photo Jan van de Laar

KickStart question: How can you
persuade your target group to play
a game with the medium and so
experience the benefit for themselves?

Please answer the following questions for our research:

☐ *Do you read the same subway posters over and over again?*
☐ *Do you read the same subway posters over and over again?*
☐ *Do you read the same subway posters over and over again?*

Thank you. You've been a big help.

TRANS AD

Your product *goes* here.

Client Trans Ad
Agency Roche Macaulay & Partners,
Toronto
Creative Direction David Rosenberg
Art Direction Gerald Schoenhoff

KickStart question: What playful strategy
could arouse the target group's curiosity
and grab their attention?

'Scratch your head over the opposite page,
and see whether you need to read this ad.'
Campaign for an anti-dandruff shampoo.
Client Triatop
Agency DM9 DDB, São Paulo
Creative Direction Walter Miranda,
Fabio Saboya
Art Direction Luiz Toledo, Diego Zaragoza
Photo Moa Sitibaldi
Source Lürzer's Archive 1/1995

KickStart question: How can you exploit
the medium so that your target group
can see the benefit right away?

As long ago as 1948, Allen Funt had the idea of secretly filming
unsuspecting victims in stage-managed situations as a source of
entertainment. *Candid Camera* laid the foundation stone of Reality TV,
and a trend to present the product in everyday situations can now be
observed in advertising too. But Reality Advertising only works if it's
sustained by an extra idea – pure reality could get a little boring.
The examples on the following pages illustrate ways in which
an everyday story told around the product can be brought to life.
Think of some everyday situations in which the product could play
a central role. Give normality an unexpected or exciting twist that
involves the product. Show the target group a new angle on things,
invent situations for comic effect, or show the funny side of things
we take for granted. This section is another that contains an
enormous field of undiscovered ideas, just waiting for your team
to start digging.

Client Adidas
Agency Leagas Delaney, San Francisco
Creative Direction Scott Wild
Art Direction Peter Nicholson
Photo Eugene Richards

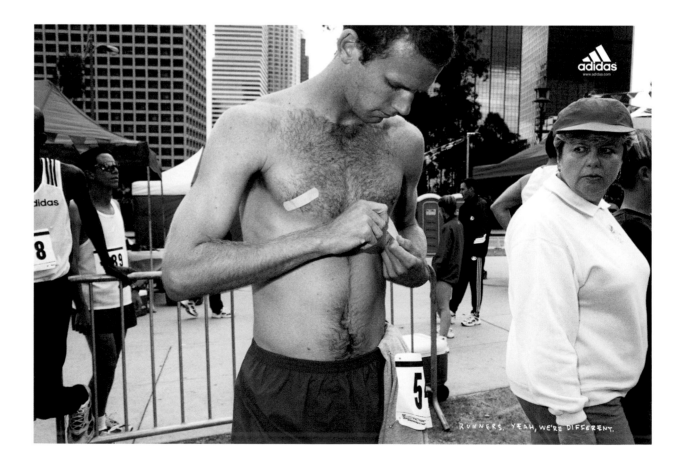

Client smart
Agency Weber, Hodel, Schmid, Zurich
Creative Direction Liliane Lerch
Art Direction Jürg Aemmer, Patricia Zaugg, Thomas von Ah
Photo Georg Schunharting

KickStart question: How can you stage an everyday situation that makes your product the centre of attention?

This Sony campaign uses the words of well-known songs which are suddenly replaced by everyday chatter when the Walkman's batteries run out. In this example, a song by the band Shalimar turns into the words of passers-by on the street.

Client Sony
Agency BMP DDB Ltd, London
Creative Direction Andy McLeod
Art Direction Richard Flintham
Photo Steen Sundland

KickStart question: Can the product be placed in an everyday situation so it will attract attention wittily or provocatively?

Energy-absorbing door padding.

Just one of over 40 features now standard
on the totally redesigned Golf.

Drivers wanted. Ⓥ

The new Golf.

Client VW
Agency Arnold Communications, Boston
Creative Direction Carl Loeb
Art Direction Paul Renner
Photo Melodie McDaniel

KickStart question: Are there any everyday
situations in which a feature of the product
can be demonstrated in an unexpected
or humorous way?

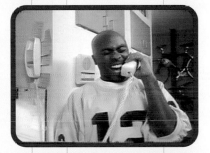

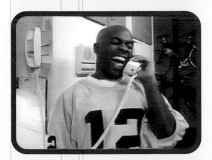

Open on Guy 1 watching sport on TV, bottle of Bud in hand. Phone ringing.
Cut to Guy 1 picking up cordless phone.
Guy 1: Hello....
Cut to caller. He also has a Bud.
Caller: Yo! What's up?
Guy 1: Watchin' the game... havin' a Bud. What's up with you?
Caller: Nothin'. Watchin' the game. Havin' a Bud...
Guy 1: True, true.
Guy 2 wearing yellow jersey enters room.
Guy 2: Whazzzup!
Guy 1: Whazzzup!
Cut to caller.
Caller: Yo, who's that?
Guy 1 to guy 2: Yo! Pick up the phone!
Cut to Guy 2 picking up extension in kitchen.
Guy 2. Hello!
Caller: Whazzzup!
Guy 2: Whazzzup!
Guy 1: Whazzzup!
Cut to Guy 2 in kitchen.
Guy 2 to caller: Yo, where's Dookie!
Cut to caller.
Caller shouting: Yo, Dookie!
Cut to Dookie sitting at his computer picking up extension.
Dookie: Yo!
Guy 2: Whazzzup!
Guy 1: Whazzzup!
Caller: Whazzzup!
Dookie: Whazzzup!
Intercom buzzer
Cut to Guy 2 pressing intercom button.
Visitor: Whazzzup!
Caller: Whazzzup!
Guy 1: Whazzzup!
Dookie: Whazzzup!
Guy 2: Whazzzup!
Caller: Whazzzup!
Guy 1: So, what's up?
Caller: Watchin' the game. Havin' a Bud.
Guy 1: True, true.

Client Anheuser-Busch, Inc./Budweiser
Agency DDB Chicago
Creative Direction Don Pogany
Art Direction Justin Reardon, Chuck Taylor
Copy Vinny Warren, Charles Stone

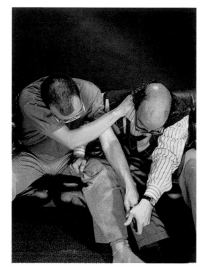

This story is told in a row of five posters,
and advertises a cable TV network.
Client UPC
Agency Lowe Brindfors, Stockholm
Creative Direction Mitte Blomqvist
Art Direction Björn Hjalmar
Photo Henrik Halvarsson

KickStart question: What everyday story could
you invent with the product at its centre?

'And suddenly Heinrich goes from Assistant
Junior Designer to head of Volkswagen
Product Development.'
Client VW
Agency Arnold Communications, Boston
Creative Direction David Weist
Art Direction Paul Renner
Photo Hans Gissinger

KickStart question: What everyday scene
could you depict to place the product
centre-stage in a surprising way?

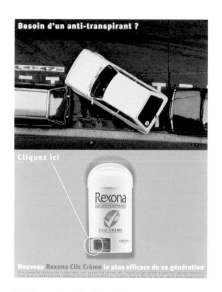

'Need an anti-perspirant? Click here – Rexona Clic
Creme. The most efficient of its generation.'
Client Rexona
Agency Lowe Lintas & Partners, Paris
Creative Direction Richard Cador
Art Direction Eric Lespagney
Photo Daniel Schweizer, Vincent Tessier
Source Lürzer's Archive 5/2000

KickStart question: In what kind of everyday
situation could the product be a lifesaver?

'Lean back for a minute and look around the room you're in. Summon up all your mental energy and try as hard as you can to stop the furniture from laughing at you.'

Plunging into the world of the absurd, the surreal and the bizarre is fascinating in itself, and it also opens up a rich source of ideas. Contradiction, exaggeration, distortion, fantasizing and zany ideas are the tools you need to create something absurd or surreal. If you want to develop this sort of idea, it helps to be a little crazy yourself. And since this kind of madness is far from routine, you need to trust the team 100 per cent in order to gain the freedom to plunge into this world.

Discuss it, and make a pact with the team that for the rest of the meeting you'll create a locked-door, laboratory situation, where each of you will be free to reveal an absurd, surreal or bizarre piece of him or herself. If your team is brave enough to take part in this exciting experiment, you'll be astonished by the results. The examples on the following pages are just a small window into the neverending richness of the absurd and the surreal.

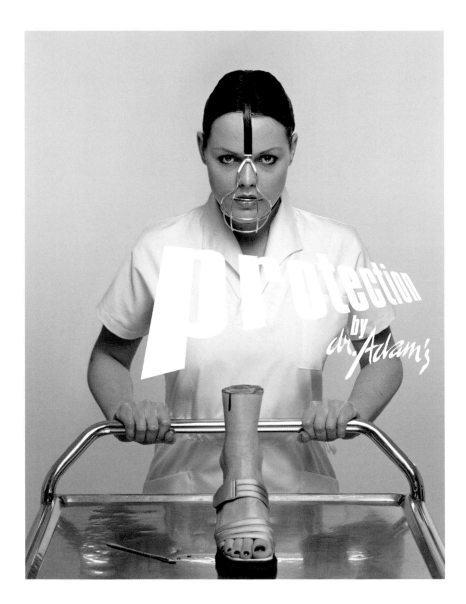

Campaign for a shoe brand
Client Dr Adams
Agency Stempels & Oster, Amsterdam
Creative Direction Christian Visser
Art Direction Christian Visser
Photo Wendelien Daan

Harvey and Hibby, two knitted toys who starred in an earlier print campaign for the department store Harvey Nichols, are seen here in a very simple animation. On the soundtrack, electronic muzak and the toys' mumbles, with subtitles. The story begins with Harvey and Hibby making another shopping trip to Harvey Nichols. Suddenly a lift door opens and another toy staggers out with his suit on fire. The voiceover tells Harvey to beat the flames out, using one of his new purchases, but the toy flatly refuses. Then Hibby is asked to do the same, but also refuses. Meanwhile another toy appears on the scene and puts the fire out with a bucket of water. The man in last season's coat is saved.

Client Harvey Nichols
Agency Mother Ltd, London
Creative Direction Robert Saville
Art Direction Cecilia Dufils
Copy Markus Bjurman
Production Arden Sutherland Dodd
Directors ACNE International

KickStart question: What stylistic conventions can you use to spin the most absurd story possible around the product?

'Snowboarding withdrawal. It's so sad.'
Client Blades Board & Skate
Agency J. Walter Thompson, New York
Art Direction D. J. Pierce
Copy Scott Duchon
Photo Bob Scott

KickStart question: What absurd or bizarre
situation can you devise to make the product
the focus of attention?

Client Dunlop
Agency BBDO, Düsseldorf
Creative Direction Walter Campbell, Tom Carty
Art Direction Werner Gerhard, Frank Weißmüller
Photo Hans Kroeskamp

KickStart question: How can the benefit best
be illustrated in a surreal or fantastic situation?

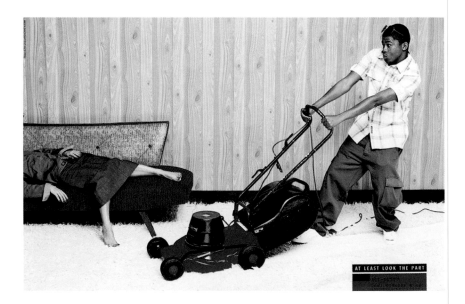

Client Levi Strauss & Co
Agency TBWA Hunt Lascaris, Cape Town
Creative Direction Peter Engelbrecht
Art Direction Alexis Beckett
Photo Kevin Fitzgerald

KickStart question: What absurd idea would
attract lots of attention to the product?

la brouette *(feminine)*
wheelbarrow

THE LYNX EFFECT

la bétonnière *(feminine)*
cement mixer

THE LYNX EFFECT

Client Lynx/Axe
Agency Bartle Bogle Hegarty, London
Creative Direction Dave Monk, Matt Waller
Art Direction Dave Monk, Matt Waller
Photo Malcolm Venville

KickStart question: What clichés can be
adapted to absurd effect in order to put
the product centre-stage?

BOCAGE
PARIS

Client Bocage Paris
Agency Devarrieux Villaret, Paris
Creative Direction Pierre-Dominique Burgaud
Art Direction Stéphane Richard
Photo Cédric Buchet

KickStart question: How can absurd, bizarre or surreal ideas be used to draw attention to the product, or give it a certain image?

Animal Planet is a wildlife documentary series on the Discovery Channel.
Client Animal Planet
Agency Saatchi & Saatchi, Singapore
Creative Direction Jagdish Ramakrishnan
Art Direction Edmund Choe, Addy Khaotong
Photo Michael Corridore

KickStart question: How can absurd and surreal situations be used to tell a story about the product?

ANYTHING'S POSSIBLE

If you want to make space for your team to spread their wings, invite them all to play this game: Assume that anything is possible and ask yourselves 'What if...'.

Shaking off the normal limitations of our own rules, standards, values and belief systems for a while, in order to enter virgin territory in our own heads, can be extremely exciting and open the way to fantastic ideas. Try it out in the team, under the DreamTeam rules, and allow a little more time than usual for the first meeting of this kind. You'll soon notice that the little phrase 'What if...' helps to lift the burden of reason and unleash everyone's imagination.

State your initial ideas in 'What if...' form, and then begin to develop and elaborate them. Think your stories through to the end, because the best things often lie a bit more deeply buried. Do it all with a twinkle in your eye, and remember to keep these meetings fun!

A few possible versions of 'What if...':

- What if...
  the product could defy gravity?
- What if...
  the product could make animals talk?
- What if...
  the product could let you read minds?
- What if...
  the product made it possible to see into the future?
- What if...
  the product was made for walking, talking dolls?
- What if...
  the product could give you an orgasm?

*'What would you say
to a cold beer?'*

*'Well, that depends on
what it said to me.'*

Every day we use familiar phrases, metaphors, slang expressions or combinations of words which, if we stop to look at them, contain buried jokes, absurd images or paradoxical situations. Try taking everything literally for the next two hours and see what happens! You'll notice that

the word-for-word translation of language into direct pictures often leads to comical, absurd or surprising ideas that can be turned into hugely successful campaigns. Have a shot at simultaneously translating all the words you hear or read directly into pictures or short film sequences.

As well as being the name of a cocktail, 'margarita' is the Spanish word for daisy.
Client Midori
Agency Leo Burnett, Puerto Rico
Creative Direction Olly Fernandez
Art Direction Christianne L. Cruz
Photo Clay Humphrey

" food"

McDrive

Client McDonald's
Agency Leo Burnett Annonsbyrå AB, Stockholm
Creative Direction Tom Nilson
Art Direction Gustaf Hultberger
Copy Mattias Öberg

KickStart question: What words or phrases associated with the product can be translated literally into a picture?

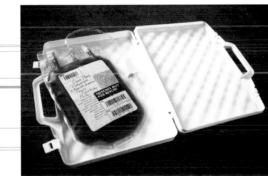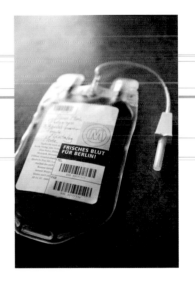

'Fresh Blood for Berlin' is a promotional mailshot for the photographer Oliver Mark.
Client Oliver Mark Fotografie
Agency Delikatessen Werbeagentur, Hamburg
Creative Direction Robert Neumann
Art Direction Robert Neumann
Photo Frank Jacob

KickStart question: What slang phrases, metaphors or turns of phrase could be translated literally into a visual image that will get the product or service noticed?

Nude Furniture

We make some of the most beautiful nude furniture in the Metroplex. Desks, tables, chairs and custom-made pieces. But please recognize that for people, shirts, shoes and pants are required.

ARLINGTON • N. RICHLAND HILLS • LEWISVILLE

Client Nude Furniture
Agency Gilliatt Paris, Dallas
Art Direction Braden Bickle, Chuck Paris
Copy Rob Baker
Photo Mike McKee

KickStart question: Are there any concepts associated with the product that can be translated literally into visual images?

Packaging for the soft drink Lucozade NRG
Client SmithKline Beecham
Agency Haines McGregor, London
Creative Direction Jeremy Haines
Art Direction Jeffrey Steventon
Copy Mattias Öberg

KickStart question: Are there any names, slogans or other verbal concepts that have a double meaning if taken literally?

ON THE ROCKS.

Client The Famous Grouse
Agency Abbott Mead Vickers BBDO,
London
Creative Direction Mary Wear
Art Direction Damon Collins
Photo James Balog
Zitaiquelle Lürzer's Archive 3/1996

KickStart question: How can common
expressions associated with the product
be converted literally into a picture?

ideas is the name of a marketing and
promotions magazine.
Agency Trickett & Webb, London

Client JEDAA
Agency The Hot Shop Design Group, Detroit
Art Direction Frank Brugos, Gloria Ajlouny

Client Adventure
Agency Mires Design Inc., San Diego
Art Direction José Serrano
Illustration Dan Thoner

As these two logos for Palm Springs show,
there is often more than one way to take
things literally.

TRAIN YOUR EARS TO SEE THINGS

The best way to develop the ability to take things literally is by
immediately converting spoken words into literal images in your head,
as soon as you hear them said. This could be in creative meetings or
brief discussions, or even when you're listening to a speech or a news
report. For example, if you hear someone complaining 'He's always taking
me for a ride', take it literally and imagine the scene. Give it as much
colour and emotion as you can. You'll have made good progress if, after
a little time, you can conjure up a picture or a film sequence for every
phrase you hear (or read) word for word, without needing to stop and
think. Try it with the following:

- I'm over the moon.
- His ideas were shot down by the art director.
- Posters attract people like flies.
- He's a bit dim and lives from hand to mouth.

For example, if you hear on the news that a minister 'flew to Tokyo
yesterday for a crisis summit', you might visualize the minister getting
into a plane at the airport and flying over a map to Tokyo, then climbing
out of the plane directly on to the summit of a volcano surrounded by
little clouds that represent the crisis. See what pictures come into your
head if you take the following passage from a sports magazine literally:
'The true sports fan is a number-cruncher and lives on statistics and
points tables. He often surfs the Net, stuffing himself with all the
information he wants.'

Exercise

Altering the product means changing its shape, cutting it into pieces, adding things, subtracting things, bending it, squeezing it, bringing it to life, blowing it up, making it transparent, transplanting it to another body or letting it rot. You'll find there are endless possibilities of changing it physically or giving it a new meaning. Get the team to think about all the things that could be done with the product, without asking first if the answers are 'right' or what they mean. Talk nonsense and really take off. You can't judge whether what you have is good and appropriate until you've gathered as many ideas as possible to choose from. All you need to do is let the ideas flow without criticizing any of them. Do the craziest things you can think of to the product and change it exactly as your fancy takes you. The examples in this section are just a few of the possibilities.

'We've been having trouble with too much green.' Campaign for a Japanese wine producer, based on using recycled glass.
Client Suntory Ltd
Agency Daiko Advertising, Tokyo
Creative Direction Hideo Kato, Jun Nishiwaki
Art Direction Kazunori Kitayama, Ryota Sukumo
Copy Jun Nishiwaki
Photo Naohiko Hoshino
Typography Naoko Seki, Kanata Ikemizu, Takashi Nagi

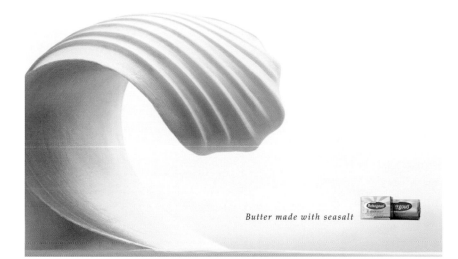

Butter made with seasalt

Client Campina Melkunie B.V.
Agency Ubachs Wisbrun, Amsterdam
Creative Direction Wim Ubachs,
Kees Sterrenburg
Art Direction Pim van Nunen, Eddy Besselink
Copy Annemiek den Uil
Photo Simon Warmer

KickStart question: How can the product be
altered to show the USP at a glance?

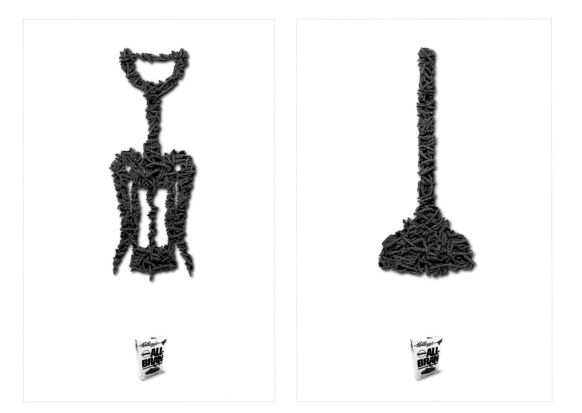

Campaign for a breakfast cereal that
prevents constipation
Client Kellogg's Mexico
Agency Leo Burnett, Mexico City
Creative Direction Tony Hidalgo
Art Direction Jorge Aguilar, Tony Hidalgo
Copy Gustavo Duenas

KickStart question: How can the product
be reshaped to communicate its benefit
on a metaphorical level?

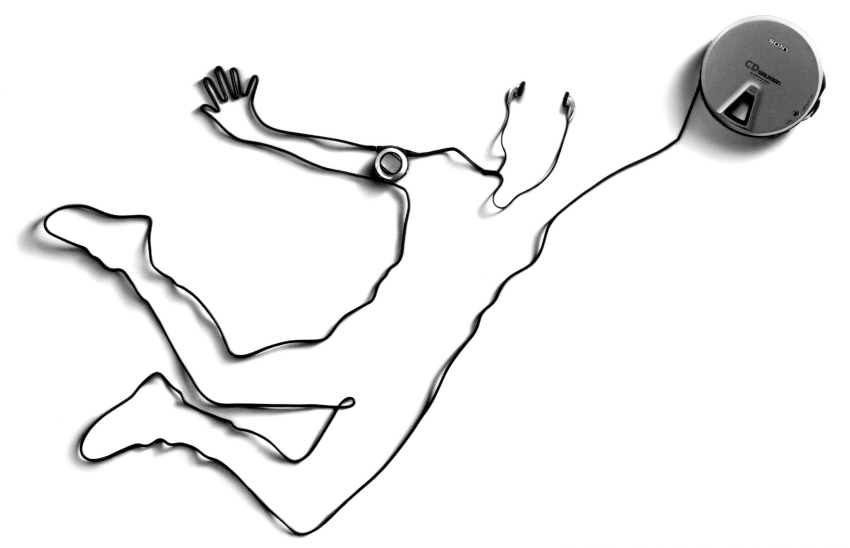

New CD Walkman from Sony. **The only one that doesn't kip while playing s**

Client Sony España S.A.
Agency Tandem Campmany Guasch DDB, Barcelona
Creative Team Tandem Campmany Guasch
Photo J. M. Roca

KickStart question: How can the product be depicted
differently to show its benefit at a glance?

 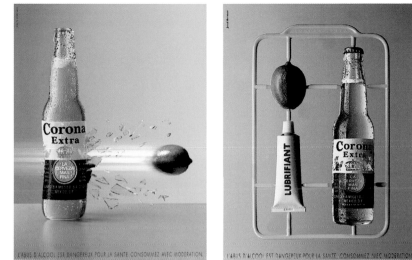

Campaign for Corona beer, usually served
with a piece of fresh lime in the bottle
Client Corona
Agency Jean & Montmarin, Paris
Creative Direction Gérard Jean
Art Direction Thierry Fèvre
Photo Paul Goirand
Copy Loïc Froger
Source Lürzer's Archive 1/2000

KickStart question: How could the product
be altered to communicate one particular
feature through exaggeration?

Client Land Rover
Agency WCRS Ltd, London
Creative Direction Nick Kidney
Art Direction Kevin Stark
Photo Max Forsythe

KickStart question: How can the
product be depicted differently to
put particular emphasis on one of
its selling points?

BE WARNED

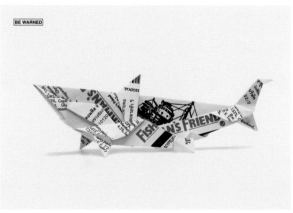

BE WARNED

Client Fisherman's Friend
Agency Ogilvy & Mather, Bangkok
Creative Direction Saranya Maleipan
Art Direction Wisit Lumsiricharoenchoke,
Sompoirn Laokittichok
Photo Fahdol Na Nagara

KickStart question: How can separate parts of
the product or packaging be altered to depict
the benefit in metaphorical terms?

The wrapper for a packet of Bahlsen
biscuits shows a continuous chain of
figures holding hands.
Client Bahlsen
Agency Lewis Moberly, London
Art Direction Mary Lewis
Photo Robin Broadbent

KickStart question: How could the product
be depicted differently to give it a special
appeal to the target group?

'Le Papillon [Butterfly] Roquefort.
What else could we call a Roquefort
matured in a cocoon?'
Client Le Papillon
Agency Young & Rubicam Kaena, Paris
Creative Direction José Doblas
Art Direction Jean-Pierre Mialon,
Patrick Chaubet
Photo Paul Goirand

KickStart question: How could you adapt
the product so that it represents the USP
metaphorically?

This section is about playful (lateral) approaches to the idea of finding new uses for the product. Where could the product be used, outside of its original context? What new situations could it be put in to emphasize the benefit, highlight a feature through exaggeration, or reveal a new perspective or an unexpected function? This section of the KickStart catalogue is an open invitation for you and your team to come and play.

So how about it? Anything is allowed, so long as it shows the team the way to new ideas, more time and fresh resources. You can even let yourselves get diverted from the original question to explore completely different pastures. The most important thing is that you stick with the KickStart questions and try to come up with as many original ideas as you possibly can.

Other papers still have their place.

Client   Sports Only
Agency   Bryant, Fulton & Shee, Vancouver
Art Direction   Jeffrey Hilts, Eric Howling
Photo   Robert Earnest

A waterskier pulls on his protective gloves and takes off on his wakeboard. Fantastic photography shows that he is master of the board in every situation. Not until halfway through the spot does it become clear that he is being pulled through shallow water at the sea's edge by an Audi Quattro with four-wheel drive.

Client Audi
Agency Bartle Bogle Hegarty, London
Creative Direction Will Awdry
Art Direction Alasdair Welsh
Copy Nick O'Bryan Tear
Production Spectre
Director Daniel Kleinman

KickStart question: In what unusual contexts could the product be used to promote its strengths?

IS YOUR PRODUCTION LINE
WORKING HARD ENOUGH?

Client Gintic
Agency Saatchi & Saatchi, Singapore
Creative Direction Calvin Soh
Art Direction Tay Guan Hin, Francis We
Photo Charles Liddall, Peter Canns

KickStart question: How could the
product itself represent its benefit
or the problem situation?

Client Sony
Agency Leo Burnett, Warsaw
Creative Direction Michael Long,
Lechoslaw Kwiatkowski, Kerry Keenan
Art Direction Michael Long,
Lechoslaw Kwiatkowski, Kerry Keenan
Photo Carli Hermes

KickStart question: Where and how could
the product be put to a surprising new use?

Campaign for a motorbike brand
Client Benelli
Agency Wieden & Kennedy, Amsterdam
Creative Direction Glenn Cole
Art Direction Robert Nakata
Photo Hans Pieterse

KickStart question: What new context could the product be placed in to underline the benefit?

Client Aspirina
Agency Almap, BBDO Comunicações, São Paulo
Creative Direction Ricardo Chester
Art Direction Marcello Serpa, Julio Andery
Photo Manolo Moran

KickStart question: Where or how could you use the product to show its benefit simply and clearly?

Client Chasecult
Agency Saatchi & Saatchi, Singapore
Creative Direction Rowan Chanen
Art Direction Edmund Choe
Photo Sebastian Tan

Client Ansell Condoms
Agency Whybin TBWA & Partners,
Melbourne
Creative Direction Paul Hastings
Art Direction Alex Fenton
Photo Eryk Fitkau

KickStart question: What unorthodox ways
of using the product would give a striking
demonstration of its USP?

'Because you're made of milk.'
Client Salute
Agency Almap, BBDO Comunicações,
São Paulo
Creative Direction Cassio Zanatta,
Marcello Serpa
Art Direction José Carlos Lollo
Photo Fernanda Tricoli

KickStart question: How can the shape
of the product be changed to show
its benefit at a glance?

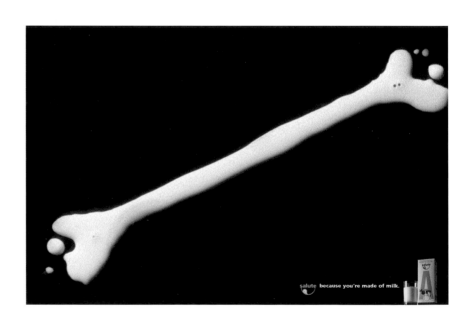

The questions in this section refer to visual as well as verbal double meanings. Most visual ambiguity is based on optical illusions which are a playful way to attract the viewer's attention. Most verbal ambiguity, on the other hand, makes its point by wordplay or suggestion, leading the reader along a path that usually ends in an alternative meaning. Both types involve people playfully by inviting them to see both meanings in a context that makes sense.

'Angry farmers from Diepenholz drove pigs to the Federal Parliament. Agriculture Minister Jochen Borchert spoke with them.' From an article in the Wolfsburger Nachrichten.

The best films in the air.

Client TAM Airlines
Agency DM9 DDB, São Paulo
Creative Direction Manir Fadel
Art Direction Sibely Silveira, Eugênio Duarte
Photo Rogerio Miranda

It's no good having power without control.

The new Audi A4 1.8 known where it stands on the major issues. Its 20 valve 125 bhp engine, makes it unequalled in its class. But, with the same four-link front suspension as the revolutionary A8 there's no doubt who's in charge. That should silence the sceptics. For more information call 0800 30 30 77.

Client Audi
Agency Bartle Bogle Hegarty, London
Creative Direction Jon Lilley
Art Direction Andy Bunday
Source Lürzer's Archive 6/1995

KickStart question: How can previous statements about the product be given a double meaning?

Client Malcolm R. Ward
Agency Colenso, Auckland
Creative Direction Ben Handy
Art Direction Ben Handy, Stu Hinds

KickStart question: How can ambiguity be used to advertise a product or a service in a humorous way?

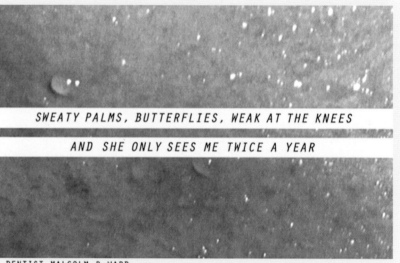

SWEATY PALMS, BUTTERFLIES, WEAK AT THE KNEES

AND SHE ONLY SEES ME TWICE A YEAR

DENTIST MALCOLM R WARD
FLOOR 10   SOUTHERN CROSS BLDG   CNR VICTORIA / HIGH ST   AUCKLAND PH 373 5521

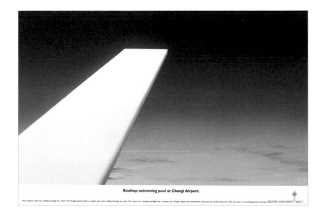

Rooftop swimming pool at Changi Airport.

Client Changi Airport, Singapore
Agency Saatchi & Saatchi, Singapore
Creative Direction Rowan Chanen, Peter Moyse, Renee Lim
Art Direction Rashid Salleh, Maurice Wee

KickStart question: How can the benefit be illustrated in a picture with a double meaning?

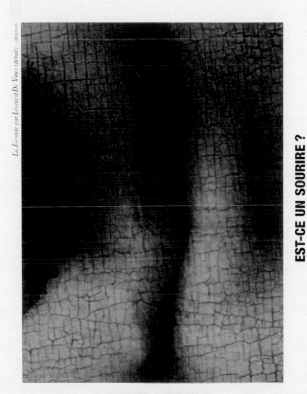

EST-CE UN DOS ?

EST-CE UN SOURIRE ?

Client Literacy Council
Agency Corporate Design Associates, Orlando
Designer Joe Krawczyk

Client Inner Beauty Dieticians
Agency Winston Advertising
Designer Dan Magnussen

'Is is a back? Or a smile?'
Client BMW
Agency BDDP, Paris
Creative Direction Noel Rémy
Art Direction Eric Holden
Photo Paul Wakefield
Source Lürzer's Archive 6/1994

KickStart question: How can you create the kind of visual ambiguity that will communicate the benefit?

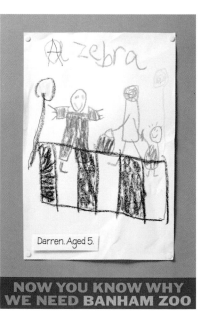

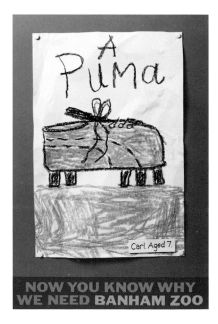

Campaign for the computer game
Earthworm Jim
Client Gameboy
Agency TBWA London
Creative Direction Graeme Parsons
Art Direction Phil Martin
Illustration Phil Martin

KickStart question: What puns and
double meanings can be created
from terms linked to the product?

Client Banham Zoo
Agency Bates Dorland, London
Creative Direction Tom Burnay
Art Direction Stef Jones

KickStart question: How can the problem
situation be summed up strikingly through
double meanings?

This web banner shows a couple getting friendly when suddenly something stirs in the young man's trousers. 'Is it her dress? ...her perfume?' Surprise! He pulls out his Motorola CD 930 with vibrating alarm.

Client DeTeMobil GmbH
Agency I-D Media AG, Hamburg
Creative Direction Hartmut Junker
Art Direction Hartmut Junker
Technical Direction Jan Oliver Kessler
Production Art Stefan Heilemann

PLAINLY AMBIGUOUS

The following exercise should improve your skill in detecting ambiguity in speech and generating it for yourself. The first step is to think of a process, an event or a situation (for example, making love), but then describe it so that other people might think you're talking about a political debate or a boxing match. It's a verbal no man's land, where the listener is always uncertain whether it's meant one way or another. As ever, practice makes perfect. Try it with these two examples:

○ How might a rapid parcels service be described in words that would allow it to be understood in a different sense: as a proposal of marriage, as an Olympic sport, or something else?

○ How might a new car be described so that it sounds like a toy for (big) children?

Exercise

Playing with words means making pictures with them. It's an invitation to experiment with type, so that the copy turns into pictures and the typography becomes the message. Ask yourself how you can break down the bounds of normal copy to make the content leap out. Could a word be integrated or transformed into an image? Could a word be depicted as the product or its packaging? Could it be merged with a pictorial element? Remember that there are many different forms of text to use. Could you style your words like a clue in a crossword puzzle, an entry in a dictionary, an appointment in a diary, an invoice or a receipt? This section should inspire you to scrutinize your ad copy as a source of ideas about design (preferably fun ones) and present the message even more clearly and effectively.

Client Mercedes-Benz Canada
Agency Roche Macaulay & Partners, Toronto
Creative Direction Geoffrey B. Roche,
Graham Lee, Dave Crichton
Art Direction Chris Harrison
Copy Mike O'Reilly

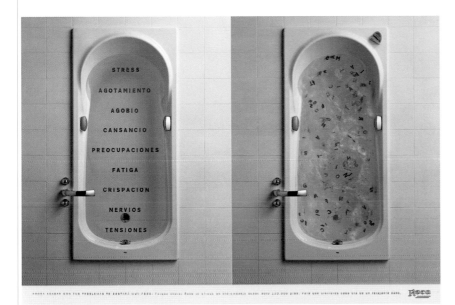

'Stress. Exhaustion. Aggravation. Tiredness. Worry. Fatigue. Anxiety. Nerves. Tension – It doesn't cost much to dissolve your problems. Roca now gives you a hydromassage for only 135,000 pesetas. So you can enjoy a relaxing bath every day.'

Client Roca
Agency Publicis Casadevall Pedreño & PRG, Barcelona
Creative Direction Jose Maria Roca de Vinalo, Jaume Rodríguez, José María Pujol
Art Direction Eva Terradas, Ramón Roda, Josep Marin
Photo Ricardo Miras

KickStart question: How can you play with the typography to represent the USP in an effective visual image?

Client McDonald's
Agency K. Trevino & Asociados, Mexico City
Creative Direction Carlo Olivares-Paganoni, Erre Cavazos
Art Direction Angie González
Photo Javier Broker

KickStart question: How can words, symbols or logos be integrated into the picture without using the usual typographic techniques?

?regnancy test

1 test • 99% Accurate • Result in 4 minutes

superdrug

Client Superdrug Pregnancy Testing Kit
Agency Williams Murray Hamm, London
Creative Direction Garrick Hamm
Art Direction Clare Poupard
Copy Richard Murray

KickStart question: How can the central advertising message be reinforced by altering the typography?

Client Mr and Mrs Aubrey Hair
Agency Pentagram
Designer Woody Pirtle

'Reliable. The Sanyo front-loader.'
Client Sanyo
Agency Lowe & Partners, Monsoon Advertising, Singapore
Creative Direction Mandy Siow
Art Direction Thomas Yang

KickStart question: How can ad copy be combined typographically with the product itself, to convey the USP in a clear and original way?

'I like it – 879,993 hairs can't be wrong.'
Client Phytoervas
Agency DM9 DDB, São Paulo
Creative Direction José Henrique Borghi
Art Direction Erh Ray
Copy Paulo Vainer, Alexandre Catan

KickStart question: How can central
elements of the picture be adapted to
show the message typographically?

Client L.A. Cellular
Agency BBDO West, San Francisco
Creative Direction Kathy Hepinstall,
Harold Einstein
Art Direction Chris Robb
Photo Geoff Kern

KickStart question: How can words be
integrated into the picture in an unusual
way, attracting attention and underlining
the central advertising statement?

Banner campaign for an eye bank. As
the mouse moves over the banner, the
braille script is converted into letters of the
alphabet so that sighted people can read it.
Client São Paulo Eye Bank
Agency AgênciaClick, São Paulo
Creative Direction PJ Pereira,
Eduardo Martins
Art Direction Edwin Veelo
Copy Mauro Alencar
Production Claudia Obata
Programming Marcelo Siqueira,
Miguel Castarde

This section of the KickStart catalogue spotlights the use of wordplay, popular sayings, quotations, rhyme, catchphrases, proverbs or maxims to trigger new ideas. Think of all the ones you know, or look for them in reference books such as dictionaries of quotations. The point is not so much integrating a quotation or idiom word for word into your ad, as putting it forward at a meeting as a stimulus for new ideas. Play with it in the team, pretend you've never seen it before, alter it, change the context, or use it as the launchpad for a completely new idea. Here are some examples of the huge array of opportunities that language offers.

'Between men'/'Underpants'
This ad plays on the multiple meanings of the German word 'unter' (between, among, under). The boys' faces are saying that, between themselves (man to man), the underpants are great.
Client Sanetta
Agency RG Wiesmeier, Munich
Creative Direction Joerg Jahn
Art Direction Gudrun Mullner,
Marie-Louise Dorst
Photo Rainer Leitzgen

○ *Rhymes:*
For mash, get Smash.
Once you pop, you can't stop.

○ *Sayings or proverbs:*
Good things come to those
    who wait.

○ *Quotations:*
One small step for man, one
    giant leap for mankind.
Play it again, Sam.

○ *Alliteration:*
My mate, Marmite.
If anyone can, Canon can.

○ *Triplets:*
Healthy. Happy. Huggies.
World problems. World solutions.
    World class.

○ *Chiasmus:*
Say no to no say.

○ *Neologism:*
Guinnless isn't good for you.
You know when you've been
    Tango'd.

○ *Non sequitur:*
The surprising alternative to
    armadillos.

○ *Adapt an existing expression:*
Head over Heal's.
Menswear buy it.

○ *Adapt a proverb:*
Think small.
Thirst come, thirst served.

○ *Personification:*
Let your fingers do the walking.
The car that talks your language.

○ *Synaesthesia (two or more
    senses combined):*
Taste the rainbow.

Client Coleman
Agency TBWA, Brussels
Creative Direction Paul van Oevelen
Art Direction Jan Macken
Photo Peter De Mulder

KickStart question: Can you construct
rhymes, puns or other kinds of wordplay
from the product or brand, which will
underline the USP?

Client BMW
Agency Fallon Worldwide, Minneapolis
Creative Direction Tony Rosen
Art Direction Tom Lichtenheld
Photo Mark Laita

KickStart question: How could a feature
of the product be represented, using the
widest possible spectrum of wordplay,
familiar expressions, onomatopoeia
or exclamations?

Fortunately, it's covered by Accident **General Accident**

Client   General Accident
Agency   Strathearn Advertising, Edinburgh
Creative Direction   Don MacAskill
Art Direction   Don MacAskill
Illustration   Frank Langford

KickStart question: How could exclamations, onomatopoeia, and cartoon images be used to communicate a problem situation or the USP in a striking way?

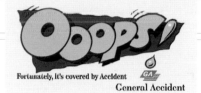

Mineral water packaging specially designed for a hotel
Client   The Germain Group
Agency   Paprika Communications, Montreal
Designer   Francis Turgeon
Art Direction   Louis Gagnon

KickStart question: How can terms associated with the product or brand be integrated into wordplay, in the widest sense, so that they become the centre of attention?

A man pushes his shopping trolley, laden with a solitary banana, across the shopping centre car park and up to his Opel Agila. He pushes down the rear seat, at which point, in view of the small bulk of his purchase, a voiceover goes 'ha ha'. But the laughter turns to 'aha!' when the man puts the whole trolley into his car and then drives it round to the trolley park.

SEX, DRUGS & R

imagine
a world without
MTV MUSIC TELEVISION

vote before 15th august

Client MTV
Agency BBDO A/S, Copenhagen
Art Direction Martin Bo Kristensen,
Lars Schmidt Hansen

KickStart question: How can familiar expressions, quotations or proverbs be adapted to foreground the product?

Client Opel
Agency McCann-Erickson, Brussels
Creative Direction Johan de Witte
Art Direction Anneke Rombaut
Production Velocity
Director Lizelle Mes

KickStart question: How can a story be developed around a phrase, rhyme or play on words to demonstrate the benefit?

This ad, highlighting the fuel capacity of the car, uses a pun on the German word 'wart' which means 'wait', while 'Tankwart' means 'pump attendant'.
Client Mercedes Benz
Agency Springer & Jacoby, Hamburg
Creative Direction André Kemper
Art Direction Kurt Georg Dieckert
Copy André Kemper
Photo Peter Lavery

KickStart question: How can the copy describing the benefit be emphasized through wordplay?

Client Oy Sokos Ab
Agency Hasan Partners, Helsinki
Art Direction Anu Igoni
Copy Sari Manninen-Mikkola

KickStart question: How can wordplay be used to describe the benefit in an entertaining way?

'An optimist says a glass is half full, a pessimist says it's half empty. They're both right, they're just putting a different interpretation on the same thing.'

REFRAMING IS THE SERIOUS SIDE OF JOKING

Now it's time to introduce the concept of reframing, devised by John Grinder and Richard Bandler, as a key to creative thinking. You'll notice that it is basically very similar to the concept of altering frames of reference in the section on jokes and punchlines in Part 3. The important difference, however, is that in this case we are not talking about reframing with the intention of creating a punchline but instead trying to show something familiar from a new perspective, giving your target group a startling new insight or a positive 'Aha' experience.

HOW DOES REFRAMING WORK?

The way we interpret events, statements or behaviour depends on the context, or frame, in which they are placed. For example, if you hear the sound of squeaking shoes behind you in a busy shopping street, you don't pay it any attention. But if you hear the same noise outside your window, at night, when you're alone in bed, the difference in the framing gives the sound a quite different significance. Here's an everyday story that provides a splendid example of how to turn something negative into something positive. A man complains that his wife takes too long to make up her mind about anything: 'She has to look at every dress in the shop and compare them with each other before she can choose one.' His friend turns this around and provides a positive interpretation: 'So she goes around choosing things very carefully. Doesn't it feel great that out of all the men on earth she chose you?' The examples on the following pages show how you could develop effective reframings in a similar way, in order to put a new interpretation on objects or events.

1. ONE WORD IS ENOUGH

Surprise your target group by showing them a new perspective on something familiar. The two print ads on this page show that a word or a simple sign is often all it takes to change the context and therefore the meaning. Each of the three suggestions posits a completely different interpretation of the situation in the picture. Each alters the viewer's perception and triggers a new reaction to an everyday scenario.

Client Red Envelope
Agency Leagas Delaney, San Francisco
Creative Direction Matt Rivitz
Art Direction Steve Mapp
Photo Daniel Proctor, Peggy Sirota

Client Canon
Agency TBWA/H Neth-work, Amsterdam
Creative Direction Guus Vonk
Art Direction Rob Sikkink, Matthijs Bakker
Photo Jacek Soltan

2. ONE PICTURE IS ENOUGH

These examples show how the meaning of a situation or an object can also be changed without words, by adding or altering a visual sign or symbol. A perfectly ordinary object acquires a new interpretation which may be funny or enlightening and we see a new side to a familiar thing.

Simple repetition of the muddy imprint of a football in the top left-hand corner of this poster puts a new meaning into the viewer's mind, and the billboard becomes a goal mouth. The second example also uses a very simple visual image to enhance the meaning. Four red stripes added to the rim of a rolled-up condom make it look like a lifebelt.

Client Adidas
Agency BBDO A/S, Copenhagen
Art Direction Mads Ohrt

Client Durex
Agency McCann-Erickson, Barcelona
Creative Direction Josep M. Ferrara
Art Direction Jaume Badia
Copy Josep M. Ferrara, Alfredo Binefa
Photo Josep M. Roca

EXPERIMENT WITH REFRAMING FOR YOURSELF

The examples on the following pages demonstrate some different types of reframing to help you develop a feeling for the technique. Try to put a new interpretation on objects, situations or forms of behaviour by experimenting with the context. The meaning of a sign relies entirely on the context in which it occurs: change the context, and the meaning changes automatically.

Client NRMA and NSW Rural Fire Service
Agency Saatchi & Saatchi, Sydney
Creative Direction Michael Newman
Art Direction Steve Carlin, Scot Waterhouse
Photo Mark Lang – Wildlight

KickStart question Is there a larger or different frame or context within which an item or object (cigarette ash) will acquire new meaning?

Campaign for a mail-order catalogue
Client 3 suisses
Agency CLM/BBDO, Paris
Creative Direction Virginie Lepère
Art Direction Frédéric Van Hoof
Photo Iris Brosch
Source Lürzer's Archive 1/2000

KickStart question: What sort of context will make a particular feature or function appear worthwhile and useful, and so show something in a new and positive light?

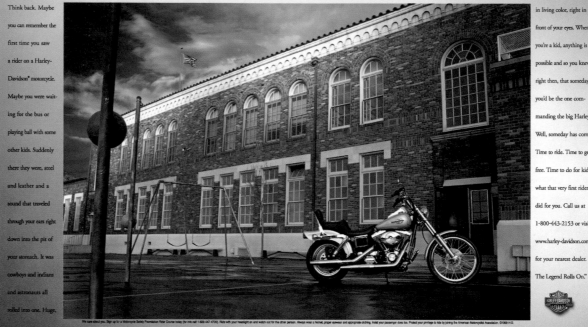

RIDE. BECAUSE CHILDREN NEED HEROES.

Think back. Maybe you can remember the first time you saw a rider on a Harley-Davidson® motorcycle. Maybe you were waiting for the bus or playing ball with some other kids. Suddenly there they were, steel and leather and a sound that traveled through your ears right down into the pit of your stomach. It was cowboys and indians and astronauts all rolled into one. Huge, in living color, right in front of your eyes. When you're a kid, anything is possible and so you knew right then, that someday, you'd be the one commanding the big Harley.® Well, someday has come. Time to ride. Time to get free. Time to do for kids what that very first rider did for you. Call us at 1-800-443-2153 or visit www.harley-davidson.com for your nearest dealer. The Legend Rolls On.™

Client Harley-Davidson
Agency Carmichael Lynch Inc., Minneapolis
Creative Direction Jim Nelson, Sheldon Clay
Art Direction Paul Asao, Peter Winecke
Photo Todd Johnson, www.tjphoto.com

KickStart question: How can you alter the frame or context from within which events are seen, and so change their meaning?

Campaign for motorcycle safety
Client Minnesota Motorcycle Safety Center
Agency Martin/Williams Advertising, Minneapolis
Creative Direction Tom Kelly
Art Direction Randy Hughes
Photo Shawn Michienzi

KickStart question: Can you give something a new name with positive or negative connotations, and so put a new perspective on familiar things?

Tattoo remover.

ALWAYS WEAR FULL PROTECTIVE GEAR. SAFETY CENTER

'All carmakers have some kind of quality control. But we think we should double check.' These two double-page ads appeared on consecutive pages in magazines.
Client VW
Agency Almap, BBDO Comunicações, São Paulo
Creative Direction Eugenio Mohallem
Art Direction Marcello Serpa

KickStart question: How can you add something to a familiar object or symbol to make it take on a new meaning?

Client VW
Agency Verba DDB SRL, Milan
Creative Direction Enrico Bonomini
Art Direction Gianfranco Marabelli
Photo Mario Cassetta

KickStart question: Are there any key words which could give the product a new meaning in the viewer's eyes?

For simplicity's sake, metaphor and analogy are used as synonyms in this section. In the broadest sense, metaphors can be regarded as simple analogies, but not all analogies are metaphors. Rather than overload the text with explanations and definitions, I do not differentiate the two as strictly as a dictionary.

Metaphors have always been one of the most effective forms of communicating meaning in a subtle and elegant way. The underlying operation is the search for similarities, because the best way to understand the significance of something new is to compare it with something we already know. For example, the first steam locomotives were often called 'iron horses', while vehicles which can run both in water and on land are known as 'amphibians'. We constantly make comparisons and transfer meanings from one living creature to another ('fox', 'foxy'), from one inanimate thing to another ('riverbed'), from the animate to the inanimate and vice versa ('caterpillar tractor'), or from the material to the spiritual ('burning love'). Comparisons like these conjure up mental images which express a thing in terms of another thing, so creating a new layer of meaning. Here's a little metaphor to show what I mean: imagine that you're flying to Paris for the first time in your life and your travel agent has sold you a week's season ticket for the Metro as part of the package. Sitting in the plane, you unfold the map of Paris to familiarize yourself with the transport network, the most important buildings, the sights, the course of the Seine and the location of the Eiffel Tower. Now of course the map is not really the area it represents, but simply an image of the layout of Paris, drawn to scale. This is how to think about metaphors: they function as mental maps, making it easier to understand new and complex content in an elegant way.

Client Levi Strauss & Co
Agency TBWA Hunt Lascaris, Cape Town
Creative Direction Paige Nick
Art Direction Michael Ipp
Photo Jan Verboom

KickStart question: How can one thing be expressed in terms of another, so that the connection casts new light on the thing described?

The basic principle of metaphor and analogy

When trying to construct a metaphor or analogy, take two elements from different spheres (e.g. technology or nature) and see if they have any similarities, such as a similar function or a shared physical characteristic (e.g. shape). The Volvo ad below is an excellent demonstration of this basic idea.

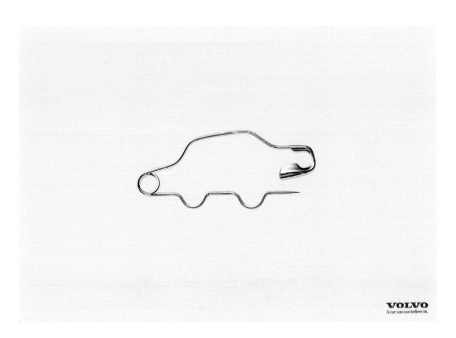

Client Volvo
Agency Young & Rubicam, Tokyo
Creative Direction Minoru Kawase
Art Direction Masakazu Sawa
Photo Megumu Wada
Source Lürzer's Archive 4/1996

Client Kraft
Agency J. Walter Thompson, Melbourne
Creative Direction John Mescall
Art Direction Simon Greed
Illustration Bill Wood

Client Boeri Sport USA
Agency Mullen Advertising, Wenham, MA
Creative Direction Stephen Mietelski
Art Direction Mary Rich
Photo Craig Orsini

KickStart question: How can the problem situation be dramatized by comparison with something different but similar, so as to highlight the USP?

Client Superdrug
Agency Turner Duckworth, London
Creative Direction Bruce Duckworth
Art Direction Janice Davison
Illustration Sam Hadley

KickStart question: How can a metaphor help to illustrate the benefit at a glance?

Client Playstation
Agency TBWA, Paris
Creative Direction Jorge Teixeira,
Luis Christello
Art Direction Marcus Kawamura
Copy Jorge Teixeira
Photo João Trabuco

KickStart question: How can a metaphor
be used to grab the viewer's attention
and emphasize the associations of
a product feature?

Client S.O.S. Mata Atlântica
Agency F/Nazca S&S, Brazil
Creative Direction Fábio Fernandes
Art Direction Sidney Araújo
Copy Victor Sant'Anna
Photo João Caetano

KickStart question: How can metaphor
or analogy present a problem situation
so that it can be seen at a glance and
needs no explanation?

Innovative packaging for a fertilizer

Client CDA Malaysia, Plant Aid

Agency Grey Worldwide, Malaysia

Designer Edwin Leong, Andy Soong, Richard Chin

Art Direction Edwin Leong, Jeff Orr

Copy Edwin Leong

Illustration Richard Chin

Photo Jack Shea

KickStart question: How can you represent a new product by comparing it with something familiar, so that the benefit is immediately obvious?

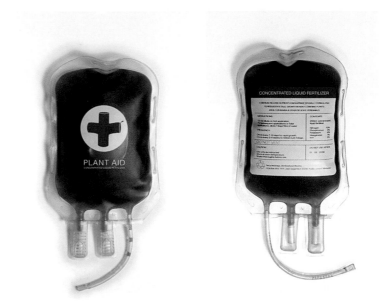

Client Shimano cycling shoes

Agency Sawyer Riley Compton, Atlanta

Creative Direction Alex Bogusky

Art Direction Tony Calcao

Copy Scott Linnen, Stefani Zelmer

Photo Mark Laita

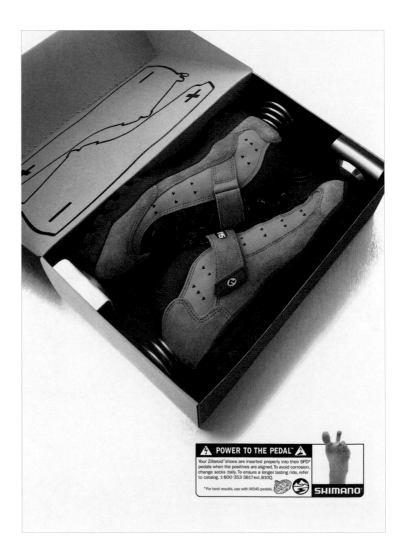

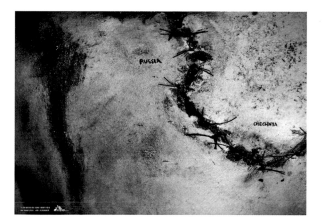

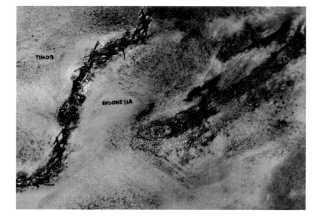

Campaign for a charity that works in war zones
Client Médecins Sans Frontières
Agency McCann-Erickson, Madrid
Creative Direction Nicolás Hollander
Andrés Martínez
Art Direction Mary Rich
Photo Santiago Esteban

KickStart question: How can a metaphor help to
present a problem situation with the utmost immediacy
and emotional impact?

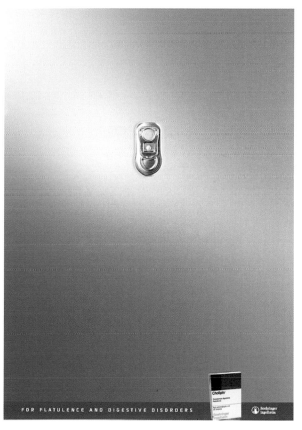

Logo for Persimmon Books
Agency Pentagram

Client Boehringer Ingelheim
Agency Young & Rubicam, Lisbon
Creative Direction Jorge Teixeira,
Luis Christello
Art Direction João Nobre
Copy Maria Pedro
Photo Picto

MAKING METAPHORS MEANS RECOGNIZING PATTERNS

When you want to invent a metaphor for a engine, for example, and you study things from different fields – such as nature or technology – to find something that works on a similar principle, you are looking for a pattern. To find patterns of this kind, you need to focus on function, form, materials, actions, or a combination of other features.

We come across simple and complex patterns every day, in every part of our lives. For instance, you may well have seen two dogs go running up to each other, then start sniffing and growling suspiciously. When the weaker of the two starts to feel threatened, it lowers its forequarters, stretching out its legs and pawing the ground, then runs away, barking. The bigger dog takes up the chase, and corners the runaway. Once again the smaller dog bows and paws, and the scene is repeated over and over again. You are witnessing a specific pattern of behaviour, which dog-owners see every day but have been unable to unravel until very recently. Behavioural scientists now interpret this pattern of 'obeisance' as a trigger for play, which automatically suppresses aggression in members of the same species.

The ability to recognize patterns, in the similarly constructed plots of thrillers, for example, or in the way an engine functions or an umbrella is folded, or in the rules of board games, is essential to the construction of simple or complex metaphors. These two exercises illustrate the structure of this type of pattern and are intended to sensitize your ability to perceive them.

→ *Exercise 1*

The following exercise demonstrates the basic principle of constructing metaphors: 'Prudence is the mother of wisdom' expresses the idea that wisdom relates to prudence as a daughter does to her mother. Now try to work out which of the four possible answers to the question in example 1 is the right one, and try to think of three or four words that would fit appropriately in example 2.

1. Books are to libraries as videos are to...

a) video recorders   b) cinemas

c) video cameras   d) video shops

2. Water is to a ship as .... is to business.

a) ....   b) ....

→ *Exercise 2*

Find the parallels in the patterns shown below. Work out how A relates to B, and then try to see which pattern (D, E or F) relates to C in the same way.

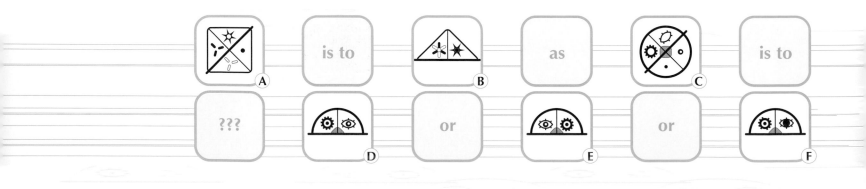

A METHODICAL WAY TO BUILD METAPHORS

The following five steps are a useful guide to building metaphors. Try to find your own variations on the metaphor depicted on the right. The most important thing is to stay with it and not give up after the first ten ideas that occur to you. If you take the time and effort, you will come up with some really new and original ideas.

→ 1. First of all, express your goal as a 'single-minded proposition'. In the case of this ad, the goal might be as follows: How can we show in a story that these tyres provide optimal safety in all conditions? Or: How can we depict the safety these tyres give the driver in a single image? Let these two goals work together and you'll notice the subtle way that different goals can shift the focus of your thoughts in particular directions.

→ 2. If you are looking for ideas in a team setting, follow the DreamTeam rules.

→ 3. Next, break down the subject of safety and car tyres into its component parts and examine it from every angle: from the viewpoint of the driver, the vehicle, the family, the manufacturer, the road surface, or even the tyre itself. Ask yourself what safety means in connection with tyres and what the consequences are. If you analyse the subject properly you will discern patterns which you will be able to use as blueprints in the next stage.

→ 4. Now that you've worked out the patterns that link safety and car tyres, look for similar patterns in other subject fields. Let your associations run free and try to find similarities in, for instance, motor racing, medicine, watchmaking, biotechnology, politics or botany. When searching for metaphors to use, set no limits on your imagination or the themes you choose. You might find it useful to ask questions such as these: What does a safe tyre resemble? Where is safety always the first priority? Where and how does nature ensure safety? How can safety be portrayed?

→ 5. A tip: Do you want to use this metaphor in an print ad or a TV spot? Depending on its destination, let the metaphors in your head take the form of a still photo or a short film sequence. Try to manage without written or spoken copy − let the pictures do the talking.

Do not treat this exercise as a recipe to be followed step by step, but as a basic framework for constructing metaphors. Read this section, think about the function and purpose of the points in it, and then try simply to forget the whole thing. Sticking too closely to the rules is the best way to block the natural and intuitive flow of ideas.

Client Nokian Tyres
Agency Paltemaa Huttunen Santala TBWA, Helsinki
Creative Direction Mira Leppänen
Art Direction Unto Paltemaa
Photo Markku Lahdesmaki

WORDS PAINT PICTURES IN YOUR HEAD

Purely verbal metaphors are especially effective when you want to generate vivid pictures in the reader's head with a minimum of words, in all kinds of slogans, captions, headlines, or advertising copy.

- ○ Put a tiger in your tank
- ○ Let the train take the strain
- ○ Go to work on an egg
- ○ Fly the friendly skies

Storytelling metaphors

Metaphorical stories have been used over the millennia to pass on religious teachings, cultural attitudes and practical knowledge from generation to generation. Metaphors which tell stories have lost none of their power even today: concepts, ideas and ways of looking at life are not communicated directly but in the form of something else comparable which stirs the imagination. Using metaphor in a story can make the listeners compare something new with something they already know and give them new insights. There are countless examples of really successful metaphors in TV spots which take only 30 seconds to explain why an innovative product is indispensable, how it makes life easier, what fantastic features it has, and what uses you can put it to that you never dreamed of before.

This TV spot shows a game warden driving his truck through the African savannah. He is speaking in Afrikaans with subtitles and seems to be on his way to release a wild animal.

'It's all wrong. The city is no place for them. Stood all day. Crammed up with no space to move around. They should be out here in these wide-open spaces where they can run free the way they were meant to.'

The lorry stops and the gamewardens open the back of the lorry. They peer cautiously into the lorry and beat the wall to tempt the supposed beast out, to no avail. After a few more attempts there is a growl – at last it has seen the way to freedom. The Freelander charges down the ramp into the savannah, where it immediately meets another of its kind, as the gamewardens cheer. The two Freelanders gambol about in high spirits then run over to join a large herd of other Freelanders living in the wild. The gamewardens watch from a distance, smiling benevolently.

Client Land Rover, Freelander
Agency WCRS Ltd, London
Director Ivan Zacharias
Art Direction Andy Dibb
Copy Steve Little
Production Blink Productions

BIONICS – NATURE AS A MODEL

Bionics is a modern term for an age-old technique. It means taking ideas from nature – especially living creatures – and adapting them for use in technology and other areas. The word itself, appropriately, comes from combining 'bio-' and 'electronic'. Velcro, for example, was inspired by the mechanism that burrs use to cling to passing animals. Cross-country skis, meanwhile, have scales on their underside which allow forward motion but prevent the ski from sliding backwards; the model for this was the unusual structure of scales on the belly of a South American snake.

In advertising and marketing, too, bionics can be a great source of creative ideas, all based around analogies in nature. Innovative products, packaging and optimal design are only part of the story: the product message can also be communicated very effectively using ideas from bionics.

A bionics session:

→ Phase 1. Begin by looking for analogies in the animal or plant world. Can you find any phenomena that resemble the problem you want to solve? Sort them according to shape, structure, method of control, function, appearance or location of use. Ask yourselves what these solutions look like. Are there several different solutions, and if so, is there a common denominator underlying the differences?

→ Phase 2. Once a study of the analogies has uncovered structures, patterns, functions, forms and conditions, the team can now begin to relate these to the original problem in order to develop possible solutions and evaluate them. If one analogy does not fit the problem properly and produces a meagre crop of ideas, feel free to select others. To make it easier to analyse a direct analogy, team members could try to identify with the analogy and ask themselves: How would I feel if I were X?

Good ideas do sometimes grow on trees – or in fields. In this example, nature demonstrates an ecologically sound method of packaging which takes up very little space: the model for the raincape pack is the bud of the oriental poppy.

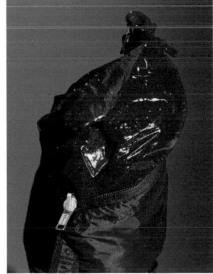

Client Mares, Neoprene diving suits
Agency McCann-Erickson, Barcelona
Creative Direction Josep M. Ferrara
Art Direction Xavi Cubero
Copy Josep M. Ferrara, Sergi Zapater
Photo Joan Rigau

*'Only the stupidest mouse
would hide in the cat's ear
But only the cleverest cat
would think of looking
there.'*

RULES ARE MADE TO BE BROKEN

When you use the KickStart questions in this section with the team,
the crucial factor is breaking rules in order to burst out of the frame
of standard advertising formats or integrate them creatively into the
message. Overstep the physical boundaries of posters, newspaper ads
or mailshots; don't just design your message creatively but integrate
the entire medium into your idea. This section shows that creativity isn't
always constructive, but often requires destructiveness too. No rules
are meant to last forever. Look around and you'll see that a large
proportion of all innovations in fields such as technology, marketing,
the arts or advertising only came into existence after previously
existing rules were broken!

Exercise

TACIT ASSUMPTIONS: WHAT DO YOU TAKE FOR GRANTED?

Try this interesting experiment which may help you to be more aware
of your own restrictive rules and assumptions. Try to join all nine spots
on the diagram below with at most four straight lines; the only condition
is that you mustn't lift the pencil from the paper!

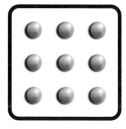

When (or if) you've found a solution and want to see what ideas other
people might have, turn the page. You'll be surprised at how many tacit
assumptions stopped you thinking of alternatives.

3D billboard campaign for insecticide
Client Juan Demergasso
Agency Pragma/FCB Publicidad, Buenos Aires
Creative Direction Pablo Poncini, David Bamballi

Campaign for a brand of workwear
Client Kansas, Work & Casual Wear
Agency Grey Worldwide, Copenhagen
Art Direction Tobias Rosenberg
Copy Thomas Asbaek

KickStart question: How can an unusual
advertising format be used to integrate
the setting and the message?

Client Duracell Batteries
Agency Wurmser Ogilvy & Mather,
Guatemala City
Creative Direction Ramiro Eduardo
Art Direction José Acevedo,
Ana Luisa de Redondo, Carlos Soto
Copy Estuardo Juárez
Photo Ramiro Eduardo

KickStart question: How can the context of
the medium be integrated into the message
in a meaningful way?

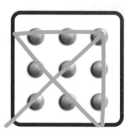
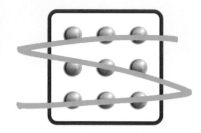

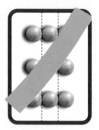

Assumption 1: The lines must not go outside the square frame.
Before you set about solving the problem, you probably took certain things for granted which significantly restricted the number of possible solutions. For example, many people assume that the lines must not go outside the square frame. However, this was not a stated condition, so you are free to ignore the frame and solve the problem as shown above.

Assumption 2: The lines must go through the middle of the spots.
If you draw the lines so that they only just touch some of the spots, you can even solve the problem with three lines.

Assumption 3: The lines must be thin.
Join the spots with one very thick stroke.

Assumption 4: The paper must not be folded.
Fold the paper so that the spots touch each other in threes. Once again you only need one thick stroke to join them all.

The message in the doll's briefcase says 'Don't be satisfied with toys. Demand the original.'
Client N-Design
Agency Delikatessen Werbeagentur, Hamburg
Creative Direction Robert Neumann
Art Direction Robert Neumann
Copy Marco Steinbuss
Photo Rolf Seife

KickStart question: How can objects from other contexts be used in place of traditional media?

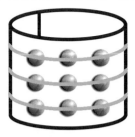

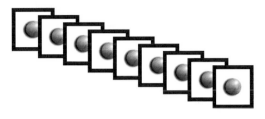

Assumption 5: The paper must lie flat.
Roll the paper into a tube. Now you can join the spots with a spiral, which is a straight line on the curved surface.

Assumption 6: The paper must stay in one piece.
Cut the spots out, lay them on top of each other and pierce through the pile with the point of the pencil.

Assumption 7: The lines must not go over the edge of the paper.
If the line were long enough, it could go all the way around the world. One line that made just over two full circuits of the globe would solve the problem.

Campaign for the Renault Kangoo, which has sliding doors on both sides. The photo shows the doors open and you can see straight through the poster.
Client Renault Nederland
Agency Publicis, Amsterdam
Creative Direction Peter Clercx, Victor Silvis
Art Direction Monique Pawirosemito
Copy Yvo Bronsvoort
Photo Hans Hiltermann

KickStart question: How can standard media be altered to give the benefit more impact?

Client KoolAid
Agency Young & Rubicam, Toronto
Creative Direction David Adams, John Farquhar
Art Direction Marc Melanson
Copy Stephen Stahl

KickStart question: How can the frame of a standard medium be broken to draw more attention to the product?

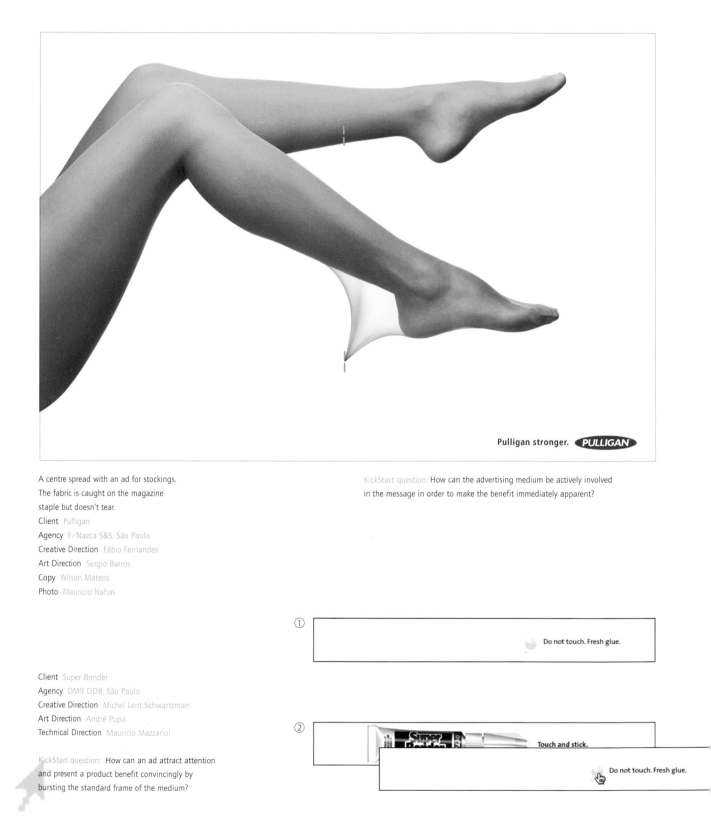

Pulligan stronger. **PULLIGAN**

A centre spread with an ad for stockings.
The fabric is caught on the magazine
staple but doesn't tear.
Client Pulligan
Agency F/Nazca S&S, São Paulo
Creative Direction Fábio Fernandes
Art Direction Sergio Barros
Copy Wilson Mateos
Photo Mauricio Nahas

KickStart question: How can the advertising medium be actively involved
in the message in order to make the benefit immediately apparent?

① Do not touch. Fresh glue.

Client Super Bonder
Agency DM9 DDB, São Paulo
Creative Direction Michel Lent Schwartzman
Art Direction André Pupo
Technical Direction Mauricio Mazzariol

KickStart question: How can an ad attract attention
and present a product benefit convincingly by
bursting the standard frame of the medium?

② Touch and stick.

Do not touch. Fresh glue.

Double-page ad for WD-40 lubricant
Client Eival, S.A.
Agency Publicis, Lisbon
Creative Direction José Trabucho,
Francisco Vasconcelos
Art Direction Rogério Serrasqueiro
Copy Marcelo Dolabella, Rui Bernardo
Photo João Palmeiro

KickStart question: How can the medium be involved
in the message in a playful and intelligent way?

③ Touch and stick.

'One Drop' banner campaign for superglue.
The order 'Do not touch' tempts the viewer
to run the mouse over it. The banner then
sticks to the cursor, and as it follows its
movement the tube of glue can be seen
behind the first banner.

Do not touch. Fresh glue.

These two photos show an ad for a security lighting system. An infra-red sensor on the hoarding reacts to movement and immediately switches the light on.
Client Kinshield
Agency BMP DDB Ltd, London
Creative Direction Tony Davidson
Art Direction Tony Davidson

KickStart question: What means can be used to overstep the normal boundaries of a medium and grab the attention of the target group?

BREAKING DOWN BARRIERS

As discussed in the section on reframing, things take their meaning from the context in which they are placed. A paperclip makes you think, first and foremost, of holding letters, memos and other pieces of paper together. Have some fun breaking down boundaries by thinking of twenty other uses for a paperclip or another everyday object. The purpose of the exercise is to train your ability to discover new ways to use something familiar and so enhance your creativity in handling standard media.

Alternative uses for a paperclip:

- ○ Turn a broken pair of spectacles into designer frames
- ○ Mend the altimeter while the plane is nosediving
- ○ Make a One-Way Street sign for ants
- ○ A necktie for an elephant

Exercise

Client La Mote
Agency Bold TBWA, Oslo
Art Direction Stéphanie Dumont
Copy Egil Alv Andreassen
Photo Nils Vik

KickStart question: How can you attract attention to the product by playing with the medium?

*'Anyone can look for fashion
in a boutique or history in a
museum. The creative explorer
looks for history in a hardware
store and fashion in an airport.'
Robert Wieder*

When did you last deliberately look for alternatives to the press,
billboards, TV or direct mail for your ads? The following questions are
intended to awaken the explorer in you and encourage you to discover
new and exciting possibilities in the world around you. Make the world
your advertising stage and don't forget that human beings have four
other senses as well as sight. If it works, do it!

The message of a German charity called
'More Time for Children' was conveyed by
escalator. Photos of children were fixed to
the risers in order to drive home the message
that 'Children don't simply disappear like
this' and 'If you worry about them soon
enough, then it won't be too late'.
Client Mehr Zeit für Kinder e.V.
Agency Boebel/Adam Werbeagentur,
Frankfurt
Creative Direction Harald Schmitt
Art Direction Marco Fusz
Copy Jens Daum
Photo Jens Görlich

This live installation in the centre of Stockholm is a spectacular ad for Kraft's Gevalia coffee. The theme of the campaign was coffee for 'unexpected visitors'.

Client Kraft Sverige AB
Agency Hall & Cederquist/Young & Rubicam, Stockholm
Art Direction Lars Hansson
Copy Henrik Haeger

KickStart question: How could an outsize installation be used to tell a story about a product in the open air or in a large space?

'Just stay like that! Tom's Saloon for Gays. 50 metres from here.'
Client P.i.t. the new generation
Agency Jung von Matt Werbeagentur, Hamburg
Creative Direction Roland Schwarz
Art Direction Marcel Fässler
Copy Jan Kesting

KickStart question: How can an outdoor location be used in a fun way to attract and involve the attention of passers-by?

Ja, genau so bleiben!
TOMS SALOON
FOR GAYS
50 Meter von hier.

This campaign for a recruitment website wants
to make people think about their careers.
Client careerbuilder.com
Agency The Martin Agency, Richmond, VA
Creative Direction Joe Alexander
Art Direction Jamie Mahoney
Copy Marc Deschenes, Jamie Mahoney
Photo Ruedi Hofmann

KickStart question: Are there any new
perspectives you could try that would provide
new advertising opportunities? On top of
something? Underneath, behind, in front,
outside, inside?

Client Auckland Regional Council
Agency Saatchi & Saatchi, Auckland
Creative Direction John McCabe
Art Direction Andrew Tinning, Andy Blood
Copy Andrew Tinning, Andy Blood
Illustration Ali Teo

KickStart question: How can street furniture or other outdoor features be used or integrated into the message, in order to attract attention?

These coins were dropped on pavements so that passers-by would pick them up.
Client Brad Wilken, chiropractor
Agency Cramer-Krasselt, Chicago
Creative Direction David Nien Li Yang
Art Direction Bill Rogers

KickStart question: How can the target group be involved in an amusing way to give them a direct impression of the benefit of the product or service?

An anti-drug campaign for the toilets of nightclubs and youth centres. The stickers say 'Drugs – Piss on them'.
Client Office of the Polish President Anti-Narcotics Programme
Agency RMG, Warsaw
Creative Direction Michal Imbierowicz
Art Direction Slawek Rogowski

KickStart question: How can an advertising message be integrated into an everyday location in an attention-grabbing way?

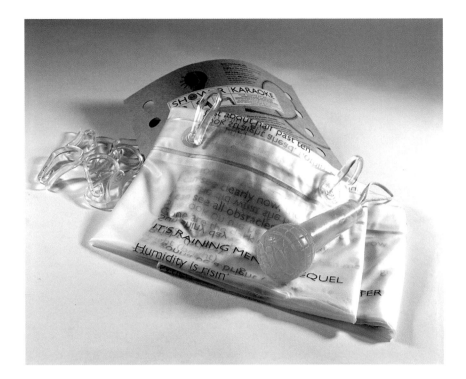

This Shower Karaoke Kit is a promotion for
the company Musica. The pack contains a
shower curtain printed with the lyrics of well-
known songs, and a soap microphone.
Client Musica
Agency The Jupiter Drawing Room,
Cape Town
Creative Direction Ross Chowles
Art Direction Jenifier Ireland,
Schalk Van Der Merwe
Copy Ahmed Tilly
Photo Caroline McClelland

KickStart question: What everyday objects
could be used for advertising, to put
the message across in an amusing
or original way?

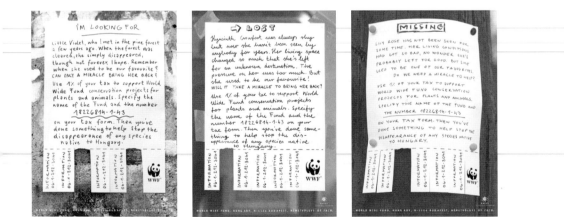

Client World Wide Fund for Nature
Agency Saatchi & Saatchi, Budapest
Creative Direction Ed Jones

KickStart question: What unconventional
ad formats could be used to grab your
target group's attention?

Campaign against private ownership and misuse of firearms. The 'KFM Gun-free Automat' was placed next to drinks machines in shopping centres and universities. Any coins inserted went straight into collection boxes.

Client KFM Radio
Agency The Jupiter Drawing Room,
Cape Town
Creative Direction Ross Chowles
Art Direction Graham Lang
Copy Anton Visser
Photo Wayne Rochat

KickStart question: What familiar places or objects can you use for your ad, to attract attention in a provocative way?

Client Smint International
Agency Tandem Campmany Guasch DDB,
Barcelona
Creative Direction José Maria Roca de Vinyals
Art Direction Juan Ramón Alfaro

KickStart question: What public places or objects could you put to amusing use for your ad?

'Tear it out and try it on.'
Client Ingemar Tärnskär
Agency BBDO Allansson Nilsson Rififi,
Gothenburg
Creative Direction Christer Allansson
Art Direction Hans-Erik Andreasson
Copy Håkan Larsson

KickStart question: How can you give people a
playful way to try the product out for themselves?

'This is how to get your foot in the door'.
Campaign by an agency trying to recruit
in student residences.
Agency Springer & Jacoby, Hamburg
Creative Direction Christoph Everke
Art Direction Axel Thomsen
Copy Alexander Schill
Source Fischer's Archiv,
www.fischers-archiv.de

This campaign uses cows grazing by
the roadside as billboards.
Client The Vegetarian Society
Agency Poulter Partners, Leeds
Creative Direction Paul Moran,
Graham Doran
Art Direction Paul Moran
Copy Graham Doran
Photo James Johnson

KickStart question: What unusual
locations can be used to grab attention?

Campaign for a car repair workshop that
specializes in repairing dents and scratches
Client Pacific Dent Removal
Agency Acme Advertising, San Francisco
Creative Direction Brian West
Art Direction Sakol Mongkolkasetarin
Illustration Theera Vasabhuti
Photo Peter Samuels

KickStart question: What alternative locations
can be used to dramatize the benefit of a
product or service in an entertaining way?

3

PART 3   COPY WITH PUNCH: USING WIT AND HUMOUR

*'The thing about being
a humorist is that if you only
get one laugh, if you only get
one smile, if you can make only
one person happy, then you
know your act stinks!'*
Gene Parret

A joke is a compliment to the intelligence of your fellow human beings.
It lightens the atmosphere and guarantees that people will retain
a positive impression of you. Short jokes are best, of course, because
people do have more important things on their minds. If they can
see the punchline coming long before you reach it, however, then they
will feel sorry for you, at best. It makes no difference whether your ad
is destined for print, the web, TV or cinema, it's always the target group
that decides whether a line has punch or not.

WIT: YOU EITHER HAVE IT OR YOU DON'T

Used properly, wit is one of the most effective instruments of human
communication. Unfortunately, there is a myth of unaccountability –
you either have it or you don't – which still clings to humour, even
today. However, the American comedy industry demonstrates exactly the
opposite. Qualified professionals provide consistently high-quality material
for sitcoms, movies or the autocues of talkshow hosts, and in recent years,
many excellent schools have been set up to train these people, such as
the one at Ohio University School of Journalism. In this part of the book,
I want to show you some examples of jokes that really hit the mark and
how you can get the most from great punchlines or develop them yourself.

Client SBP
Agency DM9 DDB, São Paulo
Creative Direction Manir Fadel
Art Direction Mariana Sá
Photo Manolo Moran

I see Hilary's found the Beaujolais.

Next time, may we suggest Loxton de-alcoholized wine?

Don't worry darling. From here they'll think it's rain.

Next time, may we suggest Loxton de-alcoholized sparkling wine?

Client Loxton
Agency Palmer Jarvis DDB, Vancouver
Creative Direction Marc Stoiber
Art Direction Bradley Wood
Illustration M. D. McKinnell

Radio campaign for Hamlet cigars
Client Gallaher
Copy Noel Hasson, John Cook
Production CDP, Katherine Blom
Technician Nick Angell

Car horn

Husband: Sweetheart, cab's here.

Wife: Darling, do you think these trousers make my bum look fat?

Husband: No, no, they look all right.

Wife: All right, just all right. So you're saying my bum is fat.

Husband: No, no. You said that, I didn't.

Wife: So you think it looks fat?

Husband: No love, you look gorgeous. Now come on, the cab's waiting.

Wife: You don't think they look too tight?

Husband: No, maybe you could wear something different underneath.

Wife: What?

Husband: Well, I mean, your underwear – it's all folded and creased up.

Wife: I'm not wearing any.

Strike match and Hamlet theme.

Voiceover: Happiness is a cigar called Hamlet. The mild cigar.

3.02 A PRACTICAL GUIDE TO JOKE-MAKING: CONSTRUCTING AND DISRUPTING FRAMES OF REFERENCE

Although humour plays an incredibly important role in our lives, it is astonishing how little has been written over the years about the way it functions or about the techniques of joke-making. This section provides a practical guide to the way that jokes work – one which explains a substantial proportion of all jokes and shows how to make new ones, and how to disrupt the frame of reference. There are also some exceptions to the model, including situation comedy, black humour, slapstick and knockabout, as well as many forms of wordplay.

JOKE STRUCTURE 1:

DISRUPTING THE FRAME OF REFERENCE

According to Gestalt psychology, the process of observing an object is not linear, taking in one detail at a time, but involves grasping the most conspicuous elements simultaneously. The observer automatically supplements these obvious elements with their own stored experience, and so completes the process of perception.

This presupposes the existence of certain patterns of perception within the observer's memory, which enable him to fit individual elements into an established context or frame of reference. These allow observers to make assumptions and draw conclusions which do not exist in the observed object itself but only in the act of perception.

Consequently, simple, conspicuous elements (clichés) can be used to call up a clearly defined frame of reference in a person's power of perception. This can produce an effective flash of humour if the obvious, easily accessed frame of reference is disrupted by the introduction of a new and wholly unexpected frame of reference. The simultaneous reference to two different levels functions like an explosion, with the fallout being laughter.

What did you see first, a donkey or a seal? The optical illusion in this drawing is a clear illustration of the pattern described above: the viewer is never able to see both animals at the same time; instead, the drawing switches to and fro between them. The transition from one to the other is like a surprising re-evaluation which simultaneously suspends the first frame of reference and establishes the second. It is essential to the process, however, that both figures, donkey and seal, are represented by the same drawing.

An everyday example of disrupting a frame of reference

If we saw an unusual light moving in the night sky, most of us would at first assume it was from an aircraft or some other kind of flying object. We tend to assign it straight away to an established frame of reference, although there is no evidence to confirm that the source of the light actually is something flying. If, on closer observation, the mysterious light is suddenly found to be the lamp on the moving arm of a crane, realization of our original mistake may well make us laugh. The solution to the mystery instantly disrupts the frame of reference that our power of perception first set up. The crucial factor is that the more convinced an observer is that the source of the light is something flying, and the longer he puzzles over it, the greater will be the surprise. In other words, the more rigid the frame of reference called up, or the more firmly it is established in the observer's power of perception, the more effective a change in the frame of reference will be in creating an 'aha' experience or, in this case, a laugh.

That is precisely the pattern underlying the TV spot shown below. The behaviour of the boys calls up a cliché that makes us jump to conclusions about what they are doing. Once we discover that they're comparing chocolate biscuits, the frame of reference is disrupted, and we find ourselves laughing.

Here's a joke which involves disruption of the frame of reference:

'Mum,' says the boy who's just turned eighteen, 'I should have listened to Grandpa, and stayed away from that strip club. Grandpa said I'd see something I'd wish I hadn't.'
'And what did you see?'
'Grandpa.'

TV spot for Cadbury's Finger biscuits
Client Premier Brands
Agency FCB France, Paris
Creative Direction Thomas Stern
Art Direction Anne Joly
Production Cohenband
Director Lyèce Boukchitine

Two boys are standing side by side, fiddling with something out of camera shot. The impression is created that they're having a lot of fun talking about their most prized possession. When a third boy suddenly interrupts them, with an even larger specimen, they burst out laughing.

Here's another joke that
involves disruption of the
frame of reference

Uproar in the theatre. Tomatoes
and rotten eggs fly towards the
stage. After the curtain falls,
just one spectator is left
clapping. His neighbour says
indignantly, 'I can't believe
you're applauding these no-
hopers.' 'Yeah, I want them to
take another bow, I've still got
a dozen tomatoes left.'

JOKE STRUCTURE 2:

CONSTRUCTING THE FRAME OF REFERENCE RETROSPECTIVELY

The second kind of joke works by giving away very little about the
meaning and future course of events. The listener can't construct a
reliable frame of reference to begin with. The information lacks a
recognizable focus until the punchline brings everything together at once.

For example, a viewer can't make much of the picture above until he
can slot it into a specific frame of reference. He can only do this when
told that it represents a giraffe passing the window.

So the picture alone does not construct a frame of reference; the
observer's power of perception must play a part. Jokes of this type
are especially effective when, following a very small amount of given
information, the punchline calls up – or overthrows – the largest
possible portion of the listener's store of acquired knowledge.

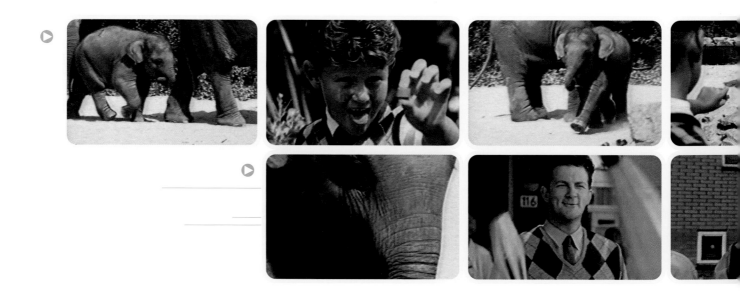

We see a small boy at the zoo, taking the
last Rolo from the pack. He's just about to
put it in his mouth when his eyes light on
the elephants. He holds out his last Rolo
temptingly and a baby elephant comes
trotting over eagerly. But before the
elephant can take hold of the Rolo,
at the very last minute the boy pops
it into his own mouth with a jeering laugh,
and the baby elephant is left forlorn. (Cut)

Years later, the boy is a grown man,
watching the circus parade through the
town, when suddenly he gets a tap on
the shoulder: it's an elephant's trunk.
Biff! Wham! – and the man goes flying.
The elephant has also grown up, and now
gets his revenge. He trumpets jeeringly
as he walks off.

Slogan: 'Think carefully about what you
do with your last Rolo'.

Client Rolo
Agency Lintas, Amsterdam
Creative Direction Diederick Koopal, J. P. Nieuwerkerk
Art Direction Marcel Frensch
Production Czar
Director Rogier van der Ploeg
Source Lürzer's Archive 2/1996

A grasshopper walks into a bar and orders a drink. 'My God,' says the bartender 'A talking grasshopper. Did you know, we have a drink named after you?'

The grasshopper looks at him in amazement and asks, 'What, Irving?'

The most basic rule for developing punchlines is: stick with it, and don't stop on any account before you've come up with twenty different versions of the payoff. Otherwise, your attempts will never get beyond mediocre, and the best reception your joke will receive is a pitying smile. The following exercises give some useful tips on techniques that even professional comedy writers use.

1. Use different styles

Here is a list of essential styles that will help you to generate punchlines. Go through the headings one by one and see whether, for example, 'supercharged reality' or 'comparison' can help you come up with punchlines that fit your goal. Use this list for the next two exercises.

- Exaggerate
- Be hostile
- Spin some insane nonsense
- Invent something fantastic
- See it from a child's point of view
- Use comparisons
- Bring out a conflict
- Use similes
- Shock people
- Question the truth
- Involve the target group
- Attack authority
- Supercharge reality
- Take a comic perspective

2. Set-up and punchline

First formulate the central message of your ad as a single-minded proposition, as briefly as possible. Use this as the set-up, as in the examples below. In the second stage, develop the payoff itself so that it reveals a new, unexpected perspective. Don't struggle to find the perfect punchline – just let the ideas flow, quantity before quality. This is your best chance of finding a really good one.

Using the list of styles given above, try to complete the following set-ups with your own punchlines.

- Customers are so demanding that...
- Men love their cars so much that...
- I wouldn't say he drives fast, but...
- This insurance is so safe that...
- This packet is so full, it looks like...

Try to finish the story below with as many different payoffs as you can think of. Don't try to work out which ones hit the bull's eye and which ones don't until you've accumulated enough. Don't forget that your raw material will need to be polished if you want the maximum punch.

- A woman is out walking her dog, when she passes a homeless man in the street. The man looks up and says 'That's the ugliest pig I've ever seen'. 'What do you mean? You must be drunk,' says the woman. 'It's a dog, not a pig.' And the man replies: ...

3. How to improve the set-up and punchline
- Get rid of all repetition and anything else unnecessary.
- Boil it down to one sentence: really good punchlines don't need any more than that, and often need less.
- Try to tell the joke more succinctly, using different words.
- When you can't think of any more punchlines, try reformulating the set-up.
- Don't force the humour, it will only fall flat.
- Tell the truth and try to stay believable.

Sleepless nights

The following cartoons were developed around the subject of sleepless nights, and illustrate how many different punchlines can be milked from a single theme. Try to add to them with versions of your own.

I'd like to show you how to adapt existing punchlines or use them as sources of fresh ideas. Remember, copyrights should never be infringed by using protected names or characters. Only the structure of the punchline should be used as the inspiration for great ideas for campaigns. These could take the form of print ads, web banners, direct mailings or TV spots. It's important that the original structure isn't altered too much in the process of adaptation, or there's a risk of losing the mechanism of the joke. Below are three key procedures with questions to ask yourself when you're trying to work out how a punchline is constructed and considering potential variations.

→ *1. Analyse the most important elements*
What are the key elements on which this comic strip depends, and which must therefore remain the same? At what point does the frame of reference change?

→ *2. Adapt the cartoon to the product or service*
What elements can be altered or replaced by others without spoiling the payoff? Could the structure of the punchline be used in a different context?

→ *3. Synthesize the old and new elements*
What is the best way to introduce the product? How can the product or service be made the focus of the joke? Does the punchline still stand up and does the joke work after all the changes?

HOW FAR CAN EXISTING JOKES BE ADAPTED?

While thinking about this cartoon, you may well come up with completely new ideas and turn the whole thing on its head. The variations shown here stick fairly close to the original. Below are four categories which are the key components of the cartoon. Each gives examples of elements you can change to make the cartoon suit your purpose. Try to find other variable elements to give the cartoon a surprising change of direction, and keep experimenting to develop your instincts about punchlines.

→ *1. Instead of cows or sheep, use:*
Dogs, birds, plants, animals disguised as people, statues, figures on posters, dolls, houses or anything else that is not supposed to behave like a human being.

→ *2. Instead of vehicles and their drivers, use:*
Cyclists, walkers, runners, pensioners, wheelchair users, parachutists, sewage workers on the job, etc.

→ *3. Use a different setting.*
Stables, a zoo, a dog-training class, a town centre, a dolls' house, a garden centre, etc.

→ *4. Change what the animals are doing:*
Reading newspapers, using the product, partying, plotting world revolution, having a pedicure, etc.

ADAPT THE JOKE FOR A TV OR CINEMA SPOT

Take the comic strip on the right and adapt it into an ad for one of the following products. This will help you to exercise (a) your ability to recognize the essential elements of a payoff and (b) your skill at making new use of existing punchlines. Stay with one theme until you've come up with at least twenty variations. Then choose the one with the most potential and refine it until it's ready to use.

- ○ A dairy product
- ○ A pizza delivery service
- ○ A computer game

CREATIVE TECHNIQUE: USE PUNCHLINES AS TRIGGERS

Start building a little archive of humour to which everyone in your agency has access. It should contain joke books, a wide range of cartoons, stories in picture form, comics, humorous books, anthologies of proverbs, anecdotes, punchlines, idioms or quotations. Team members will be able to come to a meeting already equipped with punchlines that they've found in the archive beforehand, with an eye to their relevance to the task in hand. These five steps show the course that this kind of creative meeting should take:

1. The meeting should follow the DreamTeam rules.

2. Each team member should go to the archive before the meeting to dig out a few good cartoons, jokes or anecdotes that they find appealing, and which could spark off some good ideas.

3. One of the team presents one of their chosen cartoons, jokes or quotations to the meeting. Together the team looks for ways of using its structure in the campaign, without adopting it exactly as it stands. Stay with one joke as long as you can and try to find as many variations as possible. Change the punchline, turn it upside down, develop it further, or let it inspire you to find a completely new idea. Do anything, as long as it works.

4. When the first cartoon has been wrung dry, move on to the next one and once again take a lateral look at its humorous possibilities.

5. When you've got a stack of doodles and ideas, work them up until they're ready to use.

Black humour is what happens when you cancel out the serious side of socially taboo subjects like death, illness, morality or sex by approaching them playfully. Set up a tension between the fears surrounding the taboo and the message you want to put across by infringing existing social standards. You'll need a light touch and a little sensitivity, or else your punchline could backfire.

'Lying dead in the hall, Peter? That's not like you.'

Client   Heinz
Agency   Leo Burnett Ltd, London
Creative Direction   Steve Chung
Art Direction   Rob Nielsen, Neil Gillie
Photo   Kelvin Murray

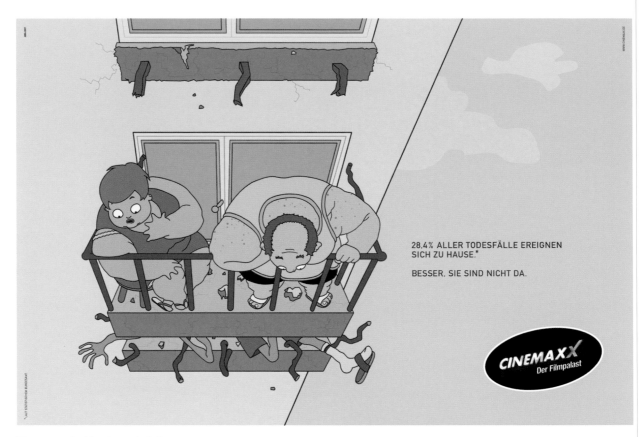

'28.4 per cent of accidents happen in the home.
It's better not to be there.'
Client H.-J. Flebbe Filmtheater
Agency Jung von Matt/Alster, Hamburg
Creative Direction Niels Alzen, Thim Wagner
Art Direction Christian Reimer, Hans Weishäupel,
Raphael Milczarek
Copy Willy Kaussen, Jens Daum
Illustration Felix Reidenbach

Mum?

Quorn™ is a completely new vegetable product that can be bought as fillets and stew. The taste is uncannily similar to chicken.

Client Signum
Agency Lowe Brindfors, Stockholm
Creative Direction Hakan Engler
Art Direction Mitte Blomqvist
Photo Wolfgang Kleinschmidt

Mother: Petra, Martin, I'm going to the supermarket.

Martin (whining): Mummy, will you buy us something?

Mother: What would you like?

Martin: Ooh, something inhumane! And something cruel to animals!

Petra: And salmonella!

Mother: Now, now, I can't possibly get you three things at once.

Voiceover: Oh yes, you can, with eggs from battery hens. Then you have inhumanity, cruelty to animals and salmonella, all in one.

Petra: Wow, Mummy, eggs from battery hens!

Voiceover: Noah. Human beings working for animals.

Client Noah
Agency Jung von Matt Werbeagentur, Hamburg
Creative Direction Hermann Waterkamp
Art Direction Götz Ullmer
Copy Vivien Hoppe, Thorsten Meier

Client Heinz
Agency Leo Burnett Ltd, London
Creative Direction Mark Tutssel, Nick Bell
Copy Rob Nielson, Jack Stephens

Background music:
'Rat In Mi Kitchen' by UB40.

There's a rat in mi kitchen
What am I gonna do
There's a rat in mi kitchen
What am I gonna do
I'm gonna fix that rat
That's what I'm gonna do
I'm gonna fix that rat...

Repeat. Music fade.

Voiceover: Any food tastes supreme with Heinz Salad Cream.

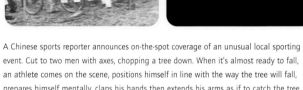

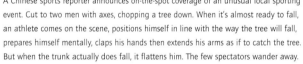

Client FOX Sports

Agency Cliff Freeman & Partners, New York

Creative Direction Eric Silver, Taras Wayner

Art Direction Rossana Bardales, Taras Wayner

Copy Dan Morales

Director Traktor

Production Cape Direct, Cape Town and
Partizan, New York

Animation Quiet Man, New York

A Chinese sports reporter announces on-the-spot coverage of an unusual local sporting event. Cut to two men with axes, chopping a tree down. When it's almost ready to fall, an athlete comes on the scene, positions himself in line with the way the tree will fall, prepares himself mentally, claps his hands then extends his arms as if to catch the tree. But when the trunk actually does fall, it flattens him. The few spectators wander away.

Campaign for extra-strong fishing line

Client Deutsche Angelgeräte Manufaktur

Agency Springer & Jacoby, Hamburg

Creative Direction Torsten Rieken, Jan Ritter

Art Direction Mathias Stiller

Copy Walter Schütz

Photo Gerd Georg

The best situation-dependent jokes do not spring from the imagination of some creative but are written by life itself. But if you want to have a go all the same, make a note of this structure: a person is in a perfectly normal, everyday situation, perhaps even rather a serious one. Suddenly, thanks to some unforeseen event, or an accident he himself caused, he is catapulted into a comic situation. The fact that the victim was completely unprepared is a key factor for unintentional comedy, and is often the crucial trigger for the payoff.

© Lappan Verlag Oldenburg, www.lappan.de, Fred & Günter

Will soon be rushing to a dentist who accepts American Express.

Accepting American Express attracts the clients you want most – those who spend more, pay dependably, and keep coming back. It's one more way to put your best patients first. And stay a step ahead of your competition. To know more, call 1-800-268-9877.

do more Establishment Services

Client American Express
Agency Ogilvy & Mather, Toronto
Creative Direction Janet Kestin, Nancy Vonk
Art Direction Mike Dietrich
Copy Brian Sheppard
Photo Craig Perman
Retouching Fellini Aerographics

Client Centre Optic
Agency Tiempo/BBDO, Barcelona
Creative Direction Siscu Molina
Art Direction Gabriel Penalva

Campaign for an anti-perspirant
Client Odorex
Agency FHV/BBDO, Amsterdam
Creative Direction Bart Oostindie
Art Direction Maxim Doornhein
Photo Phylis Schipper

BIKES FOR PEOPLE WHO LOVE TO RIDE. AND PEOPLE WHO HAVE TO.

TREK

AUTHORIZED DEALER DURHAM CYCLE CENTER

Client Durham Cycle Center
Agency West & Vaughan, Durham, NC
Creative Direction Evan Thompson
Art Direction Rob Baird
Photo Joel Sartore

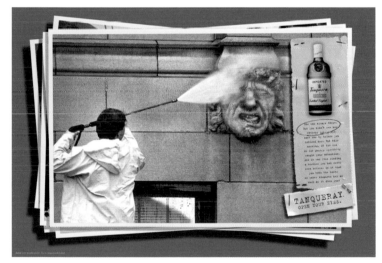

Client United Distillers
Agency Publicis Casadevall Pedreño & PRG, Barcelona
Creative Direction Pablo Rey, José María Piera, Carlos Holemans
Art Direction Ramón Roda, Eva Terrades, Maico García
Copy Pablo Rey, Carlos Holemans
Photo Dan Schlatter

'I honestly believe that advertising is the most fun you can have with your clothes on.'
Jerry Della Famina

Blue humour doesn't refer to any specific type of joke; it's just the category of humour that deals with sexuality, bodily functions and bodily fluids. The humour comes from breaking taboos, leading to an inner conflict which resolves itself in laughter. The proportion of jokes revolving around sex has always been very high – not surprising, when it's a favourite topic of the human race, touching almost every part of our lives. Make a real effort to think of a sexual side to your product or service, and ways to show this in a classy and amusing light. Once again, you'll need to develop an instinct for whether you're genuinely mocking taboos or whether you might be going too far.

'Has he gone?'/'Who?'
© Lappan Verlag Oldenburg, www.lappan.de, Fred & Günter

'Buy Vox shoes, and you can afford to hire something cute.'
Client Vox
Agency Körberg & Co., Gothenburg
Creative Direction Johan Brink
Art Direction Pelle Körberg
Photo Nina Barne

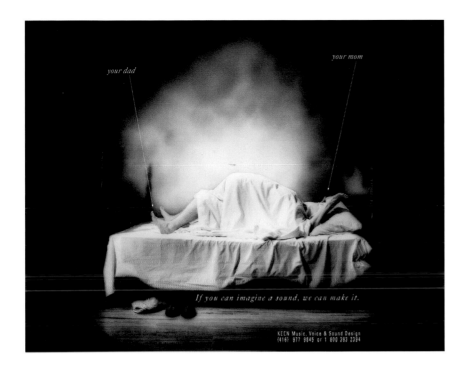

your dad   *your mom*

If you can imagine a sound, we can make it.

KEEN Music, Voice & Sound Design
(416) 977 9845 or 1 800 393 2394

Client Keen
Agency Two Cities, Toronto
Creative Direction Judy John
Art Direction Frank Lepre
Copy Chris Gordaneer

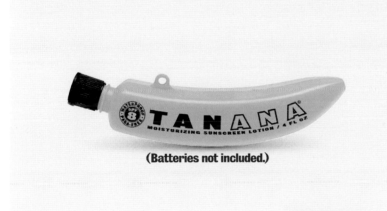

(Batteries not included.)

SPRING BREAK '95

(For external use only.)

SPRING BREAK '95

Client Tanana
Agency TBWA/Chiat Day, St. Louis
Creative Direction James Brown, Evan Willnow
Art Direction John Roberts
Source Lürzer's Archive 6/1995

DON'T WORRY,
EVERYONE WILL BE LOOKING AT YOUR HAIR.

JAMES WORRALL
HAIRDRESSING
6 Denmark St. London WC2 0171 379 0979

Client James Worrall
Agency Saatchi & Saatchi, London
Art Direction Dave Askwith, Andrew Fisher
Copy Andrew Fisher, Dave Askwith
Photo Jason Joyce

'Very very clean cars.' Campaign for a car-wash.

Client City Car Cleanic

Agency Michael Conrad & Leo Burnett, Frankfurt

Creative Direction Victor Rodriguez, Stefan Karl

Art Direction Christoph Barth, Alexandra Schneider

Photo Marc Trautmann

Client Harley-Davidson

Agency Amazon Advertising, San Francisco

Creative Direction Lynda Pearson

Art Direction Kim Schoen

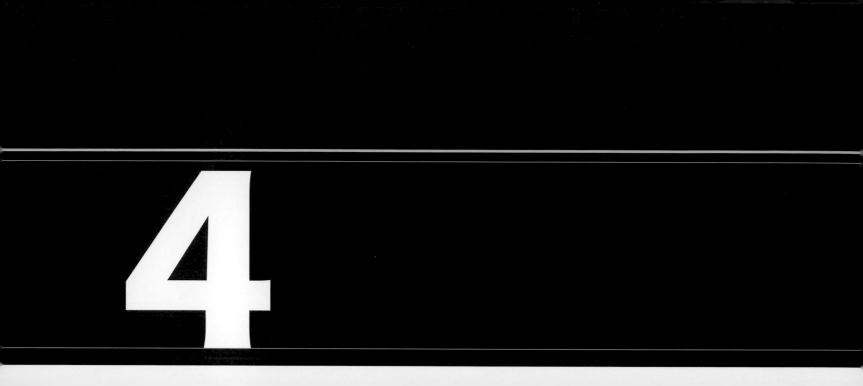

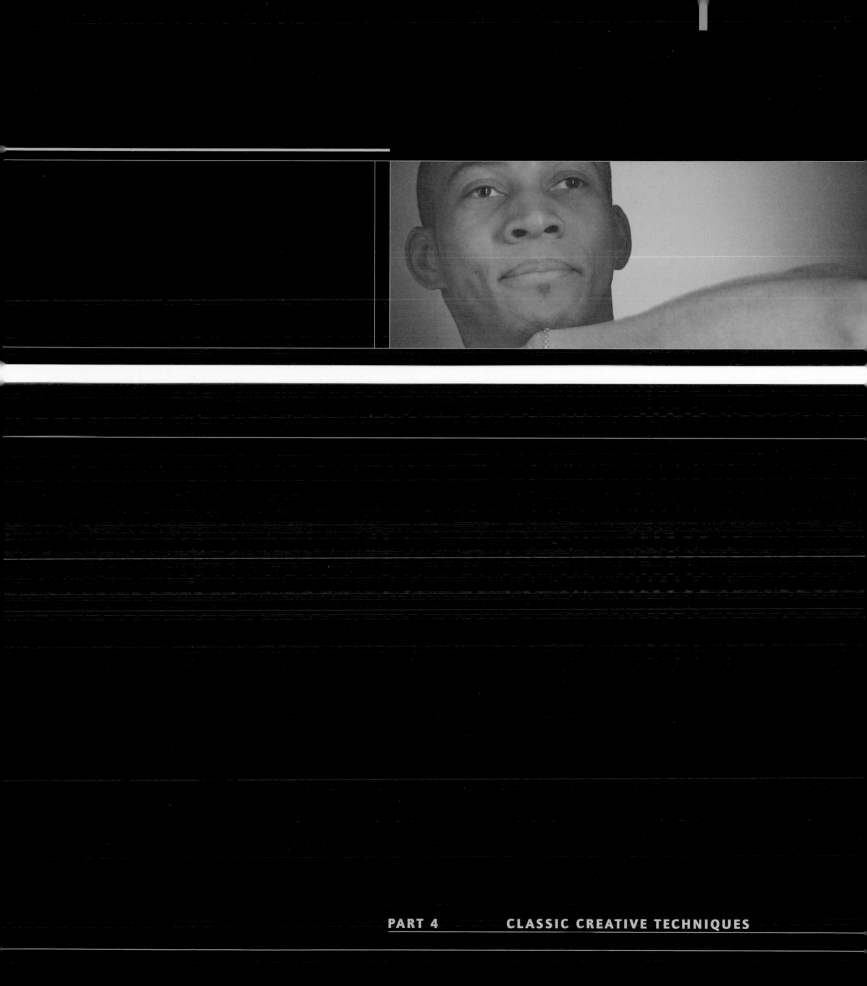

PART 4   CLASSIC CREATIVE TECHNIQUES

What's the idea behind it?

The morphological matrix is a technique for organized thinking, attributed to the Swiss astrophysicist Fritz Zwicky (1898–1974). Applied to a task or problem, the method requires you to systematically list and consider all logically conceivable possibilities, in order to obtain an overview of every aspect involved. Constructing and filling in the morphological matrix divides complex structures into manageable segments; when these segments are put back together in new combinations, new solutions to the whole emerge. It sounds complicated but after the first trial run it should prove to be astonishingly simple and effective.

When can it be used?

The morphological matrix is most helpful when you are looking for new and original ideas for packaging, brochures, folders, mailshots or logos. It provides a organized stimulus for combining materials, shapes, colours and text in entertaining ways, throwing up a large number of new possibilities.

Work with a goal

Before you go to work with this method for the first time, check to see if you and your team have a clear goal. How will you know if you've found the right logo, the most appropriate brochure or the best packaging? The first step is crucial: take the time to work out a goal, as described in Part 1 of this book. This goal will be taken with you like a compass, guiding you through the hunt for ideas. Write it across the top of your grid, and look at it from time to time to make sure you're still on target.

Follow the DreamTeam rules

Teams working with the morphological matrix will find that the DreamTeam rules from Part 1 are invaluable. However, the matrix can of course be used to good effect when you're working alone, helping you to come up with new ideas. Make sure that you just let your ideas flow at first, without being self-critical, and assemble a rich pool of ideas before you begin to evaluate, elaborate and select.

How to use the morphological matrix

There are five steps:

1. Work out a goal.

2. Break the problem down into its separate components. In the case of a brochure, for example, the components might be: material, shape, cover, texture (moulded, embossed), format, illustrations, method of folding, page layout, typography, colour and content. Add these to the matrix.

3. Next make separate notes of all possible forms that these components could take in the spaces alongside them. For example, in the case of a brochure, alongside 'material' you might write paper, styrofoam, fabric, wood, card, tin, plastic, PVC, leather, etc.

4. Now the really creative part of the meeting begins. Combine possible forms of the different components and see what new ideas come of it. For a brochure, you could combine possible materials, shapes, textures and formats at random, until some usable ideas emerge.

5. It's essential that you don't just shuffle the components and wait for a miracle to happen. Use the possibilities you create by combining them and letting them spark off real ideas. Let the endless array of possible combinations inspire you, and lead you into completely new realms of ideas. Anything is allowed!

Evaluating and developing ideas

If everything has gone well, you should have a large collection of raw ideas at the end of a meeting. Still using the basic DreamTeam rules as your guide, try to develop early ideas and potential solutions in doodle form. Do that before you start evaluating the ideas, and select the best last of all.

This example demonstrates how quickly and easily the morphological matrix can help you to tackle your problem. The diagram below shows the matrix, which you simply draw on a big sheet of paper in the meeting, and the boxes which you can gradually fill with your components and ideas. These can take the form of words or phrases as well as drawings and symbols, as shown in the example. Once the matrix is full, it's a constant reminder to the team of how many variations could be used in designing a logo on the theme of Live Aid. If the solution is not found in the matrix itself, it may still be able to provide the crucial push towards developing a really great idea.

Logo for the Live Aid rock concert to relieve famine in Africa. Designer unknown.

COMPONENTS (WHAT?)	KNOWN OR POSSIBLE SOLUTIONS (HOW?)							
Word and/or letter elements	live aid	LIVE AID	Live Aid	LIVE AID	Lᵃ	LA	La	LA	
Picture elements: instruments									
Picture elements: music									
Picture elements: Africa – globe									
Picture elements: Africa – symbols									
Picture elements: Africa – animals									
Picture elements: Africa – patterns									

The following pages contain some inspiring examples of the kind
of promotions for which the morphological matrix can used and
the results that can be achieved. These are all great ideas –
why not try and come up with even better ideas of your own?

A calendar inside a floppy disk storage case,
printed on the ribbon cables normally used
to connect computer components.
Client Japet Company, 24-hour computer service
Agency Studio A4 Bojana Fajmut, Ljubljana
Creative Direction Bojana Fajmut
Design Bojana Fajmut, Jerko Gluscevic

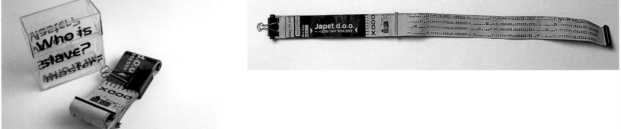

Client Thislington Cubicles
Agency The Partners
Design Direction Ester Borean
Design Tony de Ste Croix, Steve Owen,
Martin Lawless
Illustration Tony de Ste Croix

This calendar is made up 365 tiny squares of soap, that can be used one a day in the office washroom. It was sent to architects as a promotion.

These vodka bottles, designed to promote the 'Royalty' brand, all represent historical figures and institutions: an executioner, Louis XIV, a prison, the Marquis de Sade.
Client Hooghoudt Distillers B.V.
Agency Designers Company, Amsterdam
Art Direction Rob Verhaart,
Ron van der Vlugt
Source Lürzer's Archive Special, Packaging Design 1

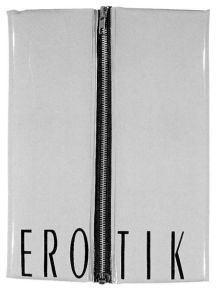

Client Wiener Stadt und Landesbibliothek
Agency Alessandri Design, Vienna
Design Cordula Alessandri
Photo Claudio Alessandri

Catalogue for a Viennese exhibition called 'Erotica
– a tentative approach'. The outer case, made of
lightly padded plastic, is opened by a zip fastener.
The cover is modelled to suggest a peephole.

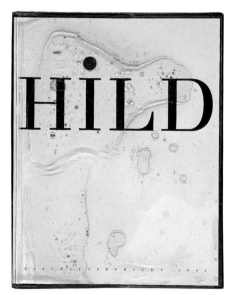

Annual Report of a sanitary and environmental
engineering company. Because all Hild products
are connected with water, the plastic cover is
also water-filled.
Client Hild
Agency Alessandri Design, Vienna
Design Cordula Alessandri

T-shirt packaging
Client K-Ration
Agency Charles S. Anderson Design,
Minneapolis
Art Direction Todd Piper-Hauswirth, Charles
S. Anderson

Metal visiting cards, stamped, embossed,
and personalized with an adhesive label.
Client KEA Pring Broker
Agency Templin Brink Design LLC,
San Francisco
Creative Direction Joel Templin
Art Direction Joel Templin

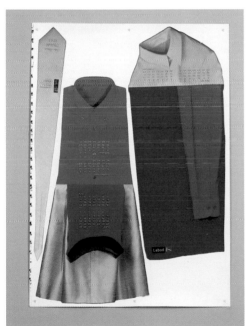

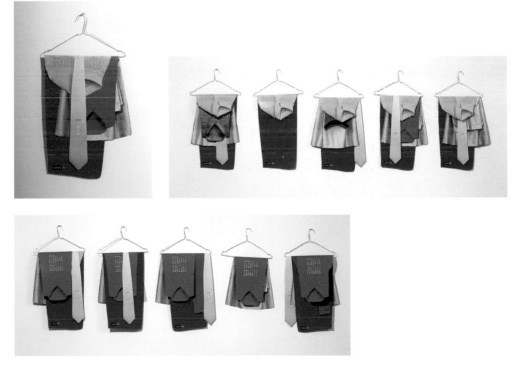

The three parts of this promotional calendar
can be combined in thirty different ways over
the course of the year. The 'clothes' are full-size
and hang on a clothes hanger.
Client Labod konfekcija Novo mesto d.d.
Agency Studio A4 Bojana Fajmut, Ljubljana
Creative Direction Bojana Fajmut, Franci Virant
Photo Franci Virant

A press release for an 'environmentally friendly'
motor scooter, packed in a sealable plastic bag of
seeds, and attached to a piece of artificial grass.
Client Aprilia
Agency Metalli Lindberg Advertising, Conegliano, Italy
Creative Direction Ester Borean
Art Direction Lionello Borean,
Francesca Spinazze
Photo Alberto Narduzzi, Gianni Sabbadin
Illustration Tommaso Alberini
Source Lürzer's Archive Special, Catalogs & Brochures 1

Invitation to a launch party held by Hong Kong's leading commercial production company. The target group were staff in the communications branch, who never left their office before 5.30 p.m. The invitation offers tips and tricks to help them get away from the office in time to go to the party.

Client Filmfirma
Agency Euro RSCG Partnership, Hong Kong
Creative Direction Nick Lim, Yvonne Ho
Art Direction Philip Lee
Illustration Philip Lee, Ronnie Hung
Photo Philip Lee

Packaging for a fashion catalogue
Client Dolce & Gabbana
Agency Bianco & Cucco, Milan
Art Direction Giovanni Bianco,
Susanna Cucco
Source Lürzer's Archive Special, Packaging
Design 1

What's the idea behind it?

In the early 1950s the American Alex Osborn drew up a checklist of ways to stimulate new ideas. Coming from advertising himself, he approached his objective back to front like a true creative, and established that the solutions to problems could have been found by restructuring the problems according to the answers to specific questions. Osborn's checklist was originally conceived as an aid to the improvement and development of products, but I have refined and added to it so that it can now lead to optimal results in advertising too.

When can it be used?

Osborn's checklist is really useful when you're looking for new and original ideas for packaging, brochures, folders, direct mailings, special forms of advertising or products.

Work with a goal

Once again, you should have a clear goal when you're working with Osborn's checklist, so that you know from the start where you're heading. For example, you could formulate the goal as follows: How can a brochure make the reader really keen to send in the coupon? Your team should keep a goal like this in front of them throughout the hunt for ideas.

Follow the DreamTeam rules

The DreamTeam rules from Part 1 of this book provide an essential basis for any team working with Osborn's checklist. But even if you are working alone with the checklist, you'll find that it makes good sense to follow some of the DreamTeam rules.

How to use Osborn's checklist

There are four steps:

1. Work out a goal.

2. Apply one of the concepts from the checklist to the goal, making sure that you keep to the DreamTeam rules.

3. Write down all the ideas suggested or make simple doodles.

4. One of the most important points for success when applying this technique is to stay with a concept once you have chosen it, and dig down deep. Get to the very bottom of every possibility, and only when the concept has absolutely nothing more to offer should you choose another concept from the checklist.

Evaluating and developing ideas

If everything goes well, you should have assembled a large number of raw ideas by the end of a meeting. Still using the basic DreamTeam rules as your guide, try to develop those initial ideas and solutions with the use of doodles. Do that before you start evaluating the ideas, and select the best last of all.

Osborn's checklist

I've taken the liberty of extending the original version of Osborn's checklist and adding new categories to it. This means you now have a tool you can use to inject new excitement into every meeting.

→ *How can the size or proportions be altered?*
Make it bigger, longer, inflatable, foldable, self-opening, wider, thicker, taller, separable, soluble, shorter, narrower, thinner, lower?

→ *How can the shape or function be altered?*
Make it more complicated, spherical, three-dimensional, more adaptable, simpler, reusable, dual-purpose, amorphous, malleable?

→ *Can the surface be changed?*
Make it smoother, silkier, softer, more slippery, more elastic, rougher, transparent, folded, embossed?

→ *How many ways are there to construct it?*
Could it have more parts, more variables, fewer parts? Could they be combined, adapted? Can you fold it, roll it up, stick bits together? Could it be simpler?

→ *Can it be made more effective?*
More rational, more economical, self-explanatory, use less energy, less material, inflatable, mobile, reversible, fun?

→ *How can the performance be improved?*
Stronger, more effective, faster, weaker, less effective, slower?

→ *Can the user do something different with it?*
Is there a puzzle to solve? Is there something to assemble, cut out, roll up, take apart, shrink, unfold – is it done by hand, semi-automatic?

→ *What materials can be used?*
Stronger, sturdier, more durable, weaker, more fragile, less durable? Combinations of materials? Synthetics, naturals?

→ *How can the information be put across better?*
Make it more obvious, scandalous, incisive, clear, discreet, concealed, understated?

→ *What style could be used?*
Conservative, traditional, historical, modern, up-to-the-minute, futuristic?

→ *What character should it have?*
Friendlier, cuddlier, funnier, more rational, more serious, cooler, grander?

→ *What about colour?*
Brighter, multicoloured, black and white, patterned, plain, transparent, opaque, adapted for the colour-blind?

→ *What sounds or noises can be used?*
Softer, muffled, silent, singing, speaking, louder, more musical?

On the following pages you will find some fantastic work showing
the kind of results you can get using Osborn's checklist. That doesn't
mean you should try to imitate these concepts – on the contrary, the
checklist should inspire you to come up with original and surprising
new ideas of your own.

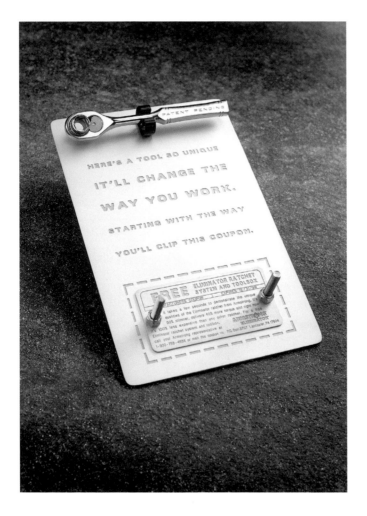

Direct mailing from a tool company,
with unscrewable coupon
Client Danaher Tool Corporation
Agency Eisner Communications, Baltimore
Creative Direction Ester Borean
Art Direction Mark Rosica
Copy Steve Etzine

How the press kit was packaged.

View through the camera's 'viewfinder'.

The inside of the press kit, and a fold-out model of an old-fashioned camera.

Press kit for Disney's animated film *Tarzan*
Client Buenavista International/Disney
Agency Zapping, Madrid
Creative Direction Uschi Henkes, Urs Frick,
David Palacios
Art Direction Uschi Henkes, Gabriel Hueso

A shoebox made from plastic
Client Exedo
Agency Minale Tattersfield Designers, London
Art Direction Evelyn Hegi
Source Lürzer's Archive Special, Packaging Design 1

Promotional handbook and CD for
a sound studio
Client The Groundcrew at John Causby
Production
Agency BlackBird Creative, Charlotte, NC
Design Direction Patrick Short
Design Brandon Scharr
Copy Patrick McLean
Photo Stock

Case for a Tom Jones CD, containing
a pair of ladies' panties
Client Granada Enterprises
Agency Tucker Clarke-Williams Creative
Manchester
Creative Direction Phil Skegg
Art Direction Phil Skegg, Dave Simpson,
Dave Palmer
Copy Dave Simpson, Sue Strange

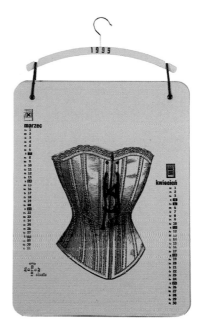

Calendar on a clothes hanger.
Client Korek Studio
Agency Korek Studio, Warsaw
Creative Direction Wojciech Korkuc
Art Direction Wojciech Korkuc

Packaging for mustard and ketchup
Client Suwary S.A.
Design Tadeusz Piechura, Lodz, Poland
Photo Christian Postl

Client The Boots Company
Agency Lewis Moberly, London
Design Shaun Bowen
Art Direction Mary Lewis
Photo Shaun Bowen

Wildbrew, an alcoholic drink in a specially designed bottle, which was sold only in pubs and bars. The drink quickly became a cult.
Client Interbrew UK
Agency Williams Murray Hamm, London
Design Direction Garrick Hamm
Design Simon Porteous, Garrick Hamm
Photo Phil Hurst

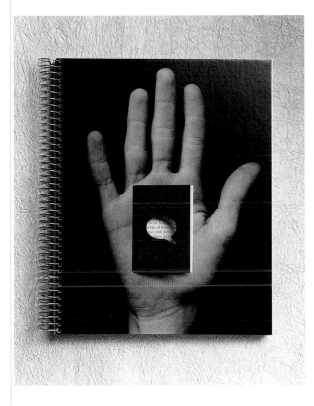

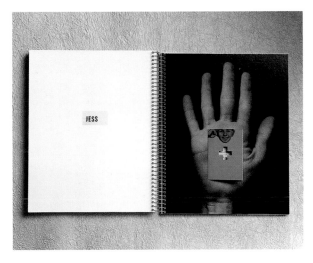

On the cover of this brochure, a small notebook
was stuck on to the picture of the hand.
Client Greater Alabama Council/Boy Scouts
Agency Slaughter Hanson, Birmingham, AL
Creative Direction Kathey Oldman
Art Direction Marion English Powers
Copy Kathey Oldman
Illustration David Webb
Photo Don Harbor

Direct mailing from a fashion firm,
made of cloth.
Client Anni Kuan Design
Agency Sagmeister Inc., New York
Art Direction Stefan Sagmeister
Photo Tom Schierlitz

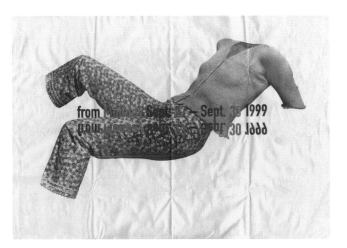

What's the idea behind it?

The word synectics comes from the Greek *synechein*, and means 'a way of combining things'. Visual stimuli are combined at random and applied to the problem in order to find out, through lateral thinking, whether their structure can contribute to the solution. Isolating the problem itself frees you from everyday thought patterns and gives you a new angle on the task. This new angle is what sparks off the creative process. Although visual synectics can lead to wonderful and unusual ideas, it is sometimes met with scepticism at first because it seems to lead along a rather absurd path. Someone with experience of the technique should introduce it to the team, because it requires practice and some flexibility from the group.

Where can it be used?

Visual synectics can help you to develop concepts for campaigns as well as individual ideas for press ads, TV spots, direct mailings, packaging or special forms of advertising. The distinctive thing about the method is that it leads to surprising and unexpected solutions.

Work with a goal

With visual synectics it is essential to work out a clear goal, because this will be the central theme of the entire creative session for your team. Any weaknesses in the brief will come to light while you are working out the goal, and this will often provide an opportunity to obtain further information and fine-tune the strategy.

Follow the DreamTeam rules

As visual synectics is a demanding and unusual method of looking for ideas, you should take time to foster a positive and open climate in the team. The fifteen DreamTeam rules are a good basis, giving your team the space it needs to develop high-quality ideas with this method. The optimal team size for this technique is between three and eight people. Experience also shows that it makes sense for one team member to act as a kind of moderator and write down all the team's ideas without passing comment.

This strip of pictures contains some motifs you could use in visual synectics. The images are not meant to relate directly to the task in hand or the product.

How to use visual synectics

→ Phase 1: Work out a clear goal and write it up where the whole team can see it.

→ Phase 2: Prepare a folder with between ten and twenty pictures (photos, slides, drawings, etc.) from which the team can choose two or three at the meeting. The pictures and their subject matter do not need to be thematically linked to each other, nor to relate to the brief in any way. Choose pictures that will have a strong emotional impact on the team, stimulate their imagination, make them angry or indignant, or make them laugh.

→ Phase 3: Put your chosen pictures in front of the team members one by one. Each member now interprets them, describing what particular appeal this picture has or what emotions it evokes. Associations, feelings, fantasies should all be freely aired. Somebody should note down everything that is said, building up a list of words that might read as follows: acceleration, integration, total chaos, hiding, heat, etc. When the list is thirty or forty words long, you can break off the search provisionally.

→ Phase 4: After analysing the pictures, study the notes and see what ideas the descriptions have in common. Select a word from the list and put it beside the goal. What ideas does the word trigger in you, what do you immediately think of? Take the word 'acceleration': what fantasies or ideas for a solution does it arouse in you? Don't cling to the word itself, let your associations run wild – that's the only way to conjure up good raw ideas for your task.

→ Phase 5: Even if the ideas flow slowly at first, stay with one word for as long as possible, until its associations are exhausted. Only then take another word from the list and use it in the same way.

Evaluating and developing ideas

Still using the basic DreamTeam rules as your guide, try to develop the ideas and solutions into doodles. Do this before you start to evaluate the ideas, and select the best last of all.

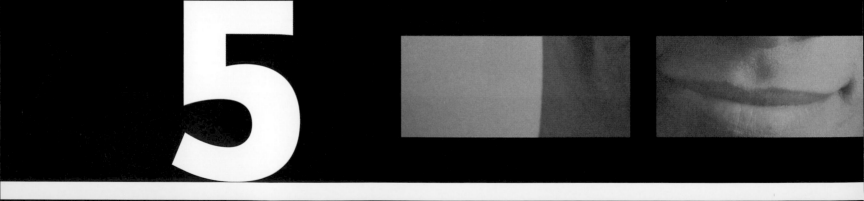

*'Creativity is an advertising
agency's most valuable asset,
because it is the rarest.'
Jef I. Richards,
University of Texas
Advertising Department*

In this part of the book, I would like to introduce a few interesting tools
and exercises which will improve your visual imagination and also make
you more aware of how you can make the 'movies in your mind' work for
you. Most of us do it everyday, automatically, without thinking about it,
but very few people realize how much control they can exercise over the
pictures in their heads. Yet psychologists estimate that we spend up to
40 per cent of our time daydreaming. The more often you do these
exercises, the more confident you will be as the director of your inner
streams of images. One of the aims of these exercises is to use the
spontaneous flow of mental images to link great ideas together
and create whole stories in your head.

DIRECT NEW WORLDS OF IMAGES

Many top creatives have excellent visual ability. They can create or change
entire scenes by running them past their inner eye. Some of the best
directors in the world seem to have a whole production studio in their
heads, in which they shoot, cut and edit their films ready for distribution.
Exploring your own imagination is probably one of the greatest
adventures of all and some people even feel a little frightened by
the possibilities it throws up. But if you set off on the adventure and
just close your eyes, you'll find you have a complete production team
of your own, at your command. Direction, editing, everything is in your
hands. There are no limits to what your imagination can do – all the
more so today, when all your ideas can be realized in computer animation.
The most recent technology enables you to create completely new worlds
of images, symbols and special effects.

Client Toyota
Agency Dentsu Inc., Tokyo
Creative Direction Shunkichi Nakazawa,
Jeffrey Keeling
Art Direction Kazunori Saito,
Mikio Takeda
Production Aoi Advertising Promotion
Director Keizo Kurita

In this TV spot, the new Toyota Estate
drives across a computer-animated
landscape by Monet.

Control a film scene

The following exercise is intended to encourage you to play consciously with a short film scene that you run before your own inner eye. Repeat your chosen film clip as often as you like; the challenge is to take conscious control of it. Try altering individual components, or manipulating the characters, setting, props or things like hairstyles, physical proportions or backgrounds.

Select one particular short scene you feel comfortable with. It could be an event from your own life, an idea for a TV spot, or a scene from a feature film. Try to call up a clear mental picture of it. It helps if you sit down comfortably to do this, and close your eyes. Now imagine that you can alter the scene in your head exactly as if you were editing video images in a studio.

- Colour the scene or make it black and white.
- Try using the fast-forward button.
- What's the sound like? Can you make it louder, deeper, higher?
- Play with the focus control, turn it from extremely sharp to very soft.
- Change the size or content of your picture.
- Stop the film and take a still.
- Let the film run backwards.
- Can you see yourself in the scene? What is your role?
- Can you zoom in or out?
- Change the perspective, alter the order of events.

- Create new special effects.
- What can you see when you turn your 'camera'?
- What else can you experiment with, what can you change?

Play with the filters of observation

The object of this exercise is to use all your senses both to prompt new ideas and at the same time allow you to handle your visualizations in a more flexible way. You can use a still picture, a scene or let a whole film run before your inner eye. Things really start to get interesting as you begin to integrate all your senses into your inner world of images. What can you hear while the film is running in your head? What can you touch, smell or taste? What changes when you alter individual elements? You'll notice that the more sensory channels you build into your visualizations, the broader your spectrum of associations will become. Every new stimulus from inside or outside will either help you keep the stream of pictures running or divert it in a new direction. Treat this exercise as a game, just waiting to see what happens and what you need to do to make the flow of images start inspiring and reinforcing itself.

The table below shows the elements you can use to stimulate your inner world of images. Experiment with it in a calm and relaxed environment where you feel comfortable. As you may know from experience, a little practice is needed before methods like this can fully take effect and be as successful as they should be.

Sight	Sound	Touch, Feel	Smell, Taste
Brightness dark – light	Volume loud – soft	Intensity hard – soft	Intensity strong – bland
Size large – small	Pitch high – low	Area, Extent large – small	Intensity sweet – sour
Colour black/white – coloured	Tempo fast – slow	Texture rough – smooth	Intensity mild – fiery
Movement fast – slow	Distance near – far	Duration constant – intermittant	
Focus sharp – soft	Rhythm fast – slow	Temperature hot – cold	
Place	Place	Weight heavy – light	

2 Exercises

5 | VISUALIZATION

The work of the imagination and the process of developing ideas can be given an extra boost if you let different sensory channels cross or merge, generating synaesthetic reactions. The following exercises show you some fun ways to develop abstract pictures or find new methods of approaching visual solutions to problems. For example, see what happens if you try to visualize feelings, moods, noises, smells or tastes. Less than one per cent of the population is born with the ability to merge sensory channels. Experiencing synaesthesia means, for example, seeing a smell, hearing a sight or experiencing smells in response to certain sounds. Figures of speech that we use every day and intuitively understand, such as 'piercing sound' or 'sweet music', demonstrate that we all have the ability to generate synaesthetic experiences.

VISUALIZE FEELINGS – JUST THE FEELINGS

Visualize a positive feeling. Imagine astonishment, or love, for example, in picture form. Discard any images of a particular face or a pair of lovers, however. Pay more attention to what an abstract, imaginary picture of these feelings might look like, and the shapes and colours they evoke. You could also visualize a wish without actually wishing for something specific. Experiment with the following feelings and allow yourself to be surprised by your inner images:

- Joy, surprise
- Love, curiosity
- Anger, pride

ABSTRACT SOUNDS, ACOUSTIC PICTURES

Try to visualize what the following sounds look like. Make whole scenes if you like.

- Harsh singsong speech
- A cry of delight
- A bittersweet noise

PICTURE THE TACTILE

Relax, lie back and convert the feel of the following things into visual compositions, but do not conjure up the concrete objects themselves.

- A soft, silk evening dress
- A steel drill
- Ice cubes

VISUALIZE TASTE AND SMELL

Relax and try to paint a clear image of the taste or smell of the following things without picturing the sources themselves.

- Spring air
- Vegetable soup
- Car exhaust fumes
- Cheese

4 Exercises

The following exercises should help you to improve the clarity and control of your inner pictures and scenes. You should play these visualization games in a relaxed frame of mind and without expecting too much at first.

FANTASY IMAGES

Try to find out the difference between images you've seen and those you've never seen. Picture these invented objects in your head, play with them and bring them to life:

- A river of chocolate with things swimming in it
- A mushroom as a guest on a TV talkshow
- A hobbit trying to resist the earth's magnetic force
- A supersonic printing press

EMOTIONAL FLEXIBILITY

Make yourself comfortable physically and take a few deep breaths to help you relax. When you're ready, visualize a chair – just a plain, ordinary chair. When you have a clear picture of the chair in your head, imagine it in a comic situation – in a hilarious scene with your favourite comedian, for example. Let your imagination draw something bizarre. Remember, nobody's watching you, nobody can censor your mental images. Keep experimenting with this exercise until you feel refreshed, enlightened and entertained.

JOIN TWO THINGS TOGETHER TO MAKE SOMETHING NEW

A large part of creative thinking involves linking two previously separate ideas and so creating something new. Gutenberg combined the idea of a die used for stamping coins with the idea of a winepress and came up with movable type and the printing press.

Look for a few interesting objects and try combining their functions, features, materials and forms in such a way that something new results. To begin with, it doesn't matter whether or not your creation makes sense or would work in practice. Wait and see, let yourself be surprised by the images that crop up. Try the following, for example:

- A shirt and a computer = ?
- A cactus and a door = ?
- A clock and a desk = ?

ASK 'WHAT IF...'

- What if gravity was switched off every morning between 7 and 9 a.m.?
- What if people could transform themselves into their favourite vegetable or plant for five minutes once a month?

Invent 'What if...' questions of your own and see where your imagination leads you. Go down into the details of your stories, and see what the effects would be in different settings and scenarios. The more often you do this exercise the more likely you are to discover some amazing visual worlds.

DISSOCIATION AND METAPERSPECTIVE

'Dissociation' is a mental state in which a person looks at a situation, or himself, from outside but without becoming emotionally involved. Adopting a kind of bird's-eye view will improve your ability to recognize larger contexts and reassess their significance. Here is an example of the course your exercise might take:

With your eyes open or closed, try to imagine yourself rising out of yourself. You might float up to the ceiling, for example, and then look down at yourself sitting on the chair. Or you might cross the room, sit down on a box behind yourself and watch yourself doing everything you did in the past twenty minutes. In another version, you could fly up into the air like a bird and then look down at yourself from this new perspective. Whichever version you choose, try to look at yourself from above, as you are now. What position are you in, where are your hands, whereabouts are you in the room? Most people find this exercise very difficult at first and need a lot of practice before they master it. It is interesting, however, that this metaperspective opens up a new angle on familiar things and so often enables us to make important new discoveries. It is also an important visualization exercise, promoting flexibility and new creative perspectives.

3 Exercises

The following three exercises are intended to help people who find it difficult to generate pictures in their heads. This isn't an innate deficiency, it only means that their strengths obviously lie in other sensory areas, such as hearing or touch. The following aids to visualization challenge you to have fun discovering all the things you can do to improve your imagination.

AFTER-IMAGES

This is a simple exercise you can practice at any time. Look at an object in all its details, let your eyes wander around it, take in every detail of colour, shape, material and other characteristics. Then close your eyes and use the remaining after-image to make the object real again, step by step. This so-called after-image is the picture that remains on your retina for a short time after you close your eyes. As soon as it fades, open your eyes, look at the object again, shut your eyes again and try to retain the after-image or enhance it. Repeat the exercise at intervals you're comfortable with and as often as you like. After some practice you will find that you can generate the after-image of different objects at will and that the pictures in your head are more concrete.

IMAGE-STREAMING

The technique of image-streaming developed by Win Wenger is a simple and effective method of encouraging the flow of pictures in your head. First of all, make yourself comfortable and don't worry about the accuracy of the images. There's no reason why you shouldn't cheat a little to begin with and act as if the pictures were perfectly clear to your inner eye. Describe your imagined picture aloud, in all its details and in the present tense. If at first you see only hazy or incomplete pictures, then exaggerate, invent things or improve on the picture, and after a while the missing pieces will appear of their own accord. If you feel good and are enjoying the images, don't leave the stream too early, stay there. One picture will lead to the next and this chain of images will take you automatically into many new imaginary worlds. The important thing is this: you should simply watch like a bystander, without passing judgement or interfering.

VISUALIZE WHILE DEEPLY RELAXED

Pictures will appear in your head more easily if you are relaxed and awake. As a first stage, get into a comfortable position, wear loose, casual clothes and breathe deeply and easily. Find somewhere pleasant to sit and don't place excessive demands on yourself. Wait and see what happens, and watch what comes up before your inner eye. The six steps listed below will show you that with a bit of practice, it's relatively easy to induce a pleasant sense of deep relaxation. After a little practice, pictures will appear that you only need to look at, as a silent observer. When a little time has passed, you can begin to intervene actively, by changing colours or shapes, for example, or by developing stories − changing them or steering them in a certain direction. Instructions like these will always sound somewhat suspect to people who've never tried this type of relaxation exercise, so beginners should try to put themselves in the hands of an experienced teacher who will introduce them to these relaxation techniques in a gradual way.

1. Sit or lie down comfortably somewhere private. Adjust your position until you feel at ease.
2. Close your eyes and focus on your breathing for a while. Let your breath flow and feel how it 'moves' you.
3. Now notice your physical sensations. What do you feel? The warmth of your body, the contact with your chair or sofa, the position of your hands, etc. Feel the tense points in your body and ease the tension by imagining that you can feel these places growing pleasantly warm and heavy.
4. All the sounds you can now hear will help you to relax and be more conscious of the peace inside you. You will become calmer with every breath.
5. If a lot of thoughts are going through your head, just let them float past, like clouds in the sky. Try not to hold on to them, simply watch and wait.
6. Let the images that appear take the lead and try to make them concrete. Try making them as clearly focused and accurately coloured as possible. When you are relaxed enough, try to alter them or steer them in a direction of your choice. Be ruled by spontaneity and only do things that are fun and help you to relax.

5.05   BRAINFLOATING

This technique, developed by Harald Braem, is an interesting exercise
to help develop visual communication. It begins with devising single
sentences that bring together thematic spheres (different professions,
topics or lifestyles) which are never normally connected. The aim is
to include, and address, as many as possible of the five senses (sight,
hearing, touch, smell and taste). It's a good method to try on your own
but it also works for teams of up to six people. Since brainfloating is
a rather unconventional technique and requires a little practice, the
DreamTeam rules should be applied, and the group should ideally
be led by someone with experience.

PHASES OF IDEA HUNTING

→ *Phase 1*

Brainfloating requires the formulation of a question, rather like a goal,
with which a team works throughout a whole meeting. The question
should bring together themes which are completely unconnected,
for example.

○ If this cola can were a mime artist, what would its movements tell you?

○ If this running shoe were a cheetah or a race horse, what emotions
would it express?

○ If this toothpaste were a plant, how would it feel?

After applying this method for a time in a spirit of playful curiosity, you
will notice that the combination of unconnected themes opens a large,
unexplored field of ideas and leads to a lot of surprising associations. It is
important to try to include as many senses as possible: the examples
above each cover two or three.

→ *Phase 2*

Let's take a campaign for Yamaha motorcycles as an example:
> *'If this motorcycle was a predatory animal, what would*
> *its acceleration sound like?'*

Describe the characteristics of different beasts of prey, such as tigers,
bears or eagles. Let your associations flow freely and concepts like
concentrated energy, rhythmic movement, perfect power transmission,
elegant musculature, optimal physical design, dynamism and goal-
directed strength are likely to come up. Keep at it for as long as you
can and see what attributes occur to you and which of these concepts
could be transferred to features of the motorbike.

→ *Phase 3*

The next stage is to ask yourself how the attributes you have thought
of could be transferred to the world of sound. The question was: 'If this
motorcycle was a predatory animal, what would its acceleration sound
like?' Is there a sound, a song (tune or words), or an animal's call that
conveys the sense of goal-directed strength, or dynamism, for example?
Can these sounds be visualized, or do they stimulate ideas that take you
further? Go through the list of attributes again and find out what ideas
they lead to. It is important not to cling too tightly to your original
suggestions, and to let your mind drift in a playful way. Wait and see
where these associations lead you and what ideas they stimulate.

→ *Phase 4*

The outcome of a session like this is usually a host of words, images and
ideas which can be converted into concrete visual ideas. Then the first
ideas and tentative solutions can be developed further in doodle form.

Creative Technique

WHAT'S THE IDEA BEHIND STORYBOARDING?

Storyboards were invented by Walt Disney and his team in the early days
of cinema. While creating their animations, they produced larger and
larger stacks of drawings, making it increasingly difficult to preserve an
overview. Then one day, Disney told his artists to stick their drawings up
on the studio walls. Now everyone in the team could see the status of
the project at a glance. The procedure not only saved the team time and
energy, but over the years it developed into an independent creative
technique, and the storyboard became the place where ideas were
developed and constantly improved.

WHERE CAN THE TECHNIQUE BE USED?

Storyboarding is especially appropriate for developing raw ideas into
TV and cinema spots, Flash animations and web banners. Moderately
good ideas need to be worked up into brilliant stories. As you will know
from experience, visualizing an idea in a meeting is often the only way
to let it survive. It has to make its way from the head of one creative into
the heads of the rest of the team if that vital spark is to make the leap.
But storyboarding is a bit more than just visualizing an idea: it creates
the space to polish early ideas and at the same time develop totally new
ones. The team works directly on the storyboard, new ideas can be seen
at once and can be developed in parallel with existing ones.

WORK WITH A GOAL

Before you go to work and begin your first experiment with this method,
you must once again formulate your goal. Even if you come to the
meeting with ideas from a previous one, you should use the new goal
as a means of deciding which of the raw ideas you want to proceed
with. Pin this goal at the top of the storyboard like a headline.

USE THE DREAMTEAM RULES

To use the storyboarding technique effectively in the team, and to enable
the raw ideas to be developed without friction, you should follow the
fifteen DreamTeam rules.

PREPARE FOR THE MEETING

Prepare all the materials you will need for the meeting in advance,
because there's nothing worse than having too few cards or no pencils.
The first thing you will need in the room where the meeting is to take
place is two or three large pinboards, unless you are actually able to
pin the cards directly to the wall. You will also need thin pieces of card
measuring 12 x 15 cm (5 x 6 in.), coloured pens and lead pencils, and
plenty of drawing pins and sticky tape.

HOW TO STORYBOARD

→   *Phase 1*

Work out a goal and pin it at the top of the pinboard.

→   *Phase 2*

The basic premise: you have already had one meeting, at which a
large number of usable ideas were developed. Now, using the new
goal, choose the three best raw ideas to continue working with.

→   *Phase 3*

Next, the whole team sets to work drawing the individual scenes
and stages of the commercial as storyboard images. The quality of the
drawings is not important, but comprehensibility and speed in getting
the ideas down are. Of course you can work with words, signs or symbols
as well, to save time. At this stage, the team can already start to
discuss individual ideas, in order to build on them and augment
them with new ideas.

→   *Phase 4*

Now the cards should be mounted horizontally, in the usual storyboard
style, so that they can be read like a comic strip. Enough space should be
left between the cards to allow for rearrangement or for inserting extra
ones. By this stage there should be quite a lot of movement in the room,
with most people standing in front of the storyboard, some drawing new
scenes, and others trying cards in different positions.

Phase 5

What follows is a process of continual alteration and embellishment of existing ideas. For example, you can try giving the spot different beginnings, middles and endings. You can follow leads to completely new ideas, or combine separate ideas or scenes in order to produce new scenes. It is important not to think only in visual images, but to call on all your other senses as well. What can be heard, what roles are played by smell and taste, and what is there to feel?

Phase 6

If an idea, sequence or scene strikes the team as interesting and usable, it should be drawn at once and added to the ideas pool. But don't throw the old ideas away; leave them on the storyboard as triggers for new ideas. Simply arrange the new scenes round the old ones. Don't accept any ad hoc solutions, but keep tinkering with them until every scene causes a 'wow!', and you have a convincing ad in front of you.

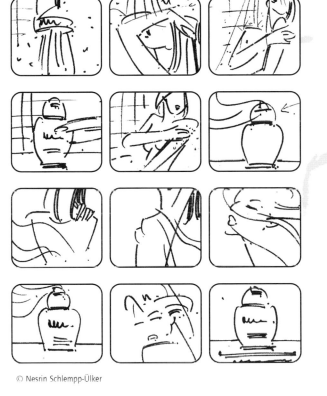

© Nesrin Schlempp-Ülker

FOUR STEPS TOWARDS A QUICK STORYBOARD

→ Keep the cards relatively small, which lets you draw a lot faster. It means the pictures are more like doodles, not finished works of art. Don't forget, you're only trying to communicate an idea, not win the Turner prize.

→ Make sure you have enough cards ready: the processing of ideas will be massively disrupted if more cards have to be cut or other materials fetched.

→ Use pencils, to make it easy to add something to the drawings, or change them. That way, you won't have to redraw the whole storyboard.

→ Write a few words at the bottom of each card, saying what is happening in it, so that everyone in the team understands exactly what the scene is about: Bob walks into the room, people appear, water pours through the ceiling. But don't write detailed stage directions or complete passages of dialogue.

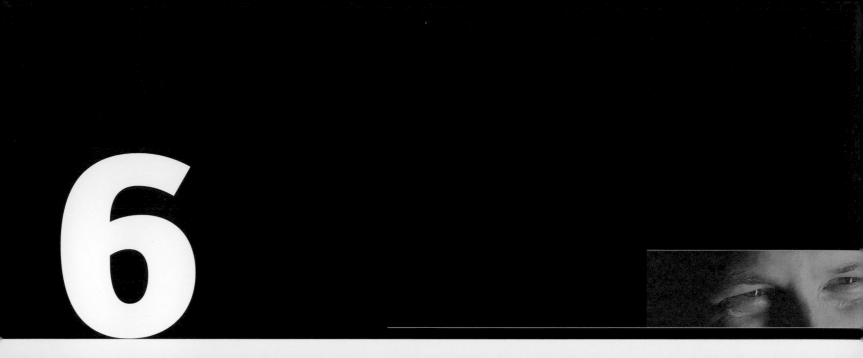

Professor Walter Lürzer is one of the most famous names in international advertising. He entered the world of advertising as a young copywriter in 1966 and was already Creative Director at Ogilvy & Mather only four years later. In the 1970s he was co-founder, partner and managing director of the agencies TBWA Frankfurt and Lürzer, Conrad & Leo Burnett Frankfurt. The first issue of his periodical *Lürzer's Archive* appeared in 1984, and it is now published worldwide. He became director of the masterclass in graphics and advertising at the University of Applied Art (Universität für Angewandte Kunst) in Vienna in 1990, and was appointed full professor in 1992.

Pricken: Professor Lürzer, you can look back on a unique career in advertising. You co-founded three advertising agencies, you are editor and publisher of the international trade periodical *Lürzer's Archive*, and you have run the masterclass in graphics and advertising at the University of Applied Art in Vienna since 1990. How do you think advertising has changed in the past ten years?

Professor Lürzer: I think questions like that always call for a little caution, because it's possible that one has changed oneself and therefore one views the world differently. I'm not sure if greater experience of life makes one more objective or more subjective. As I see it, advertising has stood still and at the same time it has changed a lot. It has stood still in that people's wishes and needs have not changed fundamentally. The proportion of advertising that says something about the product has undoubtedly fallen; today, a large proportion of it is confined to naming the product – that is to say, it's concerned with attention at all costs. I think the reason for this is that most businesses and target groups believe that coffee is all the same, whatever it is, and it's more important for the brand to have a good image, to convey prestige and confidence. The alarming thing is that asinine advertising seems to be just as effective as intelligent advertising. Since stupidity is more common and also comes cheaper than intelligence, this sort of advertising is increasing at an alarming rate. I also get the impression that, with the disappearance of personalities in business, management is adopting a pragmatic attitude; no one is ashamed of anything as long as it sells. No one shoots themselves now if they go into receivership, they just start up another company. Advertising is simply a mirror of our society. I am fascinated by the sight of so-called emancipated women grabbing straight for the object of their desire. Twenty or thirty years ago most people would probably have called them tarts, but today they're role models. And of course, the changes made by technology must not be underestimated. There are hardly any TV spots that don't use special effects or computer animation. Whether the ideas are any better for it, or whether the spots sell any better, I wouldn't like to say.

Pricken: What influence do you think your periodical *Lürzer's Archive* has on the creatives in advertising agencies?

Professor Lürzer: Role models are probably the most important motivational force there is, besides hunger and sex of course. They show what's possible, they give the imagination free rein and so provide a spur to better performance. I don't think it's *Lürzer's Archive* in itself, as an organ, that influences creatives, it's the profusion of ideas. You can see it happening, *Lürzer's Archive* activates a kind of productive envy, which drives even the lazy ones to their desks. The effect of *Lürzer's Archive*, like the effect of festivals, can be reduced to a few very human needs: people want to be admired, they want a comfortable life, they want better luck with the opposite sex, or the same sex, or they want to see their rivals spitting nails. Oh yes, of course there are still a few who want to go to heaven, but that's a different story.

Pricken: Where do you personally set the boundaries of humour, provocation and shock in advertising? What sort of ad would you not want to include in *Lürzer's Archive*?

Professor Lürzer: We are not the ones who set the boundaries, it's largely the society in which we live. Interest groups like the churches, women's associations, politicians and child protection organizations all have a say. That's already quite enough people laying down boundaries, thank God, between what's possible and what's not. Of course advertising is always trying to push the boundaries a little further and reveal a new perspective. I must admit that some advertising goes too far for my taste, but we usually publish it all the same, just to keep readers informed about all the trends in the profession.

Pricken:: What does a talented youngster need in order to be accepted as a student in your masterclass at the University of Applied Art?

Professor Lürzer: It's not all that difficult, you know. First of all, we want technical skills, secondly pleasure in creativity, and thirdly the ability to think laterally. It's true that our two-day entrance examination has the reputation of being almost impossible to pass, but that's nonsense. It's simply that, despite the number of applications, we have difficulty in finding five or six new students a year whom we believe are really gifted. Especially among the male applicants, the women are surprisingly superior.

Pricken: Why should a young person with creative talent attend your masterclass? Can creativity be learnt?

Professor Lürzer: It's not just creativity, it's also a matter of translating it into action. Believe me, if I've learnt one thing in all my years of university teaching, it's how to give my students a gentle but firm kick up the backside to get them more involved. What's the use of being creative, if you never get anything up and running? Our class is a laboratory for creatives, where our students can experiment undisturbed by the world outside, find out about their own creativity, and so mature into the next generation of creatives. I think that this freedom, combined with a broad-based cultural and educational grounding, is the reason why university is more useful in the long run than just an apprenticeship in an agency. As for the second part of your question: there are undoubtedly differences in creative ability. It can't be learned, but it can be honed.

Pricken: When you look at the students in your class today, what are the differences between them and the creatives you knew at the beginning of your career?

Professor Lürzer: Well, I think they're just as lazy as we were, and at least as obsessed with relationships. Their needs remain exactly the same, and nothing much is going to change in the phases of life that we all live through. One small difference I can see is the social pressure, which is not quite so enormous for the young nowadays.

Pricken: What would you advise a young person to do: start his or her career in a small but superior creative workshop, or go into an international organization?

Professor Lürzer: Both have their pros and cons. In general, however, I would say that an agency's big name is less important than the environment that the young creative is going into. Is it productive or destructive? Does it encourage talent or waste it? The most important thing is having someone you can look up to and use as your model.

Pricken: Are there any ideas you have been carrying around with you for a long time that you have not been able to realize up to now?

Professor Lürzer: I have built two houses, fathered two children and planted two trees. That's twice as much as is recommended for any one lifetime.

Pricken: Thank you very much for the interview.

> The alarming thing is that asinine advertising seems to be just as effective as intelligent advertising

Paulo Jorge Pereira, known as PJ, is a partner and the creative director of the new media agency AgênciaClick. Born in Rio de Janeiro, he majored in Business at PUC. He went on to become the first Brazilian ad-agency professional to work exclusively with the Internet. By 1989, he had already completed his first web project. In 1992, while in college, he wrote a best-selling business book entitled *The Streamlined Company*. Before starting at AgênciaClick, PJ worked at one of Brazil's most well-known and creative agencies, DM9 DDB. There he won the first two Brazilian Cyber Lions. PJ has represented Brazil in the most important forums and festivals around the world. He was listed as one of the top five creatives in the world by the IdeaGroup/Advertising Age International.

Pricken: Your agency wins more awards than any other new media agency on the international scene. What is it you do that enables you to reach such high creative standards?

PJ Pereira: Productivity. We try to create good stuff faster than we already can. As a result, we realize that some of those things are more than very good. But that's something that we only notice after those jobs are done. It's not as if we think 'let's create something special today'... it's more like 'the more creative work you do, the greater are your chances of creating excellent pieces'. It doesn't sound very poetic, but that's how it works here.

Pricken: What was the first fantastic idea you ever had that you still consider good today, and how old were you when you had it?

PJ Pereira: Ideas are not 'fantastic' or 'stupid'. They are just ideas. Some of them work, some don't. And by 'working' I mean 'convincing someone to do things you want'. I remember that when I was a kid I loved to convince my mother to let me do things I wasn't allowed to. And I liked to use her own arguments to let me break some rules like 'you cannot cross the road without an adult'.

Once (I was three years old, I think) I asked her:

– Mom, is God really always with us?

– Yes, he is.

– He never leaves us? Never?

– No, son, never. He's always with us.

– So you can let me cross the road. I won't be alone. He'll be going with me!

It wasn't a fantastic idea – actually, letting a 3-year-old boy cross the street alone is quite stupid – but it almost worked!

Pricken: Have you increased your creativity since then? Have you learnt to use it better?

PJ Pereira: Since my early memories, I remember myself drawing, writing stories, playing weird characters in school plays, learning to play an instrument and programming a computer. I think it all helped me to build up a creative-thinking process with lots of different artistic influences. But I think that when I graduated in business administration, I started to learn how to control this process and focus on specific results.

Pricken: How are creative meetings normally conducted at AgênciaClick? Do they have a set structure or do you prefer to leave the generation of ideas either to chance or to the mood of the participants?

PJ Pereira: I don't like to put creativity in a closed box. Creative things come all the time from virtually everybody – not only in a creative meeting or from the creative department. Some of the best things we have ever done were created by the engineering team. They know the software details that enable them to create new stuff like nobody else in the agency. The planning guys have also created fantastic opportunities that the official 'creatives' had only to lay out and write nice copy for.

My mission here is to set everybody free to speak whenever they want and inspire them to get new ideas for reaching old goals. Creativity, for me, is something you cannot think of as 'let's stop now and be creative' or 'those are the guys who create and those are the ones who think logically'. You need to think of 'creativity' as a discipline, just like 'organization', 'commitment to results' or 'responsibility'.

Pricken: Who, in your experience, delivers better ideas, an individual creative or a well-established team?

PJ Pereira: A team that knows how to work as if they were at a jazz jamming session is probably more productive than any classical virtuoso. Our everyday work is not a concert where we always play the same song. And we don't follow any sheet music. It takes more improvisation, integration and a deep knowledge of how the other players play their instruments. Of course if a great individual joins the team, he inspires the rest of the group with fresh brilliant ideas. But I have discarded dozens of people who wanted to work on their own. And believe me: some of them were *really* brilliant and yet I didn't have a minute of doubt about letting them go in order to make the creative environment more inspiring for the whole team.

Pricken: What things, in your experience, most disrupt a team's creative process?

PJ Pereira: The *'It was my idea'* disease. The first symptom is when somebody starts to claim for himself the authorship of an idea just because he was the one who put it in words first. Ideas, especially the really good ones, always come from a chain of suggestions. And they only become brilliant in the skilful hands of a team that cares about the little details during the execution. Nothing can really be perfect if one single part fails. So, when one person thinks that he or she is more important than the rest of the crew, the disaster is already there. And you are almost dead.

Pricken: In the field of new media the average age is relatively low. Are young people simply more creative, or does the advantage lie in the fact that they have a more impetuous approach to problem-solving?

PJ Pereira: I believe that they are simply more used to computers, video games and interactive thinking than previous generations. And you will see what I mean when the current Playstation2 generation joins the market. Older people still 'respect' computers. Kids now watch the *Digimon* cartoon heroes fighting against viruses spread over the internet. They look at a computer in the same way that they look at a ball or a dog. It's a funny toy, nothing more than that.

Pricken: What do you find particularly exciting about online advertising?

PJ Pereira: Online advertising is never only 'advertising'. It involves some retail thinking and sometimes it looks more like an extension of a store than a simple advertising piece. These subtle details that are being experienced and tested again and again on every different job we face are thrilling. The sensation that we are always doing something that has never been done before is what really moves the people who got touched by this profession.

Pricken: Do you feel that internet advertising is still regarded by the international advertising festivals as a rather subsidiary activity?

PJ Pereira: Not by the festivals themselves, but it is by the delegates. But this will surely change. As the Playstation2 generation joins the market, advertising people won't be afraid of the internet anymore and they will enjoy playing the game. But now, they tend to feel more comfortable ignoring it. They get mad when they notice that the points given to a gold-award-winning million-dollar TV spot are the same as those awarded to a single internet banner. But let's face it, people are moving faster and faster into consuming interactive information. These are the media your kids will be using, whether you're comfortable with it or not. And when advertising agencies realize this, they may not have enough technology to play the game.

'We must now start imagining what our work will be like in this ▲ ● ■ ✖ world. And if you don't know what ▲ ● ■ ✖ means, you should study even faster.'

Pricken: Can online advertising be compared to direct marketing in terms of the measurability of its effectiveness?

PJ Pereira: It's more than that. Have you ever seen those research girls inside a store taking notes every time somebody goes in? They are measuring the buyers' behaviour. In the online world we can measure the effectiveness of the response to marketing stimuli, as direct marketing guys do, and connect those results to the consumers' behaviour while they are browsing in your 'environment'. As everything happens inside a computer, we can follow the user from the beginning to the end. And that's when you really find great opportunities for both improving your interface (just as the researcher might suggest that you change your store layout) and your communication. Analysing media results and navigation tracks as one big picture gives you a whole new view on how your consumers react to your brand.

Pricken: Why are 90 per cent of the advertising banners on the web so boring and unimaginative? And why is it that the quality standards we are familiar with from classic advertising have not yet been matched?

PJ Pereira: Because of the books. I have already met clients who have read one or another 'important' book about online advertising with some stupid lists of dos and don'ts. When a client blindly believes in these books, you get stuck with mediocrity, unless you can convince them to break those rules. Usability issues are also a factor. Of course a 'call to action' statement in a banner can help you get faster results, the same way that clearer navigation would make your site easier to negociate. But people are not computers (thank God!) and they still enjoy clever ideas and charming approaches. Suppose these writers wrote about love, instead of the internet – like those weird books with '10 rules to make a woman fall in love with you'. Some of the advice might be good. But if you followed them all, with no restriction, you would die alone.

Pricken: Why do you invest your creative energy in this particular field? Have you ever thought of using your talent in a completely different field?

PJ Pereira: Because I love what I'm doing. Sometimes I believe that my whole life has been leading me to the internet. When I was 12, I got a computer for my birthday and two years later I started to work as a computer programmer in a company that develops hypertext systems called Telesoft. There I became a professional Information Architect. It was also there that I realized I liked advertising when I had to work, in 1989, on an interactive advertising project. Years later, I joined

DM9 DDB, where I worked in all the different areas of the agency and had the opportunity to try all the available media and participate in a highly creative process. And I really like the interactive field much more than advertising.

The time I spent in DM9 was very important for me: I developed my creative skills and learned some things about human nature (the people in front of those networked computers are the same people that watch TV). But when I started working on larger projects, I understood that the raw material of interactivity is 'software'. It means that interactive projects can't work with a process based on communications management. They need a robust software management system.

That's why I don't see my area as something smaller than advertising. It's a different thing, with the same breadth. Online advertising is just the intersection of the interactive and advertising worlds. My field is the whole interactive world, not only a part of it. It includes navigation and e-commerce skills, constant keeping-up with technological trends... Dealing with all these creative, technological and project management issues takes too much of my attention and needs a very specific approach.

Pricken: What form of internet advertising do you think has the biggest future, and how do you see it developing over the next few years?

PJ Pereira: I'm very excited about the way video games are progressing. The way they allow people and machines to interact is getting really sophisticated. The emotional bond a teenager has with a game is much higher and longer-lasting than his relationship with any Hollywood movie he might watch. I believe that these gaming experiences will turn the whole communication industry upside down: from entertainment to advertising. I suggest that all the professionals and companies in those fields pay attention to it and put it on their to-do list for the coming months. We must start now start imagining what our work will be like in this ▲ ● ■ ✖ world. And if you don't know what ▲ ● ■ ✖ means, you should study even faster.

Pricken: Thank you very much for the interview.

KesselsKramer is an international advertising and communications agency founded in 1996 by creatives Erik Kessels and Johan Kramer. Currently, around 30 people work for KesselsKramer. Half of them are Dutch, while the other half have roots in China, Germany, Spain, Turkey, Scotland, England, Sweden and the United States. The agency produces campaigns for both national and international clients like Diesel, 55 DSL, Novib and Ben. Apart from advertising, a lot of other stuff is created there, including music videos, books, documentaries and even postage stamps. Johan Kramer devotes a lot of his time to directing many of the commercials made by KesselsKramer.

Pricken: The renowned advertising journal *Lürzer's Archive* regularly features the most creative advertising campaigns on the international scene. Mr Kessels is undisputed leader in the ranking of most creative art directors and Mr Kramer occupies the number one position in the list of creative directors. How did the two of you meet?

Kramer: Funny enough, we met at a dog show in England. Since we are both big cocker spaniel lovers, we met each other at a stand over there and kept talking the whole night about advertising and dogs. A good combination. Then we started working together and tried to put a dog in every ad. For three years, it worked. Then we had to do a campaign for an English bank and the CEO hated dogs. So we gave it up. From the first moment that Erik Kessels and I worked together, we were an agency in ourselves. Both of us are 'self-made' and true fanatics. For the first two years, we worked for other agencies, but we soon discovered that we were so stubborn it was better to have our own firm. So we moved back to Amsterdam and started KesselsKramer.

Pricken: After years of working together, is there any kind of recognizable pattern to the way you generate ideas in tandem?

Kramer: The reason why we work so well together is that we don't need each other. We can both work very well on our own and do lots of stuff apart from each other. When a job comes in, we think about it for a few days on our own and then we share our ideas in ten minutes and most of the time, we crack the job there and then. Those ten minutes contain a lot of energy and always create something better than the ideas we have separately. The funny thing is that we think very much in the same way. Sometimes we do separate reviews with other creative teams here and they often say afterwards that we've given exactly the same comments. Ultimately, the reasons why we work so well together are our huge respect for one another and our ability to be really vulnerable with each other.

> 'Ultimately, the reasons why we work so well together are our huge respect for one another and the ability to be really vulnerable with each other.'

Pricken: What do you consider to be the three most important factors in creating the ideal breeding-ground for creativity within a team?

Kramer: 1. respect 2. compassion 3. humour

Pricken: And what do you consider to be the three things that most paralyse and block creativity in meetings?

Kramer: 1. fear 2. insecurity 3. too much experience (it leads to cynicism).

Pricken: Recent studies have identified stress as the number one enemy of creativity. What do your creatives do to preserve their creativity amid the hustle and bustle of the advertising agency?

Kramer: We've changed our workplace into a wooden fort that looks like a children's playground. We do everything to make our creatives feel at home and make them feel appreciated. In the end, all creatives are children who are very insecure and need constant confirmation that they are doing the right thing. Furthermore, they are in close contact with all our clients, so they understand the pressure as well. So, in the end the client is not an unknown enemy, but another human being, and is hopefully seen as a friend.

Pricken: In your experience, what role do wit and humour play in creative meetings? Does an element of fun in meetings produce better results?

Kramer: Sure. We are in the imagination business, so let's go crazy. It's important not to take things too seriously; only then do you start seeing opportunities for doing things differently.

Pricken: How would you describe a typical creative meeting at your agency?

Kramer: It's organized chaos. In our meeting rooms we have wooden picnic tables. They are there for a reason. If you sit on them longer than half an hour, you get a pain in the ass. So, we force ourselves to cut the bullshit and talk about the issues that matter. Again, we try to create a situation where insecurity and fear don't exist. Keep it relaxed, with lots of respect for everyone involved.

Pricken: Can you describe what the moment feels like when you get an inspired idea? And how are you able to tell at that moment that the idea you have had is a genuinely fantastic one?

Kramer: It's a process that never stops. You digest as much information as possible about a project and then you start thinking. A good idea is like an accidental collision of two things you normally wouldn't combine. But the really important thing is to be insecure. The moment you are sure you've come up with a great idea, it's probably shit. That's where a lot of senior people in this business go wrong. They become arrogant because they've done a few nice campaigns. If you really want to do well, you have to keep worrying and never settle for anything easy.

Pricken: Many people hold the view that the outcome of a creative advertising campaign is entirely down to the advertising agency itself. What role, in your opinion, does the client play here?

Kramer: It's very easy to make a very creative advertising campaign. It's much harder to make a very creative advertising campaign that is really effective. For this, you need an inspiring client. If your client has nothing to say, it's hard to create something that is also inspiring. So, the client is essential in all our campaigns.

Pricken: Would you be prepared to invite the client's personnel to a creative meeting in order to develop ideas in common, or would this be going too far? What do you think the result of a joint brainstorming session of this kind would be?

'Sometimes it's really good to be self-taught, because if you don't know much about something, you can think more freely.'

Kramer: To be honest, I've never ever experienced an useful brainstorming session. I think they tends to be used in big companies, where people don't have much to do. They always end up in politics with the strongest people pushing their ideas. It's much better to think in small groups and then have a bigger meeting to discuss the ideas. Groups never come up with big ideas. It's always individuals.

Pricken: Have you ever stopped to wonder whether Kessels and Kramer could have been similarly successful as a like-minded duo in any other fields, such as architecture, film or art?

Kramer: We don't wonder about it, we try. We hate to think in boxes. Advertising is much too limited. We'd rather talk about communication. Apart from that, we love to do other things and get involved in all kinds of projects. Sometimes it's really good to be self-taught, because if you don't know much about something, you can think more freely. We have done fashion and architecture projects in the past and we loved it. We also experiment with our own brand, called *do*. It's a foundation, based next to the church we work in, that does lots of different projects like creating new furniture, music, consumer goods etc.

Pricken: What are the ideas you've always wanted to realize but haven't yet had the opportunity to?

Kramer: A feature film. But keep watching your local cinema.

Pricken: Thank you very much for the interview.

K.C. Tsang has received over 150 international and local creative awards. In 1994, his television campaign for Optical 88 won the Best of the Best Award and three Spikes in the Asian Advertising Awards. At the 1995 4As Award presentation, he won five Gold and six Silver Awards. K.C. has spent thirteen years serving a wide variety of accounts including American Express, Park'N Shop, Cheung Kong Property, Hennessy V.S.O.P., Cafe de Coral, Hutchison Paging, Whirlpool and Philips, Unilever, SE Beecham, Carlsberg, Bank of East Asia and City Chain. Before joining BBDO Hong Kong, K.C. spent one year at TVB, ten years at Ogilvy & Mather and one year at Bozell Worldwide.

Pricken: Mr Tsang, you are Executive Creative Director of BBDO Hong Kong and one of the top creatives in the country. Of all your tasks and responsibilities in the agency, which do you most enjoy?

K.C. Tsang: I suppose this is a warm-up question but it is a difficult one already. Well, I must say that I enjoy everything that the post requires me to do. But I have to confess that I am not good at everything I have to do. That's a good thing, isn't it? You never know what area you need to improve in the near future. At least you know you have something to do next.

I enjoy writing ads although I do not have many opportunities to do it now. I like the process of brainstorming with those idiots who are even more stupid and crazy than I am. The jokes are definitely enjoyable. Even more enjoyable is the spirit of exploration, experiment and comradeship. And then I enjoy seeing the rough concept gradually materializing, going on air and eventually surprising the audience, newspapers and our competitors.

I also enjoy pulling a group of people together, helping them to realize their potential. I believe that there is only limited room for growth if a person is working in isolation. I think a good atmosphere is necessary for everyone to grow. Good people should stay together to stimulate each other. I like good ideas coming up here and there. You know, I enjoy recruiting new staff, because it is really important to form the right mix within the team. And it is also important for controlling the quality of our work. I don't like to dictate or 'control' the day-to-day work.

Instead, I choose my staff very carefully. Recruiting quality staff is like picking up quality stock. I am good at the former but unfortunately not the latter.

The most exciting and stimulating part of my job is, of course, making the agency grow in terms of business. It is tough but I enjoy it. People always have a misperception that creative people are not interested in or capable of dealing with figures. That is not true. Those creative people who claim that they are not good at figures are just trying to excuse themselves for doing irresponsible ads for their clients or just shoehorning themselves into a so-called 'creative' role. Being responsible for the figures means that the CD has to be much stronger and more skilful in defending the agency's work, much more visionary in leading the agency and clients to get out of the daily chaos, and much more 'into' the business so as to make 'creativity' more valuable (another way of saying making the agency more profitable.)

> 'Those creative people who claim that they are not good at figures are just trying to excuse themselves for doing irresponsible ads for their clients or just shoehorning themselves into a so-called "creative" role.'

Pricken: When did you first become aware that you were a creative person and what was your first really good idea?

K.C. Tsang: I don't think I'm a creative person. I'm just a lucky one. In my opinion, creativity, especially in advertising, is not so much about 'creating' something from scratch or making up something from nothing. It is about destroying the existing paradigm or overthrowing the establishment. Who is more likely to do so? Here is an analogy.

A fish that lives in the water is not aware of the water. It takes the water for granted. It is only a man who looks at the picture from a different perspective that knows the existence of water. In most of the societies on earth, there are far more 'fish' than 'men'.

Luckily, I am not someone who was born in the mainstream. I was educated in a 'left-wing' (pro-China) school when Hong Kong was still a British colony. This life history led me to be 'different' from most of the others, intentionally and unintentionally. This is a good fit for advertising.

My first boss thought that you don't need to be 'creative' to do creative things. All you need is to be critical. That's why he hired me. What was my first really good idea? I don't know. I guess it must be the letter that helped me find a job in advertising. To be exact, it helped me find two jobs. Two agencies offered me the post of copywriter at the same time. The second agency paid 50 per cent more than the first agency to lure me into working for them. It was so effective that it must have been a good idea.

By the way, this reflects how I think about good ideas. Some advertising men think that truly creative ads don't sell and that effective ads must be boring. I think that's nonsense. The so-called 'creative' works in their minds are actually some 'award-winning' scam ads which are bound to fail in the market. What they think of as 'effective' ads are actually mediocre ads which do neither harm nor good to the products (which do not require good ads to succeed). In other words, what they think of as creative work is not creative at all and what they think is effective is not effective either. That's why they jump to the wrong conclusions. I think that truly creative ads are truly effective ads.

Pricken: Could you imagine finding a fulfilling outlet for your creativity in some other field, such as art, science or architecture?

K.C. Tsang: When I was a secondary student, I dreamed of being a scientist. When I started selecting a university subject, I wished I could be a good doctor. When I graduated from the university, I used to think of becoming a film director. But now, I have become more pragmatic and realistic. I know that no matter how hard I learn, I am just not talented enough to be a great scientist or doctor or film director. So I give up. I prefer advertising. It's easier.

Pricken: Do you think teamwork plays a different role in your advertising agency to the one it plays in agencies in Europe or America?

K.C. Tsang: This is an interesting question. When you first mention 'teamwork', its meaning in a narrower sense pops into my mind. What I mean is that I immediately think of the 'creative team'. Of course, teamwork in this sense is extremely important for advertising. Advertising is not art. We have time pressures, and teamwork is a good approach to dealing with those. I think this is the same throughout the entire world.

However, when you elevate the term 'teamwork' to a higher level or broaden its meaning to include the co-operation between different departments, I think we have a different kind of 'teamwork' from the West.

The whole process of doing advertising in the West takes a much longer period than in Hong Kong. The strategy has to go through thorough research before it is briefed to the creative. The creative concept has to go through thorough research before it is produced. The process goes on and on forever. At every stage, a lot of people are involved. Moreover, I can imagine that clients and agencies are much more bureaucratic than their peers in Hong Kong. So the number of people involved just keeps multiplying. In this case, you really need 'teamwork'. By the way, probably because of this tiring process, many Western ads are stiff, calculated and 'professional'.

The situation in Hong Kong is different. The biggest proportion of ads are amateurish. But sometimes I think these are better than boring calculated ads because they are unexpected and you see energy in them. Why is it so? In Hong Kong, the standard length of time from briefing to the finished ad is about 1 to 2 months. Besides, the organization is much simpler than that in the West (with the exception of some really big clients). A lot of people who participate in the process are not 'professional' enough (or even well-suited to the job). Therefore, spontaneity is allowed.

In this situation, the creative department takes a leading role in the process. They are responsible for coming up with strategies, creative concepts and executions. They sell the ads by themselves. They produce them. Sometimes, they liaise with clients for the quotation as well. 'Teamwork', in this case, almost means 'how to co-operate with creatives'.

Pricken: What do you do to motivate your teams and make sure they enjoy optimum creative freedom?

K.C. Tsang: People say that creatives are hard to manage. I think this belief is wrong. Creative guys are easy to manage but hard to control. 'Manage' is not the same as 'control'. With creatives, you just need to give them a mission. They will go for it. They are already self-motivated. The best way to manage them is to free them, not to control them.

At BBDO HK, we emphasize the ideology and the value system amongst the creative staff and even the staff of the other departments. And we get rid of the bureaucracy, the rules and procedures. Then, we can see the agency take flight. This thinking is the backbone of our operations. Whose idea was this? Within the tradition of BBDO worldwide, our creative department has been striving to stay in control. Staying in creative control is the best way to let ourselves enjoy the optimal creative freedom.

Pricken: What, in your opinion, are the three worst idea killers that can disrupt a meeting?

K.C. Tsang: No. 1 killer is the hidden agenda. Some clients have the hidden agenda of keeping their jobs secure instead of performing the best they can. They don't need good ads. On the contrary, they need mediocre ads. Some clients are torn by political struggles and advertising becomes an arena for fighting. Some creatives have the hidden agenda of getting awards through short cuts instead of making the ads work harder to win awards. The doubts of each party about any hidden agenda the others may have can also kill the idea, even if there is no hidden agenda. Hidden agendas are really the most serious killer.

No. 2 killer is the hierarchy of the client. Some clients really understand the importance of advertising so the senior management gets heavily involved. They will have effective meetings with the agency, providing clear direction and important information. They are good clients. They get the good ads they are looking for.

Some clients don't trust advertising. But they delegate responsibility completely to the brand managers. They empower these managers to make decisions. They are not as good as those mentioned above but are still good clients. The brand managers sometimes do not dare to make decisions, and sometimes make the wrong decisions because of their limited view of the big picture. But most of the time, especially if the brand managers are strong enough, they approve good ads that make the brand take off.

The worst clients are those who trust bureaucracy or who take advantage of bureaucracy. They hide from meetings and avoid making decisions but make a big fuss about the decisions being made or simply kill the idea without fully understanding the idea. Bureaucracy is a weapon for shooting down good ideas.

No. 3 killer is the business pressure of both the ad agency and the client. Good ideas have to take risks. Taking risks is in turn the surest way to achieve your objective. I'd like to add one more idea killer which is our so called 'knowledge' about advertising, e.g., the grid, the format, the continuity, the white type on black background etc. What made us succeed yesterday will make us fail tomorrow. If we treat them as gospel, we will tie ourselves up. The world is changing faster than we can deal with if we still equip ourselves with yesterday's knowledge.

Pricken: How do you handle client briefings in your agency? How do you go about passing on a project to your creative team, and how do they then take it up?

K.C. Tsang: We encourage them to think without boundaries. We make them expect something totally outrageous. If we think that they are not in line with us, we will consider whether we should give it a go. Normally, we will try figure out the hidden agenda. It is not easy.

Regarding passing the project to the creative team, we will excite them with the potential outcome of the ad, and challenge them to do a better ad than their last one.

Pricken: Do you think there is a difference between the way creatives think in Hong Kong and China and the way they think in Europe or America?

> 'Good ideas have to take risks. Taking risks is in turn the surest way to achieve an objective.'

K.C. Tsang: I think we all have something in common. For example, we all do comparative ads, demonstration ads, humorous ads, emotional ads, etc. And we all know what love is. We all treasure peace. We all care about the next generation. But it's not what we have in common that makes our ads excellent. On many occasions, it's what makes us different from each other that makes the ads great. We definitely think differently from the West. We even think differently from the Chinese.

Pricken: Many people hold the view that the outcome of a creative advertising campaign is entirely down to the advertising agency itself. What role, in your opinion, does the client play here?

'Hong Kong humour is just like an unripe fruit. It is raw, dry, sour, bitter and not easy to swallow.'

K.C. Tsang: I think this is a sort of 'chicken and egg' situation. An objective answer would be: a creative advertising campaign is the outcome of good co-operation between the agency and the client.

Of course, if you are aggressive and confident enough, you might claim that a creative ad campaign can be totally attributed to the agency's efforts. In this case, you are partially right. We can easily tell creative agencies from other not-so-creative ones. It is because they believe in creativity. They know that this is what advertising is all about. So they push very hard to get work through. They'd rather struggle to survive until they get good clients, etc. Some people choose to believe this side of the story.

The other side of the story, the more pessimistic one, is that clients control the life and death of any ad campaign. Even so-called creative agencies cannot escape from this fate. If you compare the good work with the bad work, you'll find the latter by far outweighs the former, even in creative agencies, not to mention the second-rate agencies.

In my opinion, with a macroview, clients control the whole game; while with a microview, agencies can modify it a little bit. I don't mean that we should use this as an excuse for bad advertising. On the contrary, we should fight even harder to strive for excellence. I just want to stress

two points: 1. Don't glorify yourself too early. 2. Hey, this is the fun part of doing advertising.

Pricken: What kind of advertising humour do Hong Kongers like best?

K.C. Tsang: The way you ask this question seems to suggest that there are some laws regarding Hong Kong humour. But I think that humour is highly subject to the context of communication. Right at this moment, 'anti-intelligence', 'anti-middle class', 'demystifying pop culture' – those sorts of humour work better. I think 'anti-America' will become popular as the Chinese identity of the Hong Kong people becomes stronger over the coming years. Well, this is just a wild guess.

Pricken: How would you describe the humour of the Hong Kongers in general?

K.C. Tsang: Hong Kong humour is just like an unripe fruit. It is raw, dry, sour, bitter and not easy to swallow. In fact, when you put Hong Kong advertisements on a reel with other award entries, you won't find them very funny to watch. Japanese TVCs can make you burst out laughing. So can Thai TVCs. Some American and European TVCs are very funny too. Compared with them, HK humorous commercials are too controlled. They look as if some naughty primary-school students are trying to do something funny but worrying too much about being punished. It reflects the immature attitude of clients towards advertising.

Pricken: What would you have to show or say in an advertising campaign to break a taboo in Hong Kong?

K.C. Tsang: There are too many taboos in Hong Kong. That's why doing advertising is still easy. Just persuade your clients to break the taboos and the product will definitely become magnetic. Hong Kong has become a postmodern city where the distinctions between right and wrong, good and bad, fake and real, high class and low class are all blurred. In this kind of society, being able to make a noise (in whatever way) is already half way to success. Breaking taboos is just one way to make a big noise.

Showing sex is definitely a taboo. Even ads that imply sex never make it to the air. Politics is another taboo. We obviously don't touch on anything about communism, great leaders, national flags, etc. It is really strange that almost anything British is also sensitive. Even the sex scandal of the American ex-president is a political issue that is not suitable for advertising. Maybe we should be happy because this phenomenon may reflect that Hong Kong is truly an international city where all interests are present. At least someone will get to you to collect their royalty fees.

Religion is absolutely taboo. Of course, no commercial can make fun of any religion. Even glorification is not good enough for commercial use. I guess when you glorify one religion, you are actually belittling others, like FaLunGong. Someone will be left unhappy. There are probably also some other general taboos like mistreating kids and the elderly, negative portrayal of the Chinese identity, racism, sexism and so on. Comparatively speaking, violence is more acceptable in Hong Kong. Well, after all, Chinese kung fu is our cutting edge.

Pricken: Are there any ideas you have been carrying around with you for a long time that you have not been able to realize up to now?

K.C. Tsang: I have been very lucky because almost all of our ideas have had a chance at exposure in recent years. If there were any that were conceived long time ago but still remain undone, I have forgotten them. After all, I think those ideas must not have been strong enough to stand the test of time. In fact, I think any advertising idea is only valid for a short time. Classic examples are cited in textbooks, seminars or training, but it's a misconception that they still work nowadays because they are so good. I think their sell-by dates have passed. If you show them, they are bound to fail. We mistakenly believe that they still work only because of the 'framing effect' of the textbook, seminar or training itself.

It seems that I have been preaching too much. OK, I confess. I don't want to expose my unrealized ideas. I still want to sell them one day. If I tell you, will you pay me a royalty fee? I'll ask for a huge amount.

Pricken: Thank you very much for the interview.

6.05 STEFAN SAGMEISTER · GRAPHIC DESIGNER

Stefan Sagmeister was born in Vorarlberg in Austria and studied graphics and design at the University of Applied Art in Vienna. After a few years with Leo Burnett in Hong Kong and M&Co in New York, he founded Sagmeister Inc. in 1993, with the primary aim of working in the music industry. Since then he has designed, among other things, CD covers for the Rolling Stones, David Byrne, Lou Reed and countless other international bands. He has twice been nominated for a Grammy and has received many international awards.

Pricken: Your work has received many awards worldwide and attracts unusually high attention in the profession. What makes you certain that you're producing the right design at the right moment?

Sagmeister: I don't think I am absolutely certain of always doing the right thing. While I'm working on projects I'm often beset by doubt – like every one else in the profession. But over the years I've learnt that intensive research and factual detail can provide something approaching certainty – the more you know about a project, the less danger there is of coming off the rails altogether. Also, experience has shown me that it helps you sell an idea to a client if you make it clear that you've understood the background.

Pricken: What do you believe is more important in graphic design, knowledge or imagination?

Sagmeister: Pure knowledge without imagination doesn't get you far, of course, because you have to fall back on experiences you or somebody else had at some time in the past. In those circumstances knowledge would get in the way of anything new. On the other hand, imagination without strategy means that your design work isn't targeted. For me, there's a third element in graphic design, without which both imagination and knowledge are useless: it's the ability to translate ideas into action! That is, the ability to make an idea a reality. I had a wonderful experience of this with M&Co, for whom I worked for a time. The company was run by Tibor Kalman, who had no design training. And yet I believe that M&Co did the best work in the United States in the 1980s and early 1990s. Tibor had the ability to translate ideas into action both as a

businessman and as a top salesman. The ideas developed by the M&Co team were realized without any compromises. There were probably plenty of design studios at the time that developed ideas of the same quality, but we never saw them because their ability to translate ideas into action wasn't good enough. I see it all the time with designers who show me their portfolios, and then make excuses about hardly anything being left of the original idea because the client demanded so many changes. But I think the only thing that counts in the end is the idea the public gets to see.

Pricken: Are there any people, things or places you find particularly inspiring?

Sagmeister: New York! It may sound a bit of a cliché, but it's almost impossible to resist the inspirational power of this city. Creatives, especially, meet a lot of people here who simply translate their ideas into action and, even more important, it's relatively simple to get to know these people here. I think one reason for it is the basic American friendliness, which people in Europe often mistake for superficiality. But believe me, it's very useful in everyday life. In conversation with creatives and artists, you get the impression that these are people just like you and me, and that encourages you to go on with new projects that perhaps you'd never have attempted before. What I also find very inspiring is the half hour I spend in the morning with coffee and my sketchbook on the roof of my house. No telephone calls, no pressure, no deadlines. Sometimes I pick up an idea from the day before and start scribbling, or I simply begin to draw at random and wait to see where it takes me.

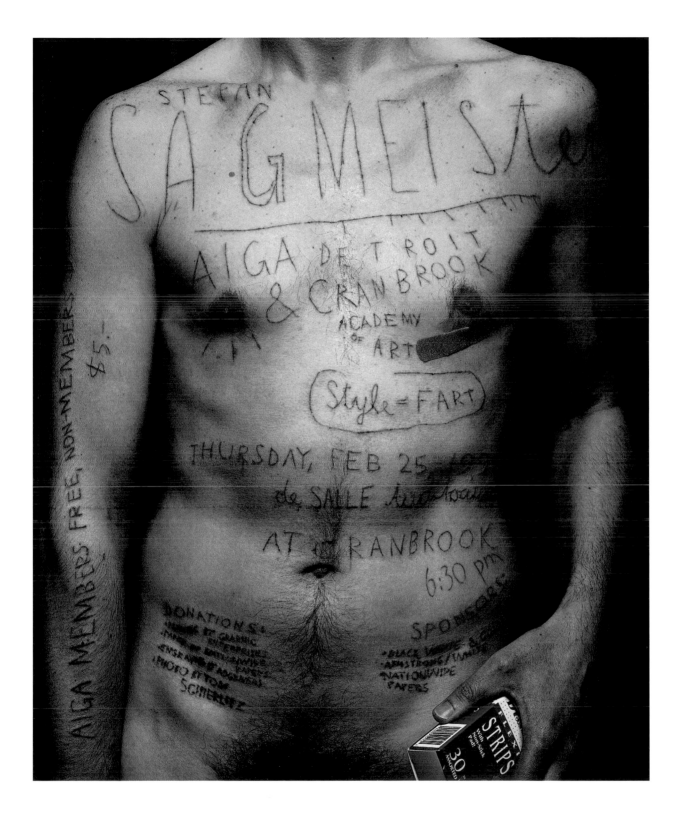

Pricken: Would you call yourself a loner, or do the best ideas come about when you're working with others?

Sagmeister: My ideas don't come into existence in a vacuum, of course, but in a field of tension with other people. There's the client, too, who of course makes important stipulations that affect the outcome of my work. When we have brainstorming sessions in the studio, it's been my experience that we get the best results when there are just two or three of us. I also think large teams don't function as well, because everyone relies on someone else to have the best idea. But deep down I think I work up the greatest number of ideas on my own.

Pricken: How much say do you allow your clients, and what influence do their wishes or views have on the outcome of your work?

Sagmeister: When we're doing a music job, for example, I talk to the members of the band as much as possible, about the band's history, the music, the lyrics, and how the album was made. Sometimes I go and visit them in the studio, too. But I always try to stop them talking about the cover itself. If a band turns up and tries to tell me how the cover ought to look, we don't normally accept the commission, because what it usually amounts to is girls with big boobs. There are exceptions, like David Byrne, for example. He's the only musician I know who has the necessary visual maturity. After all, he's made enough films and books himself. Otherwise, we take great pains to ensure that the concept comes from us. And if the clients do make suggestions, we look at them very closely to see if there's any mileage in them, or if it's just somebody wanting to satisfy their ego.

Pricken: The projects you choose are all exciting ones. How would you approach a contract that involved designing a can of fish? Would the creative results be equally surprising?

Sagmeister: I hope so! First of all I would find out about the customer and if he's interested in high-grade design at all. I've experienced often

'If a band turns up and tries to tell me how the cover ought to look, we don't normally accept the commission, because what it usually amounts to is girls with big boobs.'

enough that if the client doesn't want good design then you scarcely have a chance. Designer friends say it's possible to educate the client, but I don't agree with them. There is one tendency in graphic design that I don't welcome at all. There are international poster festivals, for example, at which the work of small theatres is entered, or posters for charity organizations, produced in-house; these are extremely creative, admittedly, but will only reach a small target group because of the scale of production. On the other hand, there are products in the supermarket which are made in millions, developed by marketing strategists who haven't a clue. And yet there are plenty of designers with the talent to make something beautiful from an object like a can of fish. I think it's a great pity, because as a matter of principle that sort of festival is degrading and becomes a kind of masturbatory circus, such as we see in gallery art too, God help us. There is a small clique in the art and design centres of this world that is working on beautiful projects, but they scarcely register with ordinary citizens on the street.

Pricken: Anything that is commonly called 'new' often turns out on closer inspection to be only a variation of something already known. What are you doing to break new ground in the sphere of graphic design?

Sagmeister: As you know, I have not accepted any commissions from clients for a year now, in order to experiment and explore new paths. For example, I'm trying to develop and produce a CD cover, including a 12-page booklet, within three hours. The time limit is not to make me more rational but to get me out of my usual rut. In three hours the parameters are completely different. For one thing, I have to make do with the materials to hand, for another, there are some tools I just can't use. I have to make decisions much faster than usual and so for that reason my decisions are different. Whether the work that results is really new, I just don't know. The public can decide, when I publish some of it in the next few months.

Pricken: Are there still any spaces today where new and original styles of graphic design could emerge, or will we only get to see more variations and repetitions of old trends in years to come?

Sagmeister: Well, if we're talking specifically about styles, these are very often influenced by the tools currently available. You see it very clearly, when a designer has new tools at his disposal, then of course something new also happens. Whether in photography, animation, film or design, when you look at work from the year 2000, a lot of it could only have been done at that time, when the necessary technical means were available. I think we can look forward to some exciting innovations in the field of technology in the future. But what interests me more is whether the future will bring anything new in the field of concepts and ways of thinking.

Pricken: What new impulses has the field of new media brought to graphics?

Sagmeister: Some of the newer ideas are just silly. Magazines, for example, are trying to adopt elements from websites into their design. I think that will vanish. What's fascinating, on the other hand, is the possibility of putting something on the net and then leaving it there to grow of its own accord. You might remember *South Park*, which originally was just a Christmas card, but it made such a splash that in the end there was even a TV series. I don't think a phenomenon like that was possible before the web. As far as design is concerned, a lot of people get bogged down trying to do everything themselves, from layout through animation to text and music. We all know the awful results. But there are also a few people in the web scene thinking along really interesting lines, especially in the field of interactivity. For example, there's the American John Maeda of MIT, who designs very simple interactive websites, which combine technology and design in an amazing way.

Pricken: Where do you draw the line between art and design?

Sagmeister: There's an excellent definition by the British musician Brian Eno, that it can be really helpful to look at a work of art not as an object but as a trigger for experience. I think that's a wonderful way of approaching art. It means I can go out in the world and ask myself, in front of every object, do I have an art experience or not? Of course that does mean that a campaign for Milka chocolate bars can trigger an art experience. On the other hand, of course, it may also happen that a Picasso triggers nothing at all. It is important to differentiate between the market for art and the market for design. But that doesn't mean automatically that something has to be purposeless to be art. That would mean that Botticelli's *Venus* wasn't art, because the Medicis chose to have a quite specific wall of a particular size in their summer palace painted, and with a particular subject.

'What's fascinating, on the other hand, is the possibility of putting something on the net and then leaving it there to grow of its own accord.'

Pricken: Are there any ideas you have been carrying around with you for a long time that you have not been able to realize up to now?

Sagmeister: Something I've wanted to do for a very long time, would be to drive a lorry from New York to Vienna. Through Canada, across the Bering Strait to Siberia and from there to Russia and finally to Vienna. We'll see. I'm working on it.

Pricken: Thank you very much for the interview.

The Team Behind This Book

Christine Klell, design, book concept and project management
The youngest member of an established Austrian family of artists, Christine Klell grew up with art. Training in design was almost inevitable, and she finished her first design projects while still a student in Vienna. Looking for new challenges, she moved through several agencies and after only four years was leading a team of creatives as art director. In 1998 she switched without hesitation to the field of new media, where she worked on some innovative CD-ROM and internet projects as art director for Wunderwerk. In 2000 she set up her own graphics studio, which carries out a wide range of projects for many international clients. She places a special emphasis on working with creatives from the widest possible range of backgrounds, including photography, new media, painting and computer animation.
www.christine-klell.com

Christian Postl, photography
Photo shoots with Christian Postl are dynamic, noisy and enthusiastic. Posing in front of his camera becomes a voyage of self-discovery and his boundless energy draws emotions from his sitters that shine through in his pictures. His body of work is as idiosyncratic as his style, and is regularly commended for its artistic and technical perfection. In the past ten years he has done countless advertising projects, as well as reportage and a select number of art exhibitions. He sees himself as a magnet for unusual projects, because without that certain 'kick' his jobs are only half as much fun!
c.postl@aon.at, www.christianpostl.com

Blagovesta Bakardjieva, illustrations
Blagovesta Bakardjieva was born in the Bulgarian capital, Sofia. Choosing the right educational track gave an early boost to her talent and led her from high school straight to the Art Academy in Sofia. In 1999 she enrolled at the University of Applied Art in Vienna, in Professor Tino Erben's graphics and design masterclass. She specializes in illustration and book design.
bbakardjieva@hotmail.com

Abbott Mead Vickers BBDO
151 Marylebone Road
London NW1 5QE
England
Phone +44 20 7616 3500
www.amvbbdo.co.uk

Acme Advertising
195 Portola Drive
San Francisco, CA 94131
U.S.A.
Phone +1 415 970 3385

Adera Nederland
Stadhouderskade 6
1054 ES Amsterdam
The Netherlands
Phone +31 20 607 1111
www.adera.nl

ADWORKS Inc.
2401 Pennsylvania Avenue
Washington, D.C. 20037
U.S.A.
Phone +1 202 342 5585
www.adworks.com

AgênciaClick
Av. Dr. Chucri Zaidan, 940, 18° andar
04583–110 São Paulo
Brazil
Phone +55 11 3017 5100
www.agenciaclick.com.br

Alessandri Design
Rufgasse 3
1090 Vienna
Austria
Phone +43 1 310 4401

Almap, BBDO Comunicações Ltda
Av. Roque Petroni Jr., 999
5°, 6° & 7° andares
São Paulo
Brazil
Phone +55 11 5181 6336
www.almapbbdo.com.br

Amazon Advertising
303 Sacramento Street
San Francisco, CA 94111
U.S.A.
Phone +1 415 433 3004
www.amazonadv.com

Angotti, Thomas, Hedge
9th Floor
320 West 13th Street
New York, NY 10014
U.S.A.
Phone +1 212 886 2100

Arnell Group
5th Floor
130 Prince Street
New York, NY 10012
U.S.A.
Phone +1 212 219 8400

Arnold Communications, Inc.
101 Huntington Avenue
Boston, MA 02199-7603
U.S.A.
Phone +1 617 587 8000
www.arn.com

Banks Hoggins O'Shea FCB
55 Newman Street
London W1T 3EB
England
Phone +44 20 7947 8000

Bartle Bogle Hegarty
60 Kingly Street
London W1R 6DS
England
Phone +44 20 7743 1677
www.bartleboglehegarty.com

Bates Dorland
(see Bates UK)

Bates Ireland
9 Upper Pembroke Street
Dublin 2
Ireland
Phone +35 3 676 0221
www.batesireland.ie

Bates Reklamebyrå
PO Box 484
Hoffsveien 1, Skoyen
Oslo 0212
Norway
Phone +47 22 87 9700
www.bates.no

Bates Scandinavia
Landemærket 29
1119 Copenhagen K
Denmark
Phone +45 33 13 7913
www.batesnet.dk

Bates UK
121–141 Westbourne Terrace
London W2 6JR
England
Phone +44 20 7262 5077
www.batesuk.com

Batey Ads
100 Amoy Street
Singapore 069920
Singapore
Phone +65 532 2288
www.bateyads.com.sg

BBDO Allansson Nilsson Rififi
Kungstorget 2
S-411 17 Gothenburg
Sweden
Phone +46 31 17 7500

BBDO A/S
Store Kongensgade 72
1264 Copenhagen
Denmark
Phone +45 33 30 1919
www.bbdo.dk

BBDO Canada
2 Bloor Street West
Toronto, Ontario M4W 3R6
Canada
Phone +1 416 972 1505
www.bbdo.com

BBDO CNUAC
16th Floor, Peregrine Plaza
1 Bao Qing Road
Shanghai 200031
China
Phone +86 21 6467 9699

BBDO Düsseldorf
PO Box 101451
Bahnstrasse 2
40005 Düsseldorf
Germany
Phone +49 211 13 7980
www.bbdo.de

BBDO Portugal
Rua das Musas Nr. 3.30
1990 Lisbon
Portugal
Phone +351 21 891 0500
www.bbdo.pt

BBDO West
Suite 1640
3 Embarcadero Center
San Francisco, CA 94111
U.S.A.
Phone +1 415 274 6200

BDDP, Paris
(see TBWA Paris)

BDDP GGT Advertising
(see TBWA/GGT Direct)

BBK Studio
648 Monroe Ave NW
Suite 212
Grand Rapids, MI 49503
U.S.A.
Phone +1 616 459 4444
www.bbkstudio.com

Benjamens Van Doorn Euro RSCG
Burg. A. Colijnweg 2
1182 AL Amstelveen
The Netherlands
Phone +31 20 547 0700
www.eurorscg.nl

BETC Euro RSCG
85–87, rue du Faubourg Saint-Martin
75010 Paris
France
Phone +33 1 5641 3500
www.eurorscg.fr

Bianco & Cucco
Via Lanzone 22
Milan 20123
Italy
Phone +39 2 805 7710

BlackBird Creative
P/704 376 8512
100 N. Tryon Street
Suite 2800
Charlotte, NC 28202
U.S.A.
Phone +1 704 376 8512
www.pricemcnabb.com

BMP DDB Ltd
12 Bishops Bridge Road
London W2 6AA
England
Phone +44 20 7258 4245
www.bmpddb.com

BOC Advertising
65 SW Yainhill Street
Portland, OR 97204
U.S.A.
Phone +1 503 222 2566

Boebel/Adam Werbeagentur
Neue Mainzer Strasse 84
60311 Frankfurt am Main
Germany
Phone +49 69 29 9620

Bold TBWA
Postboks 244 Skøyen
Karenslyst Allé 18d
Oslo 0213
Norway
Phone +47 22 12 9999
www.bold.no

Bryant, Fulton & Shee
Suite 1100
1500 West Georgia Street
Vancouver, British Columbia V6G 2Z6
Canada
Phone +1 604 669 4444
www.bfs.ca

Butler, Shine & Stern
10 Liberty Ship Way
Suite 300
Sausalito, CA 94965
U.S.A.
Phone +1 415 331 6049
www.bsands.com

Carmichael Lynch Inc.
800 Hennepin Avenue
Minneapolis, MN 55403-1803
U.S.A.
Phone +1 612 334 6000
www.carmichaellynch.com

Charles S. Anderson Design Co.
30 North First Street
Suite 400
Minneapolis, MN 55401
U.S.A.
Phone +1 612 339 5181

Cliff Freeman & Partners
375 Hudson Street
New York, NY 10014-3658
U.S.A.
Phone +1 212 463 3200
www.clifffreeman.com

CLM/BBDO
2, allée Moulineaux
92130 Issy-les-Moulineaux
France
Phone +33 1 41 23 41 23

Colenso
100 College Hill
Ponsonby
Auckland
New Zealand
Phone +64 9 360 3777
www.webnz.com/colenso

Collett Dickenson Pearce & Partners
33–34 Soho Square
London W1V 6DP
England
Phone +44 20 7292 4000
www.cdp-uk.com

Corporate Design Associates
1231 Mt. Vernon Street
Orlando, FL 32803
U.S.A.
Phone +1 407 898 8838

Courage/BDDP
Aldersrogade 6 A
2100 Copenhagen Ø
Denmark
Phone +45 39 16 0000
www.courage.dk

Cramer-Krasselt
733 North Van Buren Street
Milwaukee, WI 53202
U.S.A.
Phone +1 414 227 3500

Cramer-Krasselt Co.
225 North Michigan Avenue
Chicago, Il 60601-7601
U.S.A.
Phone +1 312 616 9600
www.c-k.com

Daiko Advertising Inc.
Shuwa-Shiba Park Bldg.
4–1, 2 Chome, Shiba-Kouen
Minator-ku
Tokyo 105 8533
Japan
Phone +81 3 3437 8213
www.daiko.co.jp

D'Arcy
Warwick Building
Kensington Village
Avonmore Road
London W14 8HQ
England
Phone +44 20 7751 1800
www.darcyww.co.uk

DDB Chicago
200 East Randolph Drive
Chicago, IL 60601
U.S.A.
Phone +1 312 552 6000
www.ddb.com

Del Campo Nazca Saatchi & Saatchi
Bogotá 973
1640 Martínez
Buenos Aires
Argentina
Phone +54 11 4836 0800

Delikatessen Werbeagentur
ABC-Strasse 2
20543 Hamburg
Germany
Phone +49 40 350 8060
www.delikatessen-wa.de

Dentsu Inc. Creative Division 1
1-11-10 Tsukiji
Chuo-ku
Tokyo 104-8426
Japan
Phone +81 3 5551 5599
www.dentsu.co.jp

Dentsu, Young & Rubicam
Kyobashi K-1 Bldg.
2-7-12 Yaesu, Chuo-ku
Tokyo 104
Japan
Phone +81 3 3278 4891

Designers Company
Stadhouderskade 79
1072 AE Amsterdam
The Netherlands
Phone +31 20 571 5670
www.designers-company.nl

Devarrieux Villaret
164, rue de Rivoli
75001 Paris
France
Phone +33 1 5329 2929
www.devarrieuxvillaret.fr

DM9 DDB Publicidade
Av. Dr. Cardoso de Mello, 1155
São Paulo 04548-004
Brazil
Phone +55 1 3040 4999
www.dm9.com.br

Doner Cardwell Hawkins
26–34 Emerald Street
London WC1N 3QA
England
Phone +44 20 7734 0511
www.donercardwellhawkins.co.uk

DPZ Propaganda
Av. Cidade Jardim, 280
São Paulo 01454-900
Brazil
Phone +55 11 3068 4000
www.dpz.com.br

Edson FCB
Rua Braamcamp, 40–7
Edifício Heron Castilho
1250-050 Lisbon
Portugal
Phone +351 21 381 1200
www.fcb.pt

Eisner Communications
509 South Exter Street
Baltimore, MD 21202
U.S.A.
Phone +1 410 685 3390
www.eisner-communications.com

Euro RSCG
Alcalá, 44 – 5ª y 6ª Planta
28014 Madrid
Spain
Phone +34 91 701 4730
www.eurorscg.es

Euro RSCG
Postfach 830, Gutstrasse 73
8055 Zurich
Switzerland
Phone +41 1 466 6777
www.eurorscg.ch

Euro RSCG Partnership
21/F Devon House
979 King's Road, Quarry Bay
Hong Kong
www.eurorscg.com.hk

Euro RSCG Works
84, rue de Villiers
92683 Levallois-Perret
France
Phone +33 1 4134 4297
www.eurorscg.fr

Fallon Worldwide
Suite 3200
901 Marquette Avenue
Minneapolis, MN 55402
U.S.A.
Phone +1 612 321 2345
www.fallon.com

FCB France
69, boulevard du Général Leclerc
92583 Clichy
France
Phone +33 1 41 06 75 00
www.fcb.fr

FCB Worldwide, Detroit
Suite 1500
1000 Town Center
Southfield, MI 48075-1241
U.S.A.
Phone +1 248 354 5400
www.fcb.com

FHV/BBDO
Amsterdamseweg 204
1182 HL Amsterdam
The Netherlands
Phone +31 20 543 7777

F/Nazca S&S
Saatchi & Saatchi Worldwide
Av. Republica do Libano
253 Ibirapuera
São Paulo 04501-000
Brazil
Phone +55 11 3059 4907
www.fnazca.com.br

Freestyle Interactive
275 Sixth Street
San Francisco, CA 94103
U.S.A.
Phone +1 415 869 7400
www.freestyleinteractive.com

Geelmuyden Kiese
Lilleakerveien 2d
Postboks 223, Lilleaker
0216 Oslo
Norway
Phone +47 22 13 0303

Gilliatt Paris
3131 McKinney Avenue
Suite 750
Dallas, TX 75204
U.S.A.
Phone +1 214 979 1177
www.gilliattparis.com

GMO/Hill Holliday
600 Battery Street
San Francisco, CA 94111
U.S.A.
Phone +1 415 617 5100
www.gmohillholliday.com

Goodby, Silverstein & Partners
720 California Street
San Francisco, CA 94108
U.S.A.
Phone +1 415 392 0669
www.goodbysilverstein.com

Grey Worldwide
Room 1804, Novel Plaza
128 Najing Xi Road
Huang Pu District
Shanghai 200003
China
Phone +86 21 6350 8660

Grey Worldwide
Kr. Bernikows Gade 1
1105 Copenhagen K
Denmark
Phone +45 33 30 0100
www.grey-kbh.com

Grey Worldwide
Sdn. Bhd. (149425 A)
28th Floor, Empire Tower
Jalan Tun Razak
50400 Kuala Lumpur
Malaysia
Phone +60 603 2723 0166

Grey Worldwide Argentina
21st/22nd Floor
Moreno 877
Buenos Aires 1091
Argentina
Phone +54 11 4344 1800
www.casaresgrey.com

Haines McGregor
250 Kings Road
London SW3 5UE
England
Phone +44 20 7352 8322
www.hainesmcgregor.co.uk

Hall & Cederquist/Young & Rubicam
P.O. Box 7838
Norrmalmstorg 14
Stockholm 103 98
Sweden
Phone +46 8 665 7100
www.hcyr.se

Hasan Partners
Pursimiehenkatu 29–31B
00150 Helsinki
Finland
Phone +358 9 8569 8569

Hoffman York
330 East Kilbourn Avenue
Milwaukee, WI 53202
U.S.A.
Phone +1 414 289 9700

I-D Media AG, Hamburg
Weidenallee 37a
20357 Hamburg
Germany
Phone +49 40 43134 8210
www.i-dmedia.com

Impiric
The Concourse
300 Beach Road #33 01/03
Singapore 199555
Singapore
Phone +65 295 0975
www.impiric.com

Jean & Montmarin, Paris
4, Rond Point Claude Monet
92300 Levallois
France
Phone +33 1 46 41 40 00

Jung von Matt Werbeagentur GmbH
Glashüttenstrasse 38
20357 Hamburg
Germany
Phone +49 40 4 3210
www.jvm.de

The Jupiter Drawing Room
21 A Tannery Park
Belmont Road
Rondebosch, Cape Town
South Africa
Phone +27 21 680 3200
www.jupiter.co.za

J. Walter Thompson
40 Berkeley Square
London W1J 5AL
England
Phone +44 20 7499 4040
www.jwt.co.uk

J. Walter Thompson Australia
Level 15
484 St. Kilda Road
Melbourne, Victoria 3004
Australia
Phone +61 3 9868 9111
www.jwt.com.au

J. Walter Thompson Company HQ
466 Lexington Avenue
New York, NY 10017
U.S.A.
Phone +1 212 210 7000
www.jwt.com

KesselsKramer
Lauriergracht 39
1016 RG Amsterdam
The Netherlands
Phone +31 20 530 1060
www.kesselskramer.com

Körberg & Co.
Box 3094, Vasagatan 45
Gothenburg 400 10
Sweden
Phone +46 317 78 9000
www.korberg.com

Korek Studio
Ul. Jagiellonska 4m3
03-721 Warsaw
Poland
Phone +48 601 20 9631
www.korekstudio.com.pl

Leagas Delaney
1 Alfred Place
London WC1E 7EB
England
Phone +44 20 7758 1758
www.leagasdelaney.com

Leagas Delaney
2nd Floor, 840 Battery Street
San Francisco, CA 94111
U.S.A.
Phone +1 415 439 5800
www.leagasdelaney.com

The Leith Agency
The Canon Mill
Canon Street
Edinburgh EH3 5HE
Scotland
Phone +44 131 557 5840
www.leith.co.uk

Leo Burnett
122, rue Edouard Vaillant
92593 Levallois-Perret Cedex
France
Phone +33 1 41 49 7300
www.leoburnett.fr

Leo Burnett
9 Karmelicka Street
00-155 Warsaw
Poland
Phone +48 228 60 9800

Leo Burnett Publicidade
Av. da Republica 139D – Algés
1499–001 Lisbon
Portugal
Phone +351 21 416 4800

Leo Burnett Annonsbyrå AB
Birger Jarlsgatan 25
Box 476
Stockholm 101 29
Sweden
Phone +46 8 412 5000

Leo Burnett Company
18th Floor
35 West Wacker Drive
Chicago, IL 60601
U.S.A.
Phone +1 312 220 5643
www.leoburnett.com

Leo Burnett Inc.
Hato Rey Tower, Suite 2200
268 Muños Rivera Avenue
Hato Rey, San Juan 00918
Puerto Rico
Phone +1 787 754 7761
www.leoburnett.com

Leo Burnett Ltd
The Leo Burnett Building
60 Sloane Avenue
London SW3 3XB
England
Phone +44 20 7591 9492
www.leoburnett.com

Leo Burnett S.A. de C.V.
Bosque de Duraznos 65-8P
Bosques de las Lomas
11700 Mexico City, DF
Mexico
Phone +52 5 596 6188
www.leoburnett.com.mx

Lesch & Frei Werbeagentur GmbH
Leipziger Strasse 59
60487 Frankfurt am Main
Germany
Phone +49 69 24 7018
www.leschfrei.de

Lew, Lara Propaganda
Av. Pres. Juscelino Kubitscheck, 1851
Vila Olimpia 3896-0000
São Paulo
Brazil
Phone +55 11 822 8519
www.lewlara.com.br

Lewis Moberly
33 Gresse Street
London W1P 2LP
England
Phone +44 20 7580 9252
www.lewismoberly.com

Lintas, Amsterdam
(see Lowe Lintas, Amsterdam)

Lowe Brindfors AB
Box 6518
Birger Jarlsgatan 57A
Stockholm 113 83
Sweden
Phone +46 8 5662 5500
www.lowebrindfors.se

Lowe Howard-Spink
(see Lowe Lintas, London)

Lowe Lintas
Bowater House 68–114
Knightsbridge
London SW1X 7LT
England
Phone +44 20 7584 5033
www.lowelintas.co.uk

Lowe Lintas
Amstelveenseweg 404
1070 CT Amsterdam
The Netherlands
Phone +31 20 573 1111

Lowe Lintas & Partners
22, quai de la Mégisserie
75001 Paris
France
Phone +33 1 4041 5400

Lowe & Partners, Monsoon Advertising
60 Martin Road
#07-23/26 TradeMart Singapore
Singapore 239065
Singapore
Phone +65 735 3339

McCann-Erickson
122, chaussée de la Hulpe
1000 Brussels
Belgium
Phone +32 2 674 1311

McCann-Erickson
Rua Visconde de Ouro Preto, 5
13° andar
22250-180 Rio de Janeiro
Brazil
Phone +55 21 533 2400
www.mccann.com.br

McCann-Erickson
15, passage Malbuisson
1211 Geneva 11
Switzerland
Phone +41 22 317 7777

McCann-Erickson Barcelona
Josep Irla i Bosch, 1–3
08034 Barcelona
Spain
Phone +34 93 252 0400
www.mccann.es

McCann-Erickson Madrid
Paseo de la Castellana, 165
28046 Madrid
Spain
Phone +34 91 567 9000
www.mccann.es

Magneto Interactive
47 Newton Street
Manchester M1 1F2
England
Phone +44 161 200 8300
www.magneto-interactive.com

Manne & Co.
Kungsgatan 48
Stockholm 111 35
Sweden
Phone +46 8 20 60 31
www.manne.nu

The Martin Agency
One Shockoe Plaza
Richmond, VA 23219-4132
U.S.A.
Phone +1 804 698 8000
www.martinagency.com

Martin/Williams Advertising
Suite 2800
60 South 6th Street
Minneapolis, MN 55402-4444
U.S.A.
Phone +1 612 340 0800
www.martinwilliams.com

Metalli Lindberg
Viale Venezia 135
31015 Conegliano, Treviso
Italy
Phone +39 438 6565
www.metalli-lindberg.com

Michael Conrad & Leo Burnett
Alexanderstrasse 65
60489 Frankfurt am Main
Germany
Phone +49 69 78 0770

Minale Tattersfield and Partners Ltd
The Courtyard
37 Sheen Road
Richmond, Surrey TW9 1AJ
England
Phone +44 20 8948 7999
www.mintat.co.uk

Mires Design, Inc.
2345 Kettner Boulevard
San Diego, CA 92101
U.S.A.
Phone +1 619 234 6631
www.miresdesign.com

Mother Ltd
200 St John Street
London EC1V 4RN
England
Phone +44 20 7689 0689
www.mother.ltd.uk

Mudra Communications Ltd
Mudra House
A-1/55, Safdarjung Enclave
New Delhi 110 029
India
Phone +91 11 616 5290
www.mudra.com

Mullen Advertising Inc.
36 Essex Street
Wenham, MA 01984-1799
U.S.A.
Phone +1 978 468 1155
www.mullen.com

Mustoe Merriman Herring Levy
133 Long Acre
Covent Garden
London WC2E 9AG
England
Phone +44 20 7379 9999
www.mmhl.co.uk

New Deal DDB
P.O. Box 7084
Majorstua Wergelandsveien 21
Oslo 0306
Norway
Phone +47 22 59 32 00
www.newdeal.no

Nova Publicidade
Av. General Norton de Matos, 65E
1495-014 Lisbon
Portugal
Phone +351 141 11200

Ogilvy & Mather
33 Yonge Street
Toronto, Ontario M5E 1X6
Canada
Phone +1 416 367 3573
www.ogilvy.com

Ogilvy & Mather
Mahalaxmi Chambers, IV Floor
29 Mahatma Gandhi Road
560001 Bangalore
India
Phone +91 80 558 4566

Ogilvy & Mather
PO Box 1396
1000 BJ Amsterdam
The Netherlands
Phone +31 20 521 6464
www.ogilvy.nl

Ogilvy & Mather
Rua Victor Cordon, 37-5°
1249-100 Lisbon
Portugal
Phone +351 1 321 8000
www.ogilvy.pt

Ogilvy & Mather
Maritime Square #12-01
World Trade 1
Singapore 099253
Singapore
Phone +65 273 8011

Ogilvy & Mather Rightford
Searle-Tripp & Makin
PO Box 1142
18 Roeland Street
Cape Town 8001
South Africa
Phone +27 21 467 1000

Ogilvy & Mather
10th Floor, Silom Center
2 Silom Road
Bangkok 10500
Thailand
Phone +66 233 8355

OgilvyOne Communications BV
Nieuwezijds Voorburgwal 37
1000 AV Amsterdam
The Netherlands
Phone +31 20 521 6565
www.ogilvyone.com

OgilvyOne Worldwide
20th Floor, Silom Center
2 Silom Road
Bangkok 10500
Thailand
Phone +66 2632 8310

Opal Publicidade S.A.
Rua de Santa Catarina 706-1º
4000-446 Oporto
Portugal
Phone +351 22 207 3660

Palmer Jarvis DDB
1600-777 Hornby Street
Vancouver, British Columbia V6Z 2T3
Canada
Phone +1 604 687 7911
www.pjddb.com

Paltemaa Huttunen Santala TBWA
Tehtaankatu 1A
Helsinki 00140
Finland
Phone +358 917 1711

Paprika Communications
400, Laurier Ouest
Montreal, Quebec H2V 3P7
Canada
Phone +1 514 276 6000

Pars-McCann-Erickson
Buyukdere Caddesi
Ecza Sokak, No. 6
Levent
Istanbul 80498
Turkey
Phone +90 212 317 5600

The Partners
Albion Courtyard
Greenhill Rents, Smithfield
London EC1M 6PQ
England
Phone +44 20 7608 0051
www.thepartners.co.uk

Pentagram
204 Fifth Avenue
New York, NY 10010
U.S.A.
Phone +1 212 683 7000
www.pentagram.com

Phillips-Ramsey Company, Inc.
6063 Friars Road
San Diego, CA 92108-1121
U.S.A.
Phone +1 619 574 0808

Poulter Partners
Rose Wharf,
East Street
Leeds LS9 8EE
England
Phone +44 113 285 6500
www.poulternet.com

Pragma/FCB Publicidad
Humboldt 1967, Piso 2
1414 Buenos Aires
Argentina
Phone +54 11 4779 4444
www.pragma-fcb.com

Publicis
7314 Beethovenstraat 198
1077 JZ Amsterdam
The Netherlands
Phone +31 20 305 1000
www.publicis.nl

Publicis
Rua Gonçalves Zarco, 14
1449-013 Lisbon
Portugal
Phone +351 21 303 5100
www.publicis.pt

Publicis
Theaterstrasse 8
8001 Zurich
Switzerland
Phone +41 1 265 3287
www.publicis.ch

Publicis Casadevall Pedreño & PRG
Avenida Tibidabo, 29 (Torre)
08022 Barcelona
Spain
Phone +34 93 418 5118

Publicis FCB
Avenue de la Couronne, 357
1050 Brussels
Belgium
Phone +32 2 645 3511

Result Advertising
17th Floor, Silom Center
2 Silom Road
Bangkok 10500
Thailand
Phone +66 662 632 8320

RG Wiesmeier Werbeagentur AG
Maximilianstrasse 30
80539 Munich
Germany
Phone +49 89 290 0890
www.wiesmeier.de

RMG Warsaw
RMG Marcom
Dluga 44/50
00-241 Warsaw
Poland
Phone +48 22 635 8188

Roche Macaulay & Partners
22 Saint Clair Avenue East
Toronto, Ontario M4T 2S3
Canada
Phone +1 416 927 9794
www.rochemacaulay.com

R. Treviño & Asociados
Avenida Roble 300
Valle del Campestre
Garza García, N.L.
CP 66220 Mexico City
Mexico
Phone +52 83 56 09 03
www.rtrevino.com.mx

Saatchi & Saatchi
70 George Street, The Rocks
Sydney, NSW 2000
Australia
Phone +61 2 9230 0222

Saatchi & Saatchi
80 Charlotte Street
London W1A 1AQ
England
Phone +44 20 7636 5000
www.saatchi-saatchi.com

Saatchi & Saatchi
Alvinci út 16
Budapest 1022
Hungary
Phone +36 1 345 9300

Saatchi & Saatchi
123–125 The Strand
Parnell, P.O. Box 801
Auckland
New Zealand
Phone +64 9 355 5000

Saatchi & Saatchi
3D River Valley Road #03-01
Singapore 179023
Singapore
Phone +65 339 4733

Sagmeister Inc.
222 West 14th Street, 15a
New York, NY 10011
U.S.A.
Phone +1 212 647 1789

Sawyer Riley Compton
3423 Piedmont Road
Suite 400
Atlanta, GA 30305
U.S.A.
Phone +1 404 479 9849
www.brandstorytellers.com

Scholz & Friends
Wöhlerstrasse 12/13
10115 Berlin
Germany
Phone +49 28 53 5300

Slaughter Hanson
2100 Morris Avenue
Birmingham, AL 35203
U.S.A.
Phone +1 205 252 9998
www.slaughterhanson.com

Springer & Jacoby Werbung
GmbH & Co. KG
Poststrasse 14–16
20354 Hamburg
Germany
Phone +49 40 35 6030
www.sj.com

SSC&B Lintas
The Phoenix Complex
Senapati Bapat Mark
Lower Parel
Mumbai 400 013
India
Phone +91 22 493 5377

Stempels & Oster
De Klencke 4
1083 HH Amsterdam
The Netherlands
Phone +31 20 301 9855

Strathearn Advertising
Silvermills House
West Silvermills Lane
Edinburgh EH3 5BD
Scotland
Phone +44 131 557 4900

Studio A4 Bojana Fajmut
Tugomerjeva 2
1000 Ljubljana
Slovenia
Phone +386 1 505 6042

Tadeusz Lewandowski, Paris
13, place Emile Goudeau
Bateau Lavoir Atelier 4
75018 Paris
France
Phone +33 1 4251 3106

Tadeusz Piechura
Zgierska 124/140 m. 168
91-320 Lodz
Poland
Phone +48 42 654 4633

Tandem Campmany Guasch DDB
Enrique Granados, 86–88
08008 Barcelona
Spain
Phone +34 93 228 3400

TBWA
8, avenue E. Van Nieuwenhuyse
1160 Brussels
Belgium
Phone +32 2 679 7511
www.tbwa.be

TBWA
1st Floor
Stadhouderskade 79
1011 LE Amsterdam
The Netherlands
Phone +31 20 571 5400
www.tbwa.nl

TBWA
Passeig de Grácia, 56, 2º
08007 Barcelona
Spain
Phone +34 93 272 3636
www.tbwa.es

TBWA/Chiat/Day
6th Floor
488 Madison Avenue
New York, NY 10022
U.S.A.
Phone +1 212 804 1000
www.chiatday.com

TBWA/GGT Direct
82 Dean Street
London W1D 3HA
England
Phone +44 20 7439 4282
www.tbwa-ggt.com

TBWA GGT Simons Palmer
(see TBWA/GGT Direct)

TBWA Hunt Lascaris
Fika Futi
51, Wierda Road West
Wierda Valley
Sandton, Johannesburg
Gauteng 2196
South Africa
Phone +27 11 322 3178
www.huntlas.co.za

TBWA London
76–80 Whitfield Street
London W1P 5RQ
England
Phone +44 20 7573 6666
www.tbwa.co.uk

TBWA Paris
162–164, rue de Billancourt
BP411
92103 Boulogne-Billancourt
France
Phone +33 1 4909 7010
www.bddp.com

TBWA Werbeagentur GmbH
Saarbrückerstrasse 20–21
10405 Berlin
Germany
Phone +49 30 443 2930
www.tbwa.de

Templin Brink Design LLC
720 Tehama Street
San Francisco, CA 94103
U.S.A.
Phone +1 415 255 9295
www.templinbrinkdesign.com

Tiempo/BBDO
Tuset 5
08006 Barcelona
Spain
Phone +34 93 306 9017
www.tiempobbdo.com

Trickett & Webb
The Factory
84 Marchmont Street
London WC1N 1RD
England
Phone +44 20 7388 5832
www.tricketts.co.uk

Tucker Clarke-Williams Creative
(see Magneto Interactive)

Turner Duckworth
Voysey House
Barley Mow Passage
London W4 4PH
England
Phone +44 20 8994 7190
www.turnerduckworth.com

Ubachs Wisbrun
Watertorenplein 4
1051 PA Amsterdam
The Netherlands
Phone +31 20 488 6888
www.ubachswisbrun.nl

Verba DDB SRL
Via Solari, 11
Milan 20144
Italy
Phone +39 2 58 19 31

WCRS Ltd
5 Golden Square
London W1R 4BS
England
Phone +44 20 7806 5000
www.wcrs.co.uk

Weber, Hodel, Schmid
Aemtlerstrasse 201
8040 Zurich
Switzerland
Phone +41 1 405 4455
www.whs.ch

West & Vaughan
One Peabody Place
112 South Duke Street
Durham, NC 27701
U.S.A.
Phone +1 919 688 2000
www.westandvaughan.com

Whybin TBWA & Partners
288 Coventry Street
3205 South Melbourne
Australia
Phone +61 3 9690 8555

Wieden & Kennedy
Elsley Court, 4th floor
20–22 Great Titchfield Street
London W1W 8BE
England
Phone +44 20 7299 6800
www.wk.com

Wieden & Kennedy Amsterdam
Keizersgracht 125–127
1015 CJ Amsterdam
The Netherlands
Phone +31 20 621 3100

Williams Murray Hamm
The Heals Building
Alfred Mews
London W1P 9LB
England
Phone +44 20 7255 3232
www.creatingdifference.com

Wongdoody, Inc.
216 First Avenue South
Suite 480
Seattle, WA 98104
U.S.A.
Phone +1 206 624 5325
www.wongdoody.com

Wurmser Ogilvy & Mather
13 Calle 2–60, Zona 10
Edificio Topacio Azul, Oficina 902
Guatemala City
Guatemala
Phone +502 332 8944

Young & Rubicam
60 Bloor Street West
8th Floor
Toronto, Ontario, M4W 1J2
Canada
Phone +1 416 961 5111
www.yandr.com

Young & Rubicam Kaena, Paris
45, rue Paul Bert
92100 Boulogne-Billancourt Cedex
France
Phone +33 1 4684 3330

Young & Rubicam Portugal
Av. Eng. Duarte Pacheco,
19-6°, 10° & 11°
1099 037 Lisbon
Portugal
Phone +351 21 381 6300

Zapping, Publicidad
Espalter, 2 (Jardín Botánico)
28014 Madrid
Spain
Phone +34 91 360 0223
www.grupozapping.com

OTHER ILLUSTRATION SOURCES:

Fischer's Archive
J & S Dialog-Medien GmbH
Bei den Mühren 91
20457 Hamburg
Germany
Phone +49 40 36 9832
www.fischers-archiv.de

Lappan Verlag GmbH
Postfach 3407
26024 Oldenburg
Würzburger Strasse 14
26121 Oldenburg
Germany
Phone +49 441 98 0660
www.lappan.de

Lürzer's Archive
Hamburger Allee 45
60486 Frankfurt am Main
Germany
Phone +49 69 247 7170
www.luerzersarchive.com

TRAINING · COACHING · INNOVATIONS POJECTS

Did the creativity techniques and thought strategies of author Mario Pricken inspire you? Are you now looking for a way to use these methods effectively in your own creative work? The author's website contains full details of flexible in-house training courses that will allow you to integrate effective creativity techniques into the work of your own team. Experience has shown that the teams that achieve the best results using these techniques are those that operate in the advertising, marketing, design, media and innovations management industries. If you would like to find out more and are interested in course contents, press reports or reference projects, please visit: www.idea-engineering.com/english